The Learning Challenge of the Knowledge Economy

The Knowledge Economy and Education
Volume 3

Scope:
The aim of this series is to provide a focus for writers and readers interested in exploring the relation between the knowledge economy and education or an aspect of that relation, for example, vocational and professional education theorised critically.

It seeks authors who are keen to question conceptually and empirically the causal link that policymakers globally assume exists between education and the knowledge economy by raising: (i) epistemological issues as regards the concepts and types of and the relations between knowledge, the knowledge economy and education; (ii) sociological and political economic issues as regards the changing nature of work, the role of learning in workplaces, the relation between work, formal and informal learning and competing and contending visions of what a knowledge economy/knowledge society might look like; and (iii) pedagogic issues as regards the relationship between knowledge and learning in educational, community and workplace contexts.

The series is particularly aimed at researchers, policymakers, practitioners and students who wish to read texts and engage with researchers who call into question the current conventional wisdom that the knowledge economy is a new global reality to which all individuals and societies must adjust, and that lifelong learning is the strategy to secure such an adjustment. The series hopes to stimulate debate amongst this diverse audience by publishing books that: (i) articulate alternative visions of the relation between education and the knowledge economy; (ii) offer new insights into the extent, modes, and effectiveness of people's acquisition of knowledge and skill in the new circumstances that they face in the developed and developing world, (iii) and suggest how changes in both work conditions and curriculum and pedagogy can led to new relations between work and education.

The Learning Challenge of the Knowledge Economy

David Guile
Institute of Education, University of London, UK

SENSE PUBLISHERS
ROTTERDAM/BOSTON/TAIPEI

A C.I.P. record for this book is available from the Library of Congress.

ISBN: 978-94-6091-257-3 (paperback)
ISBN: 978-94-6091-258-0 (hardback)
ISBN: 978-94-6091-259-7 (e-book)

Published by: Sense Publishers,
P.O. Box 21858,
3001 AW Rotterdam,
The Netherlands
http://www.sensepublishers.com

Printed on acid-free paper

DEDICATION

TO MICHAEL

TABLE OF CONTENTS

TABLE OF CONTENTS

ACKNOWLEDGEMENTS

First and foremost, my heartfelt thanks go to Michael Young without whom this book would not have been written. Michael supported me to make a transition from my previous career – a deputy headteacher mid-way through a year-long industrial placement and keen to pursue his intellectual interests rather than move on to a headship – to a new career in higher education. Michael did so by providing a 'home' for me in the Post-16 Education Centre, the centre he directed up until his retirement in 1999, where I could resolve how to pursue my interest in the theory–practice interface in professional, vocational and workplace learning conceptually, empirically and financially.

Our common interest at that time – the theory–practice interface – is the central concern of this book, and continues to inform our, all too often, highly animated, conversations about this issue. This interest is primarily a product of our shared sociological and educational curiosity about the ways in which different forms of knowledge contribute to the continuing economic, political and social development of human societies and human beings. In particular, we both agree that it is important to distinguish between forms of knowledge in terms of their similarities and differences, and to use this differentiation as the basis for addressing the theory–practice relation, rather than to elide them in an attempt to eradicate the theory–practice divide. Where Michael and I tend to differ is over the extent to which this is primarily an epistemological as opposed to a joint epistemological and ontological project.

Second, special thanks go to Chris Hayes and Nickie Fonda, from whom I have learned a tremendous amount over the last fifteen years about the way in which firms' strategic decisions influence whether they encourage or discourage people from creating epistemic cultures and practices. After an intellectually and practically full and active life into his early 90s, Chris sadly passed away in late 2008 and is therefore unable to see how he has influenced this book. Special thanks also go to David Bakhurst and Jan Derry for drawing my attention to, respectively, the significance of the concepts of reason and the inference for understanding the constitution and implications of Vygotsky's cultural–historical theory of mediation.

A considerable number of other colleagues and friends have contributed directly or indirectly to the genesis of this book even though they will not necessarily spot their influence or agree with how I have interpreted their work or our conversations. Thanks go to: Arthur Bakker, Stephen Billett, Alan Brown, Seth Chaiklin, Harry Daniels, Anne Edwards, Yrjö Engeström, Michael Eraut, Karen Evans, Alison Fuller, Andy Green, Hans Gruber, Christian Harteis, Celia Hoyles, Karen Jensen, Seppo Kontainien, Leif Lahn, Hugh Lauder, David Livingstone, Norman Lucas, Sten Ludvigsen, Reijo Miettinen, Johan Muller, Monika Nerland, Davide Nicolini, Richard Noss, Peter Sawchuk and Lorna Unwin.

I have endeavoured to use the aforementioned sociological, psychological, economic and philosophical interests and conversations with the above colleagues to identify what I believe is the distinctive nature of the learning challenge of the knowledge economy – recognising that we that we live in a mediated rather than a natural world and learning how to work with others and use different forms of knowledge to contribute to the continual transformation of that world – and to outline a framework that educational institutions and workplaces could use to support people who are working in the *rough ground* to address that challenge.

Peter de Leifde, Publisher, Sense, deserves a special mention for displaying the patience of a saint and allowing me time to complete this book. As does Octavia Reeve, who painstakingly edited several drafts and, in the process, improved the book immeasurably by helping me to develop a better understanding of the argument that I wanted to make.

An extra special thank you also go to Sarah, Alison and Joanna for tolerating over many years my tendency to slip away from our private conversations and immerse myself in some unresolved issue within the book.

Finally, I should acknowledge the influence of Roland Robertson, who was Professor and Head of Department of Sociology, and my personal tutor, when I was an undergraduate at the University of York. Although our intellectual interests were rather different, Roland's strong commitment to the study of theory as a way to understand the development of sociology and as a resource to analyse all aspects of the human condition has always been a powerful influence on my teaching and research practice.

THE KNOWLEDGE ECONOMY AND THE CHALLENGE FOR EDUCATION

INTRODUCTION

This is a book about arguments. One argument – that the emergence of the knowledge economy poses a new challenge for education – is likely to be very familiar to readers, because it has been extensively aired in a number of popular texts (Gladwell, 2005; Leadbetter, 1999; Wolf, 2002) and well-publicised policy documents (European Commission, 2000; OECD, 1996; World Bank, 2003). Though couched in quasi-Enlightenment terms that stress the importance of knowledge as the key economic resource to support the future development of societies and, as such, undoubtedly reflecting a genuine attempt by policymakers worldwide to foster a more informed populace, it is in essence a narrowly conceived economic argument. This conventional argument treats people as forms of human capital that can be rendered more or less productive in the economy depending on the extent of their knowledge, as represented by the level and domain of their qualifications.

The alternative argument, whilst accepting the premise of the former, maintains that the new role of knowledge in economies of advanced industrial societies has been unconsciously framed in terms of what the book calls, 'the two worlds view of knowledge' (that is, objective knowledge of natural, physical and social structures, or subjective knowledge of feelings, emotions and conditions), and that this framing is based on unexplicated epistemological, ontological assumptions that raise pedagogic questions and issues that have not yet been addressed by researchers and policy-makers, and so this discussion is likely to be new to readers.

In making its argument, the book draws on a number of writers from different disciplines whose work either pre-dated the discussion about the new role of knowledge in the economy, or who have never engaged with that debate, or have drawn radically different conclusions about the implications of the knowledge economy. In bringing their work together, what emerges is the cultural entailment of the economic account of the role of knowledge in the economy and in society. This argument has affinities with, yet differs from, the recent interest in Sociology (du Gay & Pryke, 2002) and Geography (Thrift & Amin, 2003) in the concept of the 'cultural economy'. The primary concern of such writers has been to argue that whilst it may be valuable analytically to separate the economic and the cultural, they are nonetheless related fields of human activity. We accept this premise into our argument, although the cultural account of the knowledge economy developed here is based on the tradition of social practice rather than an integrated system. The difference between this approach and the position adopted by the geographers and sociologists is that we maintain that individuals and societies are constituted rather than influenced by culture. This position enables us to offer a radically different angle on why the emergence of the knowledge economy poses a qualitatively different learning challenge for advanced industrial societies compared with the current conventional wisdom.

The conventional wisdom about the knowledge economy and education. The origins of the first argument lie in the widespread consensus amongst many writers that epochal global economic and technological changes have been occurring in advanced industrial economies since the mid-1950s and that, as a result, we now live in a 'risk society' (Beck, 1992), an 'information' society (Castells, 2000), a 'knowledge society' (Stehr, 1994), and so forth. The particular strand of epochalism that has fuelled the first argument is the 'knowledge economy' thesis; that is, the claim that knowledge rather than land, labour and capital is now the most important factor of production (Osborne, 1998, p. 17). The term 'knowledge economy' was first coined in the late 1960s by Drucker (1969, p. 263) to refer to the application of knowledge from any field or source, new or old, to spur economic development. The subsequent debate about the role of knowledge in the economy, which only took root from the late 1970s, has fractured over the years. One strand follows the argument first promulgated by the social theorist Bell (1973), that theoretical knowledge is the most important form of knowledge in the economy: a position that underpins the current global concern for supporting science, technology, engineering and mathematical (STEM) research. The other strand follows the argument first put forward by the management theorist Lundvall (1996), that tacit knowledge is the most important form of knowledge.

Despite the existence of these two views concerning which type of knowledge is important in the economy, policymakers internationally have tended to accept the former position. At the present time, the most obvious manifestation is the global consensus that science, technology, engineering and mathematics (STEM) subjects are critical to economic prosperity and hence should be the major recipients of research grants.

A major influence on policymakers' thinking as regards the educational response to the knowledge economy was Robert Reich's book *The Work of Nations* (1991). Reich fused the social theorists' case for the new role of knowledge in the economy and the emerging case for globalisation into a compelling argument that the challenge for advanced industrial nations was to position themselves to secure 'high skill' work, because they could no longer compete with newly industrialising nations on the basis of price alone. Reich advanced the distinctive thesis that the economies of the future would be education-led and, as a consequence, that the challenge for national education and training systems would be to develop the new forms of human capital – 'symbolic analysts' (i.e. people with the ability to manipulate abstract forms of knowledge) – which he maintained were integral to high-skill work.

The idea that we now live and work in a knowledge economy and/or society has gained increasing prominence over the last decade amongst national and supranational policymakers worldwide (European Commission, 2000; National Committee of Inquiry into Higher Education, 1997) and amongst transnational organisations concerned with economic growth (OECD, 1996; World Bank, 2003). The concept of the knowledge economy has come to constitute, paradoxically, both an 'imaginary' (Jessop *et al.*, 2008) and a 'pre-given' reality (Guile, 2006): a quasi-enlightenment vision of economic progress and a new reality that we must *adapt* to through attaining a higher level of qualification.

One of the most well-known expressions of the 'learning' policy position is found in the European Commission's Lisbon Memorandum (European Commission, 2000). This memorandum led to the concept of a knowledge economy being deployed in European Union (EU) policy literature in two senses. It provided a vision of the purpose of all future European economic activity, but also intertwined this vision with a policy for lifelong learning. The most highly influential expression of the readiness position is the development by the World Bank (2008) of its *Knowledge for Development (K4D): Knowledge Assessment Methodology (KAM)*. The *KAM* is an interactive, diagnostic and benchmarking tool that the World Bank is actively encouraging countries and regions to use, to provide a preliminary assessment of the knowledge base of their economies. This will be expressed in terms of the volumes of knowledge-based products and services generated by their economics and qualifications held by their populaces (Robertson, forthcoming).

Despite invoking lifelong learning and knowledge-based products and services as the cornerstone of educational and economic policy, the new argument presented here is that policymakers and transnational agencies have only partially understood the new role of knowledge in the economy and, as a result, only partially grasped the learning challenge of the knowledge economy.

Problems with the conventional wisdom. Policymakers and transnational agencies have only partially grasped the implications of the new role of knowledge in the economy (and by extension more widely within society) because they have both concentrated on one aspect of the account of the new role of knowledge. In the process, they have treated knowledge as an abstract entity that is separate from both the social practices responsible for its codification and its deployment as a resource to generate new products and services in the economy. Moreover, on the rare occasions when they do acknowledge the role of tacit knowledge, they quickly fall back on the language of codification to explain the purpose of that form of knowledge in the economy (Allen, 2002). This interpretation of the social and management theorists' positions about the new role of knowledge in the economy leaves the debate, at the research level, floundering. On one side is the relative importance of theoretical knowledge (Cowan *et al.*, 2000) compared with tacit knowledge (Johnson *et al.*, 2002), and on the other is the extent to which workers are empty vessels who need to be 'filled up' with more knowledge or possess 'hidden' forms of knowledge that employers are disinterested in acknowledging for financial reasons (Livingstone & Sawchuk, 2003). As a consequence, very few writers have considered the relationship that the philosopher Polanyi (1958) – the figure most commonly cited by management theorists to justify the importance of tacit knowledge – maintained exists between theoretical and tacit knowledge, nor pursued the epistemological and ontological – let alone the pedagogic – implications of that relationship.

3

At policy level, this has led, despite the concern for STEM subjects over other forms of knowledge, to an attempt to embrace the theoretical and the tacit into a coherent position. One of the best examples of this development is the EU's three-fold definition of learning: formal learning (i.e. learning that occurs in a structured context and that results in nationally recognised qualifications); non-formal learning (i.e. learning that is embedded in planned activities that are not explicitly designated as learning) and informal learning (i.e. learning that arises from daily life experiences, that traditionally does not lead to certification but may be subject to some form of accreditation/recognition; Colardyn & Bjornavöld, 2004). Although a seemingly progressive development – because it offers a way to acknowledge the importance of different types of knowledge and learning – the EU's policy amounts in practice to little more than a technical exercise of accrediting or validating forms of knowledge and skill that are gained informally and/or non-formal kinds that were previously disregarded, rather than considering the implications of the relation between these forms of knowledge (Guile, 2006).

What is argued here though is that, as a consequence, policymakers and transnational agencies, aiong with the social and management theorists, have failed to recognise that knowledge economies and societies pre-suppose the existence of 'epistemic' (i.e. knowledge) cultures and activities, which foster both the production and utilisation of knowledge, and agreement about the purpose for using knowledge in economic, social and political contexts (Knorr Cetina, 2006). Hence, it is epistemic cultures and forming agreement about economic, political and social goals, not just knowledge itself, that are central not only to the economy but also to societies that 'run on' knowledge and expertise. These cultures constitute the settings in which new theories or new forms of knowledge are produced, and where existing forms of knowledge are recontextualised in new ways to support and/or challenge economic, social and political goals. Without these cultures and goals, there would be no knowledge economy, no experts whose knowledge can be tapped into, nor any debate about the future direction of advanced industrial societies. Furthermore, once we focus on epistemic cultures and practices, we are able to see more clearly than policymakers, transnational agencies and the social and management theorists have previously seen, that what is distinctive about such cultures is that the interdependence between different forms of knowledge – theoretical and tacit, in the same or in different disciplinary fields and professions – and the relation between knowledge and outcomes (i.e. products and services), is more explicit than at any previous point in history.

Arguments for a new learning challenge in the knowledge economy. The above argument implies that firstly, we can no longer conceive of the knowledge economy or society *sui generis*. Instead we should recognise that the knowledge economy/ society exists only where there are cultures concerned with the production of new forms of knowledge, activity, and products and services. Hence it follows that the political challenge is to provide incentives for higher education, firms, professional associations, etc., to create more of these types of culture and/or to support the further spilling-over of extant epistemic cultures into more sections of the economy/society. Secondly, we can infer that the conventional wisdom about the link between the knowledge economy and lifelong learning has to be rethought. Assuming that the increased demand for the 'product' of knowledge in the economy implies only an increased demand for an existing 'educational product' – (i.e. more highly qualified people) as expressed by qualifications (Young, 2000) – is unsatisfactory. It is vital to recognise that the knowledge economy/society implies a new *learning challenge* – the creation of cultures and practices in education and work, which assist people to *mediate* between different forms of knowledge in order to create new practice and objects – and this, in turn, pre-supposes a concern for pedagogy.

This line of argument entails a new challenge for educational institutions and workplaces. This three-fold challenge is to support people to:
– consider and conceptualise the relation between different forms of knowledge
– develop the cultures and practices to use extant and/or new knowledge to create new forms of economic, political and social activity
– identify the different outcomes associated with such economic, political and social activity.

Structure of the Argument

The three points above constitute the starting issues of this book, argued through a focus on the nature of this learning challenge for three particular aspects of learning – professional, vocational and workplace learning – because these forms of learning are central to transition into, continued employment in, and the transformation of the knowledge economy in a way that primary and secondary education are not. This focus enables us to consider the general issues of the relations between theoretical and tacit knowledge, the cultures and practices that support people to mediate these forms of knowledge, and the economic, social and political outcomes of mediation, through reference to their manifestation in working life.

To sustain this focus, we adopt an interdisciplinary approach. The arguments presented in Chapters 2 and 3 introduce the reader to the social and management theorists' views about the new role of knowledge in the economies of advanced industrial societies. It also explains why this has resulted in a rather abstract focus on knowledge, separate from the forms of social practice that enable it to function in the economy in the way that the social and management theorists' claim. We identify the origins of the debate about this new role of knowledge, in Bell's (1973) highly influential argument that theoretical knowledge constitutes the 'axial principle' of innovation and economic growth in such societies. We illustrate how this argument has gained credence in the Social Sciences, as Bell's original ideas were built on and extended by other sociologists, most notably by Castells' (1996) treatise on the role of information in networked societies and to a lesser extent by Stehr's (1994) argument about the role of knowledge work within such societies, and has even informed the critique from Lash and Urry (1994) that cultural knowledge is as important as science in the knowledge economy. We then examine a contrasting view of the new role of knowledge – that it is the tacit knowledge held by workplace communities of practice that are central to economic development – that has been formulated as an alternative to the Bellian orthodoxy in the Social Sciences. Three expressions of this position, by Gibbons *et al.*, (1994), Lundvall (1996), and Nonaka and Takeuchi (1995), are considered.

Chapter 4 is pivotal in three senses. Firstly, we start to broaden the social–scientific frame of analysis by discussing the philosophical origins of the split between theoretical and tacit knowledge in order to demonstrate why the social and management theorists offered different explanations of the new role of knowledge in the economy. We then move on to explore a hitherto under-appreciated feature of knowledge economies/societies – Knorr Cetina's (1999) argument about the role of epistemic cultures to the production and utilisation of scientific knowledge, as well as knowledge in other professionals fields – and argue that if we are to understand the new role of knowledge in the economy and the learning challenge posed by that development, then we need to understand the ways in which culture is constitutive of economic and human development. Having noted that the distinction between theoretical and tacit knowledge is a marginal feature of discussions about the implications of knowledge cultures for professional activity, we return to the distinction between these two types of knowledge. We present an interpretation of Polanyi's ideas about theoretical and tacit knowledge that suggests that they should be seen as interdependent dimensions of, rather than separate types of, knowledge; and we use Zuboff's (1988) discussion of different forms of skill to consolidate this interpretation. Finally, we conclude by suggesting that we should conceive of theoretical and tacit knowledge as having a *mediated* (a term that we explain in Chapter 6) as opposed to a binary relation to one another, and arguing that mediation offers a different starting point for considering the learning challenge of the knowledge economy.

Before addressing this issue, it is necessary to consider the main measures that governments have taken to address the conventional wisdom about the knowledge economy. Using the UK government's policies and measures since the 1980s, Chapter 5 considers how they have repositioned those forms of higher education most closely associated with the knowledge economy, namely professional, vocational and workplace learning (PVWL), to support people to adapt to this new type of economy. It then acknowledges that although many people involved with PVWL have made a determined effort to introduce new pedagogic strategies, referred to here as 'pedagogies of reflection', to help people to bridge both forms of knowledge and link them to experience, these new pedagogic strategies end up perpetuating rather than solving the problem that they were designed to address.

Chapter 6 starts with a discussion of John Dewey's concept of reflection, which is the primary, if under-acknowledged, source of inspiration for the pedagogic developments considered in the previous chapter. The discussion points out that although Dewey had a much more sophisticated conception of reflection than the concept that has been operationalised in the pedagogies of reflection, he conceives of reflection in naturalistic terms. He sees reflection, therefore, as a strategy that we use to transact between the mental and the material, rather than a process that contributes to the development of mind as a conceptually structured capacity that can be exercised practically and descriptively. Crucially, this means that Dewey is unable to provide us with a way to grasp the mediated relation between theoretical and tacit knowledge.

In light of this conclusion, we turn to Lev Vygotsky's theory of cultural mediation, and the theoretical tradition that Vygotsky spawned – Cultural–Historical Activity Theory (CHAT) – to show why it constitutes a conceptual foundation that is a significant advance over Dewey's work in addressing the learning challenge of the knowledge economy. We point out that the philosophical pre-suppositions of Vygotsky's theory are based on the argument that all we live in a humanised rather than a natural world (i.e. one in which forms of experience are culturally and historically constituted). Hence it provides a way to: (i) overcome the philosophical separation and relation between both mind and world, and theoretical and tacit knowledge; (ii) explain the cultural–historical genesis of mind and action; and (iii) identify the pedagogic practices that facilitate the mediation of different forms of knowledge and action.

The implications of Vygotsky's theory of cultural mediation for our understanding of learning is extended and elaborated in Chapter 7 through focusing on a number of writers – Aleksei Leont'ev, James Wertsch, Jean Lave and Etienne Wenger, and Yrjö Engeström – who are widely acknowledged in CHAT for having made significant contributions to the development of mediated conceptions of learning. Readers familiar with the field of CHAT may feel that coining the term post-Vygotskians to reflect the idea of this unifying link between Vygotsky and the work of the aforementioned writers is pejorative, since CHAT abounds with a proliferation of terms that have been very carefully defined to demarcate a theoretical position, and there are significant differences of opinion among writers (Cole, 1996; Daniels, 2001). Nevertheless, we show that the post-Vygotskians' distinction between 'mediation by activity' and 'semiotic mediation' allows us: firstly to introduce, respectively, the role of objects, practices and discourses more explicitly into our understanding of mediation; secondly to identify a number of ways in which practice can develop and, in the process, make a link between mediation and epistemic cultures; and thirdly to broaden Vygotsky's original ideas about the mediated basis of learning. We note that in doing so the post-Vygotskians lose sight of Vygotsky's concern for the central role of reason in the process of mediation.

To restore reason to our argument about the mediated basis of learning, we consider the work of three philosophers in Chapter 8 – Evald Ilyenkov, John McDowell and Robert Brandom. Despite their historical and intellectual separation, we maintain that they have collectively addressed epistemological and ontological issues about the concept of reason that enable us to: (i) re-establish the relation between mediation by activity and semiotic mediation that was an integral, albeit implicit, feature of Vygotsky's theory; (ii) identify a number of key facets of mediation – *restructuring, repositioning, recontextualisation* and *reconfiguration* – that were either a relatively underdeveloped feature of Vygotsky's original theory or that arose from the work of the post-Vygotskians; and (iii) identify a number of expressions of the development of activity – *evolve, laterally branch* and *transform* – that emerged from that discussion.

We use these four facets of mediation and three expressions of the development of activity, along with our argument about the centrality of reason to mediated thinking and acting, to outline in Chapter 9 a conception of learning that is based on understanding the iterative relation between concepts, reasons and action. We conclude that our mediated expressions of learning will play an invaluable part in our reformulation of PVWL.

In the last chapter, we summarise the ways in which the different strands of the argument presented in the book have turned the conventional wisdom about the learning challenge of the knowledge economy on its head. We then argue that a shift has to occur in the tenets that underpin PVWL. This shift is from a concern for adaptation, reflection and qualifications, and towards mediation, objects and reason. We conclude by highlighting the challenge that those parties involved in PVWL will face if they are to enact those tenets and thus address the learning challenge of the knowledge economy.

Given that the cultural–historical tradition that informs the argument presented in this book has been viewed by some writers as having being superseded by the development of neuroscience, the book contains an Afterword. This Afterword recognises the breakthroughs made in neuroscience but reclarifies why the book's core concerns are unlikely ever to be addressed by these breakthroughs. These concerns are to support people to:

- consider and conceptualise the relation between different forms of knowledge;
- develop the cultures and practices to use different forms of knowledge to create new forms of economic, political and social activity;
- identify the different outcomes associated with such economic, political and social activity.

CHAPTER 2

SCIENTIFIC KNOWLEDGE AND THE ECONOMY

INTRODUCTION

We start our exploration of the claim that knowledge in the form of science has become the major factor in economic development by discussing Daniel Bell's book, *The Coming of Post-industrial Society: A Venture in Social Forecasting* (1973), because Bell's argument that scientific knowledge is now the 'axial principle of economic development' has shaped much of the subsequent debate in the Social Sciences about knowledge economies and/or societies[1]. We trace Bell's legacy in two major contributions to the sociological debate about the knowledge economy – Manuel Castells' treatise on the emergence of the 'information age' (Castells, 1996) and Nico Stehr's discussion of 'knowledge work' (Stehr, 1994) – before concluding by considering the case presented in Scott Lash and John Urry's book, *Economies of Signs and Spaces* (Lash & Urry, 1994) that cultural knowledge is as important as science in the knowledge economy.

Scientific Knowledge and Industrial Change

Introduction
Prior to Bell's publication, the role of science in the economy was either viewed as an enabling or potentially subversive element in the process of industrialisation (Kumar, 1995; Touraine, 1969). The more Utopian perspectives on industrial society (which are associated with Comtian-influenced sociologists) viewed science as though it constituted some form of 'enlightenment' (Osborne, 1998, p. 43). They stressed that the application of the logic of science supports the creation of a rationally organised and planned society and, moreover, that this development leads to the replacement of all irrational and particularistic forms of power. In contrast, the more critical perspectives (which are associated with Marxist-influenced sociologists) viewed science either as a form of 'exploitation' or as a form of 'emancipation' (Kumar, 1995, p. 5). The former linked science to the economic, political and military power bases in society and argued that this linking provided the ruling élite with a means to legitimate their specific interests. The latter conceived of Marxism as a form of science that provided a framework for predicting the trajectory of change within societies.

Despite the existence of these two radically different interpretations of the contribution that science could make to the development of industrial societies, both the 'Utopian' and 'critical' theories shared certain assumptions about the character of industrial societies, though they differed about the consequences for economic, political and social development. They both emphasised that land, labour and capital were the most important factors of production, that industrialisation was dependent on their exploitation to produce surplus value to fuel future investment. Where they clashed was when considering how the fruits of industrialisation should be allocated within society (Kumar, 1995). Consequently, until the 1970s, sociologists concentrated primarily on the industrial relationships that helped to shape or challenge the process of production, rather than on the 'technological application of science' that was underpinning the rapid development of new industries.

The shift from an industrial to a post-industrial society.   The shift in the sociological debates about the critical resources for economic development started to take place after the publication of Daniel Bell's (1973) book *The Coming of Post-industrial Society*. Bell used the term 'post-industrial society' to explain the trends he believed were responsible for fundamentally changing 'the social framework of Western society' in the late 1960s and early 1970s. He described his book as an 'essay in social forecasting' (Bell, 1973, p. 3), because it represented an attempt to make sense of the extensive empirical evidence he had amassed about a number of changes in industrial society. Bell drew particular attention to the gradual break-up of what he referred to as 'family capitalism' in industrial society and the changing composition of the labour force, as evidenced by growth in the 'tertiary' (i.e. leisure, travel and tourism, entertainment), 'quaternary' (i.e. education, medicine, social services, environmental health) and 'quinary' (i.e. regulatory bodies) sectors. He maintained that such, 'changes in the social structure posed questions for the rest of (industrial) society', because these changes were resulting in a highly specialised division of labour, the emergence of a new 'technical' mode of management and the escalating influence of science and technology on everyday life in industrial societies (Bell, 1973, p. 13).

Unlike Marx and many other sociologists such as Tocqueville and Weber, who, according to Bell, had sought to provide a 'general theory of social causation' (1973, p. 10) that was applicable to all industrial societies, Bell tried to develop an analytical framework that 'specified not causation but centrality'. In other words, he was positing a method of analysis that allowed him to identify the 'organising frame' that enables societies to change without pre-supposing the outcome of that change (Bell, 1973, p. 10).

To clarify his ideas about the transformation that was occurring, Bell contrasted the different types of economic problem faced by an industrial society with the problems faced by what he called the emerging post-industrial society. The chief economic problem that had confronted societies that were beginning to industrialise was that they had to, 'engage in a game against nature' (Bell, 1973, p. 116). By this he meant that the process of industrialisation involved societies using steam power to transform the 'natural environment' into a 'technical environment'. This pattern of development implied that the most important sectors in industrialising societies were primary sectors, such as mining and farming, that directly supported the transformation of the environment, rather than secondary sectors, such as engineering and technical or semi-skilled factory work, that were directly involved with product design and product manufacture. Consequently, for Bell, the chief economic problem faced by industrial societies was the generation of sufficient financial capital to produce and manufacture goods and services (Waters, 1996), since economic development in industrial societies relied on 'machine technology', that is, the application of manufacturing technology within the process of production.

In contrast, Bell argued that post-industrial societies confronted an entirely different set of circumstances. The primary reason for this change was that economic development increasingly rested on 'intellectual technology' (Bell, 1973, p. 116). Intellectual technology had, according to Bell, two distinctive features: the use of scientific knowledge to specify ways of doing things in a reproducible manner; and the substitution of problem-solving rules (i.e. algorithms) for intuitive judgements. What was distinctive about the new intellectual technology, for Bell, was the collective effort on behalf of policymakers, technocrats and managers to both define rational action and to identify a means for achieving it. Thus, social planning was, for Bell (1973, p. 30), a logical, practical and instrumental process that was determined by the accuracy and precision of the application of knowledge.

Scientific knowledge as the 'axial principle' of society. Although he accepted that some form of knowledge had always been central to the functioning of any society (in the sense that knowledge is an anthropological universal), Bell (1973, p. 164) argued that what was distinctive about post-industrial societies was the change that had occurred in the character of knowledge itself and in the role that it played. He identified this as the 'axial principle' of the post-industrial society, namely the, 'centrality of theoretical knowledge as the source of innovation and policy formation for that society'. This axial principle of the social structure of post-industrial societies refers to the application of codified knowledge, i.e. theoretical or scientific knowledge. (Bell employs the terms interchangeably.) The major change, he claims, is that societies are now dependent on theoretical knowledge as a source and mode of innovation, a development that was particularly apparent in the, 'new science-based industries... computers, telecommunications, optics, polymers and electronics' (Bell, 1973, p. 23). Such industries are, in contrast to earlier models, dependent on the codification of knowledge into abstract systems of symbols that support further innovation and hence the development of new goods and services.

Bell justified this claim by arguing that the exponential growth that had occurred in government-funded research and development (R&D) constituted evidence of the role of knowledge as the axial principle of economic development. He acknowledged that, although the conventional wisdom of the late 1960s and early 1970s accepted that expenditure on R&D constituted a 'financial' measure of the growth of science and technology within society (Bell, 1973, p. 250), there were 'analytical problems' if expenditure on R&D was related to economic growth, scientific productivity and innovation. Nevertheless, Bell (1973, p. 250) argued that it was still possible to employ 'a simple indicator' relating knowledge and economic growth. He defined

11

this simple indicator as, '...the commitment of a country to its scientific and technological potential by the expenditure on R and D [scientific research and development] and, to a secondary extent, on education'.

To illustrate this argument, Bell highlighted how expenditure on R&D in the USA had multiplied by 15 times since the end of the Second World War and argued that this increase had become a symbol to which other countries aspired. Thus Bell concluded that, despite the analytical problems associated with the measurement of knowledge and technology, the revolutionary nature of the new intellectual technology was the driving force behind the shift from industrial to post-industrial societies. This momentum would be sustained, according to Bell, because the sources of innovation were increasingly derived from the research and development agencies. In making this case, Bell extended the factors to be considered within what is referred to as the 'rational choice framework' for innovation (Lundvall, 1996). That framework, up until then, consisted of the following inputs – technology, land, labour and capital – Bell now added a fifth factor – knowledge – and, moreover, maintained that it was now the main factor of economic development[2].

Because he was primarily concerned with what he referred to as, the 'social utility' of knowledge, Bell (1973, p. 175) defined knowledge as:

...a set of organised statements of facts or ideas, presenting a reasoned judgement or an experimental result, which is transmitted to others through some communication medium in some systematic form.

This is a fairly 'restricted definition' because 'knowledge' is limited to a form of 'intellectual property' (1973, p. 175) that is either certified by copyright or through some form of social recognition (for example, a publication). This definition is consistent with Bell's (1973, p. 349) claim that modern societies only survive through a process of constant innovation and by using knowledge to anticipate the future and to plan ahead, because they now have to live by innovation and growth, and theoretical knowledge serves a dual purpose in society. On the one hand, it is central to the process of innovation; on the other hand, it is central to planning and forecasting.

One consequence of the new role of knowledge in society is the change in relative importance of different industrial sectors. Initially, Bell identified two shifts in the division of labour as a result of this trend (Waters, 1996, p. 113). The first shift was a move towards a service economy, that is, a growth in the number of white-collar employers in the 'co-ordination sectors' of the economy (for example, banking and finance) and a corresponding growth in the number of people employed in personal and leisure services. The second shift was the emergence of new, specialised enterprises such as computing companies and the corresponding development of new, specialised occupations, for example, software engineers.

Taken in combination, Bell argued that the shift towards a service-sector economy and the increased application of knowledge as a *source* of economic value constituted a profound transformation in industrial societies. He claimed that instead of the character and wealth of society being determined in terms of a labour theory of value, as traditionally accepted by social scientists, post-industrial societies are being determined by a 'knowledge theory of value':

> ...when knowledge becomes *involved* in some systematic form in the *applied transformation of resources* (through invention and design), then one can say that knowledge, not labour, is the source of value.

(Bell, 1979, pp. 167–8)

Thus, it is the application of knowledge at every stage of the production process (i.e. conception, realisation and distribution) that is responsible for determining the value of a particular good or service. Furthermore, unlike many social theorists of his time or later, Bell raised the implications of his thesis for the content of education. He argued that national systems of education would have to foster a stronger sense of scientific inquiry amongst students from primary education onwards.

Bell's thesis that knowledge constitutes the axial principle of economic development has, as we are about to see, been recast and reinvigorated over the subsequent decades. One of the most notable attempts is Manuel Castells' *The Rise of the Network Society* (1996), which moves beyond Bell's analysis and pins down the implications of the revolution in information and communication technology (ICT) for advanced industrial societies.

Technology and Societal Change Society

Introduction

Two decades passed between the publication of Bell's book and Castells' *The Rise of the Network Society*. This trilogy has been heralded as the single most important analysis of the state of the world produced by a sociologist in at least a generation (Calhoun, 2000; Lyon, 2000; Touraine, 2000; Webster, 1997a). It contains three main lines of argument[3]. The first is a continuation of Bell's argument that knowledge (in Castells' terms, information generation, processing and transmission) has superseded land, labour and capital as the fundamental sources of productivity and power[4]. Castells goes a step further than Bell and maintains that this has resulted in the emergence of a new economic paradigm – an 'informational' economy. The second extends his analysis by introducing two further propositions about this new paradigm: it is 'global' and 'networked'. Thirdly he argues that the emergence of this global and networked informational paradigm is simultaneously hastening an integration of world affairs and bringing about increased social fragmentation, since it has a very uneven impact within and between societies and regions[5].

Castells' debt to Bell. Castells traces the emergence of the 'information age' to the period of economic crisis in the 1970s, which marked the end of what has often been referred to as the 'post-war' settlement (Webster 1997a, p. 71). By taking this period as his starting point, Castells recognises that he is entering similar territory to that covered by a:

> ...well-established tradition in theories of postindustrialism and informationalism, starting with Alain Touraine and Daniel Bell, [of placing] the distinction between

pre-industrialism, industrialism, and informationalism (or postindustrialism) on a different axis than the one opposing capitalism and statism (or collectivism, in Bell's terms)... [in order to] maintain analytical distance and empirical interrelation between modes of production (capitalism, statism) and modes of development (industrialism, informationalism).

(Castells, 1996, p. 14)

Castells takes great pains to acknowledge the affinities between the theoretical and empirical basis of Bell's analysis of the contribution of theoretical knowledge to the development of the post-industrial society and his own analysis of the contribution of information to the development of networked societies. He demonstrates his indebtedness to Bell in three ways. He acknowledges Bell as a 'forebear of informationalism' (Castells, 1996, p. 26). He also adopts explicitly Bell's definition of knowledge as a set of organised statements of facts or ideas that have been worked up through a process of reasoned judgement or empirical study and communicated in some systematic form:

I have no compelling reason to improve on Daniel Bell's own definition of knowledge.

(Castells, 1996, p. 17)

Finally, he consolidates his debt to Bell's fairly traditional conception of knowledge by adopting a definition of information that is more or less congruent with Bell's use of the term, when he defines information as, 'data that have been organised and communicated' (1996, p. 17). Castells, however, relates the increased demand for knowledge and information (and also its increased production) to the revolution that has occurred in information and technology. Although he acknowledges the key role of science in generating the theories and concepts that are responsible for the 'technology revolution' (Castells, 2000, pp. 6–7), Castells is chiefly concerned with, 'the secondary elaboration of data (information) rather than its genesis in scientific activity' (Muller, 2001, p. 287).

Castells is interested in the continued application of science in the form of technology because post-industrial societies were characterised by tremendous advances in computing technology. There are similarities between his views and Bell's view of technological change, because Castells accepted Bell's definition of technology as, 'the use of scientific knowledge to specify ways of doing things in a reproducible manner' (1996, p. 30). Nevertheless, writing twenty years after Bell, Castells focuses on the impact of ICT on society rather than on the automation of production. In common with other writers (Forrester, 1985; Lash & Urry, 1994; Dosi, 1988), Castells argued that ICT was characterised by:

...incomparable memory storage capacity and speed of combination and transmission of bits... [thus, they offer] ...substantially greater flexibility, feedback, interaction and reconfiguration of data, [and] on-line communication, combined with flexibility of text, allows for ubiquitous space/time programming.

(Castells, 2000, p. 30)

It is the knowledge and information (Castells often uses the terms interchangeably or together, i.e. as 'knowledge-based information') generated by ICT that constitute the critical resource to transform economic activity.

Information as the mode of development. Castells, like Bell, firstly insists that social and economic change can be analysed by looking at the relationship between production and development, and secondly develops his position in opposition to his own Marxist past (Webster, 1997b, p. 79)[6]. He contrasts the Marxist concept of the capitalist mode of production with his own concept of the 'informational mode of development' to argue that a dual shift has occurred in capitalist economies. The first is the move away from a mode of production whose primary aim was to maximise output in order to produce surplus profit, towards a new sociotechnical paradigm – an 'informational mode of development' (Castells, 1996, pp. 61–5). Castells claims that this presents modern economies with a new way of creating a given level of wealth, because it is based upon new principles that have led to changes in the organisation of work. The second shift is that, whereas industrialism was focused on maximising output, informationalism is focused on technological development and the generation of data. In other words, 'informationalism' is concerned with the accumulation of wealth through the continuous transformation of existing technologies themselves and through the generation of data that can be used to enhance the performance of those technologies. Informationalism pre-supposes the constant development of knowledge. This process, according to Castells (1996, p. 17), not only supports technological innovation, the ever-increasing application of technology and higher levels of complexity in information processing, but also supports increased productivity and profitability.

Castells rests his case for the informational paradigm on five specific features of the new information and communication technologies. The features of these new technologies can be summarised as follows. They:
- act on information, the new raw material of economic activity, not just technology as in earlier technological revolutions;
- are pervasive: they become an integral part of all human activity since all processes (i.e. economic, social, cultural, political) are shaped by the new technology;
- extend the possibility of the networking logic to all parts of the economy;
- can be used flexibly, thus allowing organisations to fundamentally alter, re-arrange and modify technological components;
- engender industrial and technological convergence, since new integrated information systems are emerging that embody computing and telecommunication technology and are leading to the creation of new industries, new products and new forms of knowledge.

(summarised from Castells, 1996, p. 61; 2000, pp. 70–71)

Hence Castells argues that the new information technologies provide the technological basis for a new type of economy. Initially, in the first edition of *The Rise of the Network Society*, he claimed that this new economy had two intertwined and distinguishing features. It was *informational*: the productivity of the units or agents in this economy, whether firms, regions or nations, fundamentally depends on their capacity to generate, process and apply knowledge-based information efficiently. Hence, the economic challenge is to find ways to realise more of the productive potential in mature industries and economic activities, such as car manufacturing, or in emerging scientific fields, such as genetic engineering (Castells, 1996, pp. 47–50); and, it was *global*: the core activities of production, consumption and circulation, as well as their components – capital, labour, raw materials management, information technology and markets – were organised on a global scale. In the second edition of the book, Castells introduces a third feature by explicitly developing a theme that was an implicit aspect of his earlier argument. He argues that the new economy is also a *networked* economy, because in the new informational paradigm, productivity is generated through, and played out in, a global network of interaction and not just a national context. Castells acknowledges though that this informational and networked pattern is an inherently uneven phenomenon often exacerbating existing differences between regional economies (Calhoun, 2000, p. 35).

One of the defining features of the new paradigm in Castells' (1996, p. 67) view is that the products of the new information technology industries are information-processing devices or information processing itself: 'the action of knowledge upon knowledge itself (is now) the main source of productivity'. Thus, from his perspective, a decisive shift has occurred in the nature of economic activity and the role of knowledge within that activity. However, instead of perceiving economic activity as relying primarily on the theoretical knowledge produced in universities and research institutes, as Bell postulated, Castells introduces a new focus. He argues that economic activity is inextricably tied up with the tremendous advances that are continually occurring in information-processing technology. Information processing in the private and public sectors, as he explains, focuses on:

> ...improving the technology of information processing as a source of productivity, in a virtuous circle of interaction between the knowledge sources of technology and the application of technology to improve knowledge generation and information processing.

> (Castells, 1996, p. 17)

The result, for Castells, is that the spatial and temporal nature of work is being profoundly transformed because the new technologies serve as a conduit to transmit and process information in a rapid but fairly unproblematic way[7]. He points out that until the information technology revolution occurred, human experience had been historically rooted, socially organised and constrained by spatial location. He maintains that space and time have been radically transformed by the combined effect of informationalism and the new economic activities associated with that paradigm. Castells (1996, p. 412) invokes the term the 'space of flows' to encapsulate the idea of the 'material organization of the time-sharing social practices that work flows through'. By 'flows', Castells means the purposeful, programmable sequences of exchange and interaction that are experienced as occurring horizontally between communities and individuals. The phrase 'time-sharing social practices' refers to the way in which distinctive types of social practice, R&D, production and distribution, have been brought together in such a way that they come to share a work culture and instrumental goals aimed at producing new knowledge, new processes and new products.

He notes that this development has had a number of effects and is contributing to the transformation of economic activity. Instead of companies specialising in all aspects of production, distribution and marketing, corporations form strategic alliances, enter into licensing and subcontracting arrangements and either transform operating units into networks or create temporary networks to create new products and services (Castells, 1996, p. 65). It is also resulting in networks becoming the context for the exchange of commodities such as 'know-how', technological capability or a particular approach or style of production whose value is not easily measured. This is partially happening because it is not always easy in the market to exchange novel technological know-how, consequently the locus of innovation lies ever more in inter-organisational relationships that are based not on written contracts but on the norms of reciprocity that reflect the, 'complementarity of the knowledge, resources and interests of the actors' (Powell, Koput & Smith, 1996, p. 119). The space of flows is also contributing to the creation of a culture of 'real virtuality', where all manner of media are combined into a single hypertext system – text, visual image, aural communications – and become the basis of new products and/or new services; for example, MySpace, which can be endlessly reconfigured by producers and users, and Facebook, which can support virtual social networking.

The significance of the preceding discussion for our argument is to show why Castells' three interconnected concepts – informationalism, globalisation and networks – constitute a compelling series of metaphors that can be used to identify the changing character of the global economy and work in that economy. The latter issue is however treated at a very general level in Castells' trilogy (Thrift, 2004). For this reason, we now consider the work of Nico Stehr.

Knowledge Societies and Knowledge Work

Introduction
Writing, like Castells, twenty years after Bell's thesis about the onset of the post-industrial society, Stehr highlights another manifestation of Bell's argument that theoretical knowledge constitutes the axial principle of economic development. Instead of following Bell and concentrating on the current ways in which science and scientific research are applied to the organisation of production, Stehr draws attention to two subsequent developments. First, the ways in which governments and corporations have organised societies to support the further production and application of scientific knowledge. Second, the way in which this development has impacted on the organisation of work.

Knowledge and knowledge work. The outcomes of scientific research (for example, the data and systems that emerge from natural and physical sciences as much as social and human sciences) produce and reproduce the knowledge structure of society, and Stehr describes this process as the 'scientisation' of production and consumption (Stehr, 1994, pp. 10–11). The idea that theoretical knowledge has now penetrated into every sphere of modern society and, in doing so, has dramatically enlarged the available options for social action in cultural, economic, political and social life, paves the way for Stehr to discuss the role of knowledge work in advanced industrial societies[8].

The term 'knowledge work' was originally coined by Machlup in the early 1960s to distinguish knowledge work from other forms of work. Machlup is often wrongly interpreted as arguing that knowledge work was a new phenomenon; the substance of his argument was, however, that there were now more knowledge workers than ever before (Cortada, 1998, p. xvi). He defined knowledge work as those forms of work that were responsible for processing and transmitting types of knowledge, and which helped people to learn something they had not known previously. Thus Machlup operated with a very broad definition and this led him to, for example, count a clerical worker as a 'knowledge worker'.

Based on his argument about the scientisation of society, Stehr (1994, p. 179) questions whether it is meaningful to identify clerical or similar types of work as knowledge work. He further argues that we should define knowledge work by differentiating between the extent to which such work involves the production of new theoretical knowledge, or the accumulation of additional information in a given occupational field, to either improve or monitor the productive process, rather than continuing to use definitions of knowledge work that are merely concerned with the processing and transmission of such knowledge.

Although couched in different language, Stehr's ideas about knowledge work have many affinities with Beck, Giddens and Lash's argument (1994, p. vi) about the development of a much more 'reflexive' global culture. For them, national institutions such as universities, corporations and individuals use knowledge to reflect critically on their own social practices and the wider social practices in which they are inevitably bound up, as well as to continue the traditional scientific/social scientific approach of the radical problematising of pre-suppositions and practices.

For Stehr, Giddens' (1990, p. 17) notion of 'expert-systems' offers a way to pursue the implications of these developments. Giddens uses this term to explain the growth of systems of technical and/or professional expertise that are responsible for either organising large areas of the material and social environments in which we live in traditional institutional settings, for example, government agencies, or in emerging institutional settings, for example, counselling and therapy services that assist us to survive in that environment. Such knowledge workers are, according to Stehr, differentiated from other types of workers by the purpose of their work, such as the principles behind the application of knowledge, rather than broad-based measures, like job descriptions. Based on this line of reasoning, Stehr (1994, p. 183) concludes that knowledge work can be defined in terms of those who:

> ...consult, provide guidance to others, counsel, or give expert advice, as the group of occupations engaged in the *transmitting* and *applying* of knowledge.

This definition reflects not only Stehr's (1994, p. 95) idea that knowledge constitutes a 'capacity for action', but also Giddens' idea that certain forms of work have developed to assist people use knowledge reflexively (i.e. consider options) to address political, professional and personal issues – a paradigmatic example would be management consultants. As a consequence, both writers adhere to an intra-professional conception of knowledge work. From this perspective, knowledge work pre-supposes that experts use the principles that underpin the technical content of a field of knowledge to explain its relevance to the task in hand, that we use those principles to guide our application of that knowledge, and to appraise critically the implications of the course of action we adopt.

CONCLUSION

We have seen that the social theorists discussed in this chapter have generated a number of new concepts, such as post-industrial society, network society and knowledge society, to explain the new type of societies that they claimed were emerging. They have also introduced a number of new ideas about the role of knowledge in the economy, such as axial principle and informationalism, and for work. Our discussion has allowed us to see that the unifying link between Bell, Castells and Stehr's argument, that theoretical knowledge is the critical form of knowledge for economic development, is that they all assumed that knowledge is a discernible cultural object. Further, they accepted that knowledge can be transferred unproblematically from one context to another to facilitate economic, political and social development, and that knowledge workers were central to this process.

This emphasis on the primacy of theoretical knowledge as the critical resource within the knowledge economy underpins the 'strong' argument about the knowledge economy, that it is dependent on exponential investment in and exploitation of science to create the key knowledge-based industries of the 21st century such as nanotechnology and robotics (Thurow, 1997) that surfaced during the 1990s. This view is supported by the transnational consensus about the importance of supporting R&D in the fields of science, technology, engineering and mathematics (STEM). This argument is, however, hotly contested by other social theorists and in other branches of the Social Sciences.

In the case of the former, the focus on science and technology was first challenged by Lash and Urry in the early 1990s, by acknowledging the contribution that the cultural sector – for example, advertising, performing arts, film, television and new media – made to the economy, and that cultural knowledge made to production of 'design intensive' goods and services in all spheres of economic activity[9]:

> ...production has become not just more knowledge infused, but more generally cultural; that it has become not just a question of a new primacy of information-processing, but of a more generic symbol-processing capacities. In the culture industries the input is aesthetic rather than cognitive in quality.

> (Lash & Urry, 1994, p. 123)

Furthermore, Lash and Urry (1994, p. 108) argued that the growing importance accorded to such signifying practices in the production process has started to have an effect on the internal life of organisations as well. It has, in part, heralded a 'turn to culture' in the world of business and organisation, premised on the belief that competing in the global economy is influenced by the ways in which people conduct themselves in organisations and when working with clients. In making this dual argument, Lash and Urry have broadened the social theorists' argument about both the role of theoretical knowledge within the economy and within society: they have acknowledged the increased importance of aesthetic knowledge to the design of new products and services, and added a cultural dimension to Bell, Castells and Stehr's technicist account of knowledge work[10].

In the case of the latter, there is a considerable body of thought that affirms that another form of knowledge – tacit knowledge – is at least as, if not more, important than science to economic development. This issue is discussed in the next chapter.

NOTES

[1] The contribution of knowledge as a factor in production has had a fairly 'hidden' history in Economics. For a recent assessment, see the special issue of *The International Social Science Journal, 171* (Feb–March 2002).

[2] One of the main influences on Bell's thinking was the collection of theoretical and empirical studies produced by the highly celebrated American economist Robert Solow (1957) on the contribution of technology to productivity. Solow described the fundamental sources of long-run growth in terms of the link between capital accumulation, labour-force growth and technical progress. From Solow's perspective, increases in productivity are a result of the increased technological application of science in the economy that leads to shifts in the ratio between labour and capital. Thus, unlike earlier generations of economists, Solow acknowledged that factors such as technology, which are exogenous to the basic components of economic theory (i.e. investment in capital and the growth rate of the labour force), carry equal importance with those components in raising levels of productivity.

[3] It is important to note that Bell claims that Castells has not advanced significantly his thesis about the role of knowledge within the economy, nor distinguished between the different functions knowledge and information serve in the economy (Bell, 1999, pp. xxiii–xxiv).

[4] In the second edition of *The Rise of the Network Society*, Castells links his argument about informationalism to the debate in contemporary economics about the emergence of the 'new economy' (2000, pp. 77–147). His intention, as he makes clear, is to demonstrate the similarity between the two arguments. He argues that his thesis, the 'informational age', is based on three assumptions about the economy: that it is global, informational and networked. In contrast, he argues that the proponents of the new economy mainly focus on the accelerating impact of globalisation and the deployment of ICT, and tend to play down the 'networked' dimension of the new economic conditions. The exposition of Castells' analysis in this chapter concentrates on his argument around the impact of ICT on economic activity. It does not stray into the 'new economy' debate.

[5] The account presented in this chapter of Castells' thinking concentrates mainly on the implications of 'informationalism' in relation to economic activity; an argument he presented in the first volume of his trilogy, and in the revised second edition (2000).

[6] Having originally adopted a Marxist mode of analysis, Bell rejected this theoretical tradition. He conceived of his work from the early 1960s as an attempt to go beyond what he felt were the theoretical weakness of Marxist preoccupations with general theories of social causation (Bell, 1973, p. 10). Castells, however, has continually endeavoured to rethink the relationship between his developing scholarship and particular Marxist concepts, such as the mode of production. *The Rise of*

the Network Society (1996) attempts to spell out the advantages as well as the inequities and injustices of a 'networked' world.

[7] One of the main reasons that Castells often conflates knowledge and information throughout the three volumes of *The Rise of the Network Society* is that he is mainly interested in identifying the economic effects of knowledge/information. Thus, he never discusses the social practices that enable knowledge/information to support economic development; an issue that will be addressed in Chapter 4.

[8] In a later book *The Fragility of Modern Societies* (2001), Stehr discusses the implication of this development for the 'governance' (Stehr, 2001, p. 71) of 'knowledge societies' (Stehr, 2001, p. 93), for the 'policing' of knowledge (Stehr, 2001, p. 114) to protect different communities' (i.e. religious, political, etc.) interests, values and beliefs.

[9] The creative and cultural sector spans traditional craft and artisan industries, such as craft, design and fashion, as well as longstanding professionalised industries, such as TV and radio, and new-media industries, such as video games and web design. The UK is ranked third in the global creative economy, behind America and Japan. The UK's creative and cultural sector generates revenues of around £115 billion and employs 1.3 million people. They contribute over £10 billion in exports and account for over five per cent of Gross Domestic Product (GDP). Moreover, output from these sectors grew by more than twice that of the economy as a whole in the late 1990s (DCMS, 2001).

[10] Their argument has also served as a forerunner for, what became known in the early 2000s as, the 'Florida thesis' (Florida, 2002), that is, the idea that the creative and cultural sector constituted the major source of growth and renewal for advanced industrial economies, and resulted in a worldwide clamour to establish creative 'hubs' and 'cities' to provide the conditions to attract and retain 'creative' people.

TACIT KNOWLEDGE AND THE ECONOMY

INTRODUCTION

We present here the counter-argument to the claim that theoretical knowledge is the axial principle of economic development. This alternative view, which gives primacy to tacit knowledge, has its origins in the field of what we have defined as 'management studies'[1] and, as we saw in Chapter 1, constitutes the other world of knowledge. The argument presented in this chapter is much more multi-faceted than the social theorists' case for theoretical knowledge and, for this reason, we discuss a number of accounts of the role of tacit knowledge in the economy. The strands of the argument are that: (i) tacit knowledge is the most important and difficult kind of knowledge to put to work in the economy, and therefore the economic challenge facing all societies is to 'learn' how to put such knowledge to work (Lundvall, 1996; Lundvall & Archibugi, 2001; Johnson, Lorenz & Lundvall, 2002); (ii) new modes of the production of knowledge – 'Mode 2' (Gibbons *et al.*, 1994) – have emerged that are significantly determined by a firm's, or a network of firms', stock of tacit knowledge and these modes are just as important as theoretical knowledge to economic development; and (iii) there is an 'epistemological dimension' to firms' production of new products and services that renders tacit knowledge the most important form of knowledge in this process and, by extension, for knowledge work (Nonaka & Takeuchi, 1995).

Putting Tacit Knowledge to Work in the Economy

Introduction
We saw in Chapter 1 that Drucker had acknowledged the importance of tacit knowledge to economic development in the 1960s, but that the hegemony of Bell's argument that theoretical knowledge constituted the axial principle of economic development obscured the significance of Drucker's insight in social theory and sociology. Since then, the contribution of tacit knowledge to economic development has gradually been acknowledged, as the field of management studies has become more prominent in the social sciences. We start the discussion here by considering Lundvall's work, as he has provided one of the most influential and widely cited accounts of the role of tacit knowledge in the economy.

The cornerstone of Lundvall's argument is that standard economic theory and policy have become increasingly incapable of explaining economic development. He argues, following Drucker, that all forms of knowledge have to be shared more widely in firms and networks if knowledge is to facilitate economic development and social regeneration (Lundvall, 1996, p. 4). Tacit knowledge is the most important and tricky kind of knowledge to put to work in the economy, according to Lundvall and colleagues, because it is embodied in people and embedded in networks; thus it follows that the demanding challenge all economies face is to learn how to share and apply tacit knowledge. Lundvall, along with other colleagues, invokes the concept of the 'learning economy' to encapsulate the nature of this challenge (Lundvall, 1996; Johnson, Lorenz & Lundvall, 2002; Lundvall & Archibugi, 2001; Foray & Lundvall, 1996).

The concept of a learning economy.   Lundvall (1996, p. 2) employs his concept of the learning economy in two senses: as a theoretical perspective on the economy, 'where the emphasis is on explaining and understanding the process of change in technology, skills, preferences and institutions'; and to refer to, 'specific historical trends which make knowledge and learning increasingly important at all levels of the economy'. He defines a learning economy as:

> ...an economy where the success of individuals, firms, regions and national economies reflect their capability to learn (and to *forget*, which is often a pre-requisite especially for learning new skills). The learning economy is an economy where change is rapid and where the rate at which old skills get obsolete and new ones become in demand is high.

> (Lundvall, 1996, p. 2)

Lundvall's concept differs from Castells' ideas about the informational society because, although Lundvall recognises that the economy is affected by ICT, he is not concerned with information processing; his notion of a learning economy is concerned with the collective building of human competence at the micro-, meso- and macro-levels to foster and sustain innovation. The concept also differs from Bell's ideas about a science-based economy in two senses: Lundvall, unlike Bell, acknowledges the value of all forms of knowledge to economic growth, and their value in all sectors of the economy.

To clarify his argument about the link between tacit knowledge, learning and economic development, Lundvall (1996, p. 5) differentiates between the four kinds of knowledge. They are: *know-what* knowledge, for example, learning facts; know-why knowledge, for example, principles and laws of motion in nature, in the human mind and in society (a knowledge type that has been extremely important for scientific and technological development); *know-how* knowledge, for example, the capability to do something in a community or industrial context (the kind of knowledge that is kept within the borders of a firm or research team); and *know-who* knowledge, for example, the social capability to establish relationships and involve people in networks and projects.

He argues that we learn each type of knowledge in very different ways. Know-what and know-why knowledge are typically learnt through study in an educational institution or through self-directed study. In contrast, know-how knowledge is typically learnt through progressing along the novice-to-master continuum, most commonly via apprenticeship/internship/case-orientated study. Know-how is an embodied form of knowledge, built up over time through immersion in professional and organisational cultures, and rarely articulated explicitly. Following Polanyi, Lundvall (1996, p. 4) refers to the implicit dimension of know-how as tacit knowledge, arguing that it is difficult to transmit such knowledge, because it is personally and socially embedded, and it inevitably loses some of its intrinsic qualities if it is codified in order to move it from one context to another.

For this reason, Lundvall maintains that his fourth form of knowledge, know-who, is increasingly important in the economy. Instead of trying to codify and transfer know-how, he argues that a more effective strategy is for people to develop the capability to recognise, 'who knows what and who knows to do what', to establish relationships with such specialised groups and to involve them in networks and projects in order to 'draw upon their expertise' (Lundvall, 1996, p. 6). This type of knowledge, as Lundvall observes, cannot be taught in the conventional sense through attending courses; it has to be developed through social networking.

Lundvall develops his argument about the link between tacit knowledge, economic development and learning in the economy by comparing the assumptions of classical economic theory with the assumptions that underpin his concept of a learning economy. He points out that the theoretical core of neo-classical economics – the lineage from Smith via Schumpter to Hayek – is concerned with 'making choices between well-defined alternatives' and the 'allocation of scarce resources' in accordance with rational principles to establish an economic equilibrium (Lundvall, 1996, p. 7). The challenge in a learning economy, however, is to innovate in two senses: to create new products and services, and the new forms of activity to support their production. The learning-economy perspective thus differs from the standard neo-economic framework in two important respects.

> First, what is treated as a given framework for rational choice – technologies, preferences and institutions – are assumed to be in a process of flux – they are learnt and forgotten as time goes by... Second, the focus is not so much on allocating existing resources as on the creation of new use-values, products and services.

His argument is illustrated diagrammatically in the table below:

		Criteria to facilitate development	
		Allocation	Innovation
Criteria for economic development	Making choices	Rational decision	Agreeing criteria to guide creation of new products and services
	Learning	Allocation of resources	Putting know-how and know-who knowledge to work

(modified from Lundvall, 1996, p. 8)

Figure 1. Four different perspectives in economic analysis.

The global economy is, for Lundvall (1996, p. 8), in a constant state of 'accelerating change', consequently the challenge for firms is to focus on the creation of new ideas and new things, and know-how and know-who knowledge are central to this process. Lundvall acknowledges that other writers who draw the same conclusions about the importance of learning to economic development do not necessarily agree with him about the importance of tacit knowledge. In fact, Lundvall's former colleague Dominique Foray draws a very different conclusion. Working with Paul David, he advances a modern version of Bell's original argument about the role of theoretical knowledge in the economy and Castells' argument about the use of ICT to process knowledge. Cowan, David and Foray (2000) maintain that there is 'no kind of knowledge which is tacit by nature', because all forms of knowledge are susceptible to codification, and moreover that the increased deployment of ICT is accelerating the tendency towards codification, not least because, 'the testing and the design of new products occurs through virtual experiments using computer simulations'.

Lundvall highlights the limitations of this argument through reference to his knowledge taxonomy. He notes that the incentive to codify was the driving force behind the first phase of 'knowledge management' in the corporate sector, and that it resulted in the development of 'encyclopedian databases' of know-how knowledge in companies throughout the world and in Herculean efforts to simulate the mental operations of specialists in order to transfer knowledge and skill within organisations (Davenport & Prusak, 1997). These efforts have, as Lundvall presciently observes, faltered, and the second generation of knowledge management has recognised the difficulties associated with trying to codify know-how and know-who knowledge. First, work on experts systems has demonstrated that the transfer of know-how from a tacit into a codified expert-system form is far from straightforward; it is difficult to incorporate intuitive knowledge and skills into software programmes (Hatchuel & Weil, 1994), and registers of names cannot hope to capture the intricacies of social network relationships. Furthermore, some of the:

> ...tendencies emphasised by the protagonists of the codification trend have contradictory effects on the relative importance of tacit knowledge and on learning-by-doing and learning-by-interacting... [because the] ...steep increase in the amount of data to which there is public access implies that specific skills become of even greater importance than before.

> (Lundvall, 1996, p. 7)

The rapid increase in the volume of codified data and the growing importance of tacit knowledge in the economy has created a paradoxical development. The former increases the demand for people to develop the capability to recognise new patterns in the data, to select relevant and disregard irrelevant data and to learn new (and forget old) skills. By highlighting the important differences between the types of tacit knowledge developed in different fields of expertise and/or practical activity, the latter re-affirms why know-why knowledge is so critical to building teams and networks in order to collaborate to create new products and services. The ensuing learning challenge is to support people to develop the capability to do both.

Learning, trust and the market. Lundvall's (1992) background in studying national innovation systems – which always consisted of a balance between internal factors such as institutions and cultures – and external factors such as policy frameworks – led him to use Romer's (1986) work on 'endogenous growth theory' to conceptualise the relation between learning and the operation of the market (Romer, 1986)[2]. From this perspective, economic growth is spurred as much, if not more, by firms' internal and networked activities with one another, rather than on access to land, labour and capital. It is a short step from this emphasis on firms' internal activities to Lundvall's interest in the critical contribution of know-how and know-who knowledge in facilitating innovations in products and services. Trade in such knowledge and skill is, however, always difficult because there will always be an:

> ...asymmetry between the seller, who knows the information, and the buyer, who is willing to pay for it only because he does not have full access to it. There will be uncertainty involved and quite some room for opportunistic behaviour. This is why trust will play a key role as a prerequisite for successful trading in information. In more complex situations where different parties are involved in a process of interactive learning, trust will play an even more fundamental role.

(Lundvall, 1996, p. 14)

Drawing on his earlier work, Lundvall (1996, p. 14) argues that know-how and know-who knowledge are often expressed in 'local codes' and associations shared by all parties who are involved in the innovation process, and that the significance of these codes and associations lies beyond the comprehension of the traditional neo-classical perspective about the operation of markets, which tends to focus on the actual costs of land, labour and capital. Thus, they marginalise or even dismiss the significance of the more intangible factors such as 'local knowledge'. The logic of this position therefore implies:

> ...a need to generalise this special case [i.e. analyses of features of national innovation] to a broader set of interactions involving learning. While it is *difficult* to exchange information in the pure market, it is impossible to get access to tacit knowledge through ordinary market transactions. There are different prototypes of learning new skills but they all have in common their strong roots in the social system.

(Lundvall, 1996, p. 14)

Given that learning in general is affected by trust, and that the process of learning know-how and know-who knowledge is even more strongly affected by trust, Lundvall suggests the creation of a learning economy pre-supposes a premium on trust and people who can promote trust. Trust though, as Arrow (1962) presciently pointed out, 'cannot be bought, and if it could be bought it would have no value whatsoever'; and, as Fukuyama (1992) has highlighted more recently, trust depends on the creation of and sustaining of 'social capital', that is, webs or networks of people who are committed to sharing their accumulated cultural capital, rather than engaging in a zero-sum game of trying to eliminate one another from the market. Thus, Lundvall (1996, p. 17) concludes that the learning economy cannot neglect the 'social dimension of learning', that is, the ways in which societies formulate policies to assist all sections of the population to learn how to use these forms of knowledge. Realising this goal pre-supposes, for Lundvall, the introduction of a new education and training – a 'New New Deal' – to strengthen the learning capability of those who are weak in this respect.

Tacit Knowledge and New Modes of Knowledge Production

Introduction

We now move onto the second expression of the argument about the role of tacit knowledge in the economy. This expression has emerged as a result of the changing relationship between science and society in the past half-century. This can be characterised as a shift from the assumption that science was separate from society, governed by its own norms, values and methods of inquiry and that it constituted the major source of enlightenment[3], to a gradual acceptance by policymakers, scientists and philosophers of science that science is inextricably connected to society (Osborne, 1998)[4]. We can summarise the reasons for this change in the status of science as follows:

– the intensification of a tripartite alliance[5] between universities, industry and the state has significantly broadened the range of interest groups, frequently referred to as the 'triple helix' (Etzkowitz & Leydesdorff, 1997), that are concerned with the production of knowledge in advanced industrial societies;
– the process of globalisation, which has placed a far greater emphasis upon the 'performativity' (Lyotard, 1984, p. 3) of knowledge, and made the new research partnerships and the forms of knowledge they develop more responsive to the demands of business (Shin, 1999, p. 152);
– the increased 'risks' associated with the commercial exploitation of science and technology have led societies to become more distrustful of science and to contest its knowledge claims (Beck, 1987, p. 1).

A manifestation of this new relationship between science and society has been the significant change in the organisation of certain aspects of science and research practice. Michael Gibbons and his colleagues have provided in their book *The New Production of Knowledge* (1994, p. 1), the most widely debated account of this type of change. The authors state the book's core thesis in the following terms:

> …the parallel expansion in the number of potential knowledge producers on the supply side and the expansion of the requirements of specialist knowledge on the demand side are creating the conditions for the emergence of a new mode of knowledge production.

> (Gibbons *et al.*, 1994, p. 13)

Gibbons and colleagues (1994, p. 4) propose that a process of de-differentiation has been occurring between science and non-science spheres. They claim that one of the outcomes of this process is that science has begun to lose its distinctive cognitive and institutional character, and that, in the process, a new organising principle for the production of knowledge has been generated. This development, according to Gibbons *et al*. is fundamentally transforming the pattern of activity and the relationships between universities, government research institutes and private industrial laboratories[6].

The emergence of a new mode of knowledge.   Gibbons *et al*. distinguish between two modes of the production of knowledge, which they term 'Mode 1' and 'Mode 2'. The former has traditionally been associated with disciplinary-based research conducted in universities, while the latter is a mode of knowledge production carried out outside universities. Mode 2 is based on teams of university and business researchers creating a new type of knowledge that incorporates theoretical insights from many disciplines, hence the idea of transdisciplines and insights gleaned from practical experience[7]. For Gibbons *et al*. (1994, pp. 2–3), Mode 1 refers to a mode of knowledge production that has grown up to:

> ...control the diffusion of the Newton model (of science) to more and more fields of enquiry and to ensure its compliance with what is considered to be sound scientific practice.

Mode 1 has been characterised historically by the following features:
– problems have been set and solved in a context that is governed by the academic community alone;
– it seeks constantly to accumulate more knowledge in a given field either through building on or adding to the existing stock of knowledge;
– Mode 1 knowledge has been characterised historically by a high degree of homogeneity of knowledge producers;
– standards of scientific excellence have been decided in accordance with a process of rigorous, anonymous academic peer review as the main form of public accountability.

Thus Mode 1 is, for Gibbons *et al*., a convenient, albeit oversimplified, way to summarise the cognitive and social norms that have traditionally influenced the production, legitimisation and diffusion of scientific knowledge.

In contrast, Gibbons *et al*. employ the term 'Mode 2' to describe the mode of production of knowledge that they claim is being developed now in advanced industrial societies to support economic, social and political changes. Mode 2 knowledge can be distinguished from Mode 1 knowledge in a number of ways.

Firstly, Mode 2 knowledge is produced in a 'context of application'; by this Gibbons and colleagues (1994, p. 19) mean that there is a situation, '...where knowledge is developed for and put to use, while results – which would have traditionally been characterised as applied – fuel further theoretical advances'. Moreover, the actual process of research is guided by principles of design originally developed in an industrial context, rather than traditional scientific inquiry, because the outcome of the knowledge production process is a form of technologically contextualised knowledge. Contexts of application are defined by a process of continuous

29

negotiation of the needs, interests and specifications of stakeholders, such as universities, industry and government. The main issue is whether the knowledge that is produced has a utility value that meets the needs of the interest groups that were involved in negotiating the original research specification, and this will vary in accordance with their relative status in the interest group (Jacob & Hellstrom, 1999).

A second way that the production of Mode 2 knowledge is distinctively different from Mode 1, is that it involves teams of diverse specialists whose intellectual agenda is not set by a particular discipline. Mode 2 generates its own distinctive theoretical structures, research methods and modes of practice. Moreover, the solution to problems can be both empirical and conceptual (though not necessarily based on disciplinary knowledge), and results are communicated as practitioners move from one context of application (i.e. membership of a research team or an area of production) to another (Gibbons et al., 1994, p. 5). A classic example of Mode 2 knowledge production according to Gibbons et al. (1994, pp. 20–22) is the links that have been established between the aeronautical industry and university-based physics departments in the attempt to build a 'hypersonic aircraft'. The success of this project depends on solving the problem of propulsion generated by an aerobic motor that, 'uses air as the combustant rather than oxygen mass'. The formulation of the research agenda to address this issue cannot be understood, as Gibbons et al. (1994, p. 20) observe, without paying attention to prior developments in technology, which structure the context of application.

A further way that Mode 2 is different is that, in many instances, firms are the sites for research and development. Gibbons et al. (1994, p. 25) note that commercial applications are developed in the main in companies or business units rather than universities. This development means that firms have to:

> ...configure the competence of individuals into a distinct, firm-specific know-ledge base which will form the core of its capability to compete in national and international markets.

Thus, unlike Mode 1 knowledge – which tends to grow homogeneously through the acquisition of more knowledge in the same disciplinary field – Mode 2 knowledge grows heterogeneously, since an integral element is tacit knowledge held by communities of professionals and this constitutes the critical resource for its production, according to Gibbons et al. (1994, p. 45).

The challenge of producing knowledge in such contexts of application is best understood, according to Gibbons et al. (1994, p. 24), through reference to the distinction between 'codified' and 'tacit' knowledge[8]. This distinction was originally coined by Polanyi (1958) to indicate the philosophical limitations of conceiving of scientific knowledge in purely abstract, formal terms. Gibbons et al. do not explicate the way in which they have chosen to interpret Polanyi's original distinctions; they simply use the terms 'codified' and 'tacit' to clarify what is distinctive about Mode 2 knowledge. They define codified knowledge as the systematically organised, stored and retrievable forms of knowledge, which can be represented by disciplinary knowledge, a form of operational knowledge expressed in protocols and manuals, or the proprietary knowledge that is subject to licensing and commercialisation

(Gibbons *et al.*, 1994, p. 22). Tacit knowledge, on the other hand, is defined as the form of personal knowledge gained from experience of work and held by professions working in transdisciplinary teams.

Predating Lundvall by a few years, Gibbons *et al.* (1994, p. 24) developed an earlier version of his argument. They maintained that the competitive advantage of firms in the knowledge economy increasingly 'lies less in a firm's pool of proprietary knowledge than on its base of tacit knowledge', because the former can be traded in open markets whereas the latter cannot. As a consequence, the challenge for firms is to nurture and utilise their own pool of tacit knowledge to develop the internal capability to create new products and services based on modes of knowledge that are less susceptible to being traded. This development further consolidates the shift in the locus of R&D detected by Castells and Lundvall by adding a new dimension. R&D is no longer exclusively an exogenous process, carried on outside firms either in partnership with universities or separately from firms. Gibbons *et al.* note that R&D is now increasingly conceived as an endogenous process, that is, carried out inside firms and not necessarily involving universities. The challenge facing firms who engage in this new mode of knowledge production involves:

> ...not merely the reallocation of existing resources... but through experiment discovering configurations of knowledge which convey a commercial advantage on a recurrent basis. In this process new knowledge is created which provides the base for the next set of advances... [in the design and delivery of products and services.]

(Gibbons et al., 1994, p. 68)

As firms become more R&D-intensive their costs increase exponentially, in particular because the cost of maintaining an all-inclusive, in-house capability is prohibitive. This has led many firms to form partnerships with other firms and/or create alliances and enterprise webs to spread the R&D costs and risks. Gibbons *et al.* observe that this development has particular consequences for the production of Mode 2:

> Because problems and solutions cannot be defined in advance, formal meetings and agendas do not reveal them. They emerge out of frequent and informal communication among team members. Mutual learning occurs within the team, as insights, puzzles, and solutions are shared.

(Gibbons et al., 1994, p. 124)

This development puts a premium on the creation of interdisciplinary research teams, who can not only collectively share insights and learn from one another but also work in more heterogeneous settings and facilitate learning in such settings.

Whilst many writers accept that this conclusion follows from Gibbons *et al.*'s argument, there are mixed views about the feasibility of inter-firm learning and sharing of tacit knowledge. Some writers are highly pessimistic and argue that these suggestions are exceptional rather than regular features of firms' economic activity and their internal learning process (Cowan, David & Foray, 2000) while other writers maintain that inter-firm and inter-professional collaboration are critical to sustained success in the knowledge economy (Heckscher & Adler, 2007).

Tacit Knowledge and New Product and Service Development

Introduction

The case for the third expression of the role of tacit knowledge in the economy pre-dates both Lundvall's and Gibbons and colleagues' work, although its current manifestation is contemporary with their arguments. The idea that firms constitute sites for innovation started to surface in management science (Drucker, 1969), organisational science (Penrose, 1959) and evolutionary economics (Nelson & Winter, 1972) in the 1960s[9]. Up to then, most theories of the firm had been rooted in the neo-classical 'transaction cost' school of business economics (Coase, 1937). From this perspective, the cost of market entry and purchasing new technology (i.e. the transaction cost) was portrayed as more critical to economic success than R&D. Thus, the dominant idea of the firm from the 1940s onwards tended to reinforce that a firm's competitive success was dependent on controlling its transaction costs. The switch to a focus on firms' behaviour, as we are about to see, enabled writers to highlight the limitations of the 'transaction-cost' theory and the assumptions it made about firms. It gradually became apparent that resources (for example, finance and R&D) were never by themselves the most important 'inputs' in the production process (Penrose, 1959, pp. 67–87). Firms' competitive success was determined by their ability to use 'latent' knowledge, that is, knowledge about under-utilisation of resources or ideas as to how to specialise and extend the product and service range, how to reconfigure productivity or how to enhance productive operations.

Tacit knowledge and knowledge production. It does not automatically follow, however, that because firms are repositories of knowledge they can develop the capability to utilise such knowledge. A number of writers have pointed out that, because of the idiosyncratic nature of such knowledge, firms in similar lines of business can produce vastly superior or inferior products or services, and experience radically different fortunes (Nelson & Winter, 1972). Nevertheless, one result of the increased attention on firms' responses to changing market conditions and evolving customer trends and preferences has been the focus on the 'epistemological dimension' to firms' activities (Nonaka & Takeuchi, 1995).

Epistemology is normally used in the Human, Social and Natural Sciences to refer to the study of the philosophical foundations on which knowledge in different disciplines stand. However, two related arguments have been advanced to support the contention that there is an 'epistemological dimension' to firms' activities. The first argument reflects a continuation of the more pluralistic view of knowledge that has emerged with the performativity culture in science. This recasts the process of knowledge creation in terms of philosophical anthropology rather than sociology: in other words, knowledge is produced as a result of people's active engagement with the world, as opposed to being considered a highly specialised activity occurring in laboratories (Spender, 1998, p. 233). The second argument builds on the premises of the first. If people, and hence firms, develop knowledge through the way in which they engage actively with the world, it is important to understand the repertoire of strategies, processes and activities that enable people to generate, share and apply knowledge (Spender, 1998, p. 234).

Both arguments imply that one of the ways that firms contribute to knowledge economies is through adding to the wider stock of ideas about what constitutes knowledge creation and knowledge sharing in contexts other than the laboratory (Nonaka & Takeuchi, 1995, pp. 49–50). In addition, the arguments also imply that:

When organisations innovate they do not simply process information, from the outside in, in order to solve existing problems and adapt to a changing environment. They actually create new knowledge and information, from the inside out, in order to redefine both problems and solutions and, in the process, to re-create their environment.

(Nonaka & Takeuchi, 1995, p. 56)

Thus, innovation is a process of problem identification and problem-solving that occurs inside firms and this constitutes a major basis of firms' knowledge-producing activities[10]. It is widely accepted within management theory (von Krogh, Roos & Klein, 1998) that the pre-eminent exposition of the way in which knowledge is created inside organisations has been provided by Nonaka and Takeuchi (1995).

Nonaka and Takeuchi (1995, p. 32) ground their discussion of the creation of new knowledge within organisations explicitly in terms of the dualism between mind and world. They argue that the history of western organisational thought, from Alfred Marshall to Peter Senge, can be seen as repeated challenges to the 'scientific' view of knowledge by the 'humanistic' one. Moreover, they maintain that by framing the debate in terms of this dualism, irrespective of which epistemological position is adopted, organisational theorists have largely concentrated on identifying the contribution that 'existing' knowledge, usually science, makes to innovation, organisational development and wealth creation.

The challenge for all organisations in the knowledge economy is, according to Nonaka and Takeuchi (1995, p. 49), to innovate continually through creating new knowledge. Whereas the scientific view assumed that scientific methods were the sole source of the production of new knowledge, Nonaka and Takeuchi (1995, p. 60) maintain that the reservoir of 'subjective, bodily, and tacit aspects of knowledge' held by individuals in workplaces is an inescapable element in this new knowledge. Thus, from their perspective, tacit knowledge is an embodied and intuitive form of knowledge that we accumulate through practical experience, and which constitutes the basis of our personal and professional judgements. We can only share our tacit understandings, according to Nonaka and Takeuchi (1995, p. 64), by developing 'mental models', in other words, pictures or patterns that represent the significance of our experiences; and it is through the sharing of such mental models, either discursively through the use of metaphors or analogies in the workplace or through the explicit use of strategies to make the implicit explicit (see below), that we are able to begin to transform the production process.

The origin of this theory of knowledge conversion, that is, the process of making the implicit meaning explicit, lies in what Nonaka and Takeuchi refer to as the 'Japanese Intellectual Tradition' (Nonaka & Takeuchi, 1995, p. 27). They define the main features of this tradition in terms of the following three assumptions: the oneness of 'humanity and nature'; the oneness of 'body and mind'; and the oneness of 'self and other'. They argue that one of the dominant features of this tradition is the Zen Buddhist belief in the use of 'question-and-answer conversations' to clarify understanding of paradoxical issues (Nonaka & Takeuchi, 1995, p. 30). They suggest that this is akin to people coming to understand themselves more fully by undertaking a 'journey' that allows them to acquire a new perspective, a new view of the world and, ultimately, new knowledge. Nonaka and Takeuchi (1995, p. 56) maintain that the:

> ...cornerstone of our epistemology is the distinction between tacit and explicit knowledge... [and that] the key to knowledge creation lies in the mobilisation and conversion of tacit knowledge.

Drawing on their extensive experience of supporting the 'journey' of Japanese companies, such as Toyota and Honda, which were engaged in 'new product development', Nonaka and Takeuchi (1995, pp. 56–70) define their definition of knowledge creation in firms as a spiralling of interactions between explicit and tacit knowledge. The primary purpose of these interactions is to turn tacit knowledge about products, services and systems into explicit knowledge. In other words, these processes allow this tacit knowledge to be shared, to become part of the wider repertoire of knowledge held by all members of an organisation and, in the process, to create new knowledge. Nonaka and Takeuchi suggest that this new knowledge could take the form of either an entirely new product or service or a significant modification to existing ones.

The rationale for the development of their alternative conception of epistemology – and hence knowledge production – lies, according to Nonaka and Takeuchi (1995, p. 60), in Polanyi's ideas that we acquire knowledge through analysing external objects. They argue that we actively create and organise our own experiences by involving ourselves with objects, that is, through self-involvement and commitment. Hence, from their perspective, to know something is to tacitly integrate its particulars. New knowledge emerges, for Nonaka and Takeuchi (1995, pp. 62–9), from the continuous interaction between the stock of 'codified' ideas that determine the process of production, such as operating manuals and other protocols, and our practical experience of applying these guidelines. The process of creating new knowledge from the interaction between codified and tacit knowledge involves four phases. In the first phase, tacit knowledge is formed as we share experiences through the creation of 'mental models and technical skills'. In the second phase, explicit knowledge is created through:

> ...articulating tacit knowledge into explicit concepts. It is a quintessential knowledge-creation process in that tacit knowledge becomes explicit in the shape of metaphors, analogies, concepts, hypotheses or models.

> (Nonaka & Takeuchi, 1995, p. 64)

In the third phase, different types of explicit knowledge are combined through a process of 'systemising concepts' (i.e. the common understandings that have been built up) into a 'knowledge system', to construct a body of knowledge that can be used to reconfigure the process of design and/or production. The final phase involves the operationalisation and internalisation of the new form of explicit knowledge. By this they mean that, as this explicit knowledge is applied within the production process, it is converted back into a new form of tacit knowledge and thus constitutes a resource to support the process of modifying an existing, or creating a new, product.

The spiral of interaction, which Nonaka and Takeuchi (1995, pp. 62–72) claim is a universal characteristic of firm-based knowledge creation, is a dynamic process that amplifies the knowledge created in each phase. They maintain that the spiral of knowledge creation is a never-ending process, which is gradually embedded in organisational routines through the creation of special environments. In these, professionals can share their ideas, mental models and so forth, so as to pool their expertise to modify and/or create new products and services (Nonaka & Konno, 1998).

CONCLUSION

In focusing on the processes that facilitate knowledge production and the modification and/or creation of new products or services, the management theorists identified a number of different expressions of tacit knowledge and the contribution that they make to economic development. In doing so, they highlighted that the new role of knowledge in the economy is not just confined to those industrial sectors that are predominantly concerned with the applications of concepts and methods from STEM subjects. There are, however, a number of issues relating to these claims about tacit knowledge that Lundvall, Gibbons et al., and Nonaka and Takeuchi leave unaddressed, and which have theoretical consequences for their own position, for Bell, Castells and Stehr's positions, and more widely for our understanding of both the new role of knowledge in the economy and the learning challenge that this new role presents.

The first issue is that although all the management theorists discussed advocate a more pluralistic conception of knowledge to reflect the new modes of knowledge production emerging in the knowledge economy, they construct their respective positions in opposition to the strong assumptions that characterised the social theorists' case. These can be summarised as the premise that theoretical knowledge is the most important type of knowledge in the economy because it can be easily transferred across contexts to facilitate economic development. As a consequence, although Lundvall, Gibbons et al., and Nonaka and Takeuchi maintain that they have introduced a radically different perspective to the role of knowledge in the knowledge economy, we will see in the next chapter that on closer inspection their claim amounts to little more than the perpetuation of the classic split between the two worlds of knowledge that has afflicted philosophy and the Social Sciences since Descartes first conceived of knowledge in this way.

Furthermore, although it is clear that the writers discussed in this chapter, unlike Bell, Castells and Stehr, explicitly acknowledge that a knowledge economy is more than just an economy that consists of more highly qualified people and more specialised products and services, they still remain wedded to the split between the economy and culture. Lundvall, Gibbons and colleagues, and Nonaka and Takeuchi are primarily concerned with affirming the importance of the cultural as well as the economic sphere of activity, rather than exploring the way in which our society's cultural traditions constitute the economic and cultural spheres of human activity. Hence, their concern is for the 'products' of putting tacit knowledge to work – new modes of knowledge production, new types of knowledge, new products and services – rather than considering whether there is a relation between theoretical and tacit knowledge and, if there is, the implications of that relationship for supporting learning in the knowledge economy.

These observations suggest that, in order to understand the new role of knowledge in the economy and the learning challenge it presents, it is necessary to: first, appraise critically the epistemological pre-suppositions that underpin the separation of theoretical and tacit knowledge in the conventional wisdom about the knowledge economy; and, second, to consider the implications of this re-appraisal for the concept of learning. We take the first step in engaging with this challenge in the next chapter.

NOTES

[1] We have employed this term to indicate a commonality in approach in the work of all the theorists discussed in this chapter who are concerned with the implications of tacit knowledge for economic and organisational development, rather than as referring to the academic field of Management Studies.

[2] The idea that endogenous forms of innovation made significant contributions to economic prosperity first surfaced in the school of economics that has been called 'new growth theory' (Romer, 1986). The proponents of new growth theory argued that economic 'spillovers' and increasing returns constituted the fundamental sources of growth. New growth theory highlighted, in particular, that non-traditional forms of capital investment, such as company-based and company-resourced R&D, are prime examples of the types of investment that are associated with increasing returns or spillovers.

[3] That is, in the terms of the kind of knowledge science makes available and the kinds of methods of inquiry it advocates.

[4] It is important to note that the consensuality and consensibility that these writers attribute to the status of science and scientific findings within the scientific community and more widely within society is a particular characteristic of the post-World War era. There is considerable evidence that scientific findings were hotly contested in the eighteenth and nineteenth centuries.

[5] The development of the 'triple helix' has some affinities with the development of close links between universities and industries that occurred in nineteenth-century Germany. Both developments shared a concern to ensure knowledge production supported economic development. The German developments, however, were based on the principle of a state-led economy whereas the triple helix refers to the extension of the principles of 'marketisation' into the university.

[6] *The New Production of Knowledge* has received a very mixed response among academics. It has been perceived, on the one hand, as proposing a radically new relationship between science and society and a new role for science in the economy (Muller, 2001) and a new relationship between university science departments and the commercial world (Jacob & Hellstrom, 1999); and, on the other hand, as an alternative version of the 'finalization' thesis of the 1970s (Weingart, 1997), which ventured the argument that as sciences mature their potential for relevant application increases, and an over-statement that traditional scientific research is in decline (Rip, 1997; Shin, 1999).

[7] Before proceeding to discuss the differences between Mode 1 and Mode 2, it is important to distinguish transdisciplinary from multi-disciplinary knowledge production. The latter refers to the formation of new hybrid disciplines, which has been occurring in universities for some time. It involves the combination of different disciplines. Examples can be found in the Humanities (for example, the emergence of cultural studies from sociology and literary criticism) and in the Sciences (biochemistry and biophysics were both developed from biology, chemistry and physics).

[8] Polanyi (1958) distinguished between 'formalised' knowledge and 'tacit' knowledge. The former referred to those forms of knowledge that were transmittable in formal systematic or codified languages. The latter referred to the type of knowledge that was acquired by people as they created and organised their own experience. According to Polanyi, neither form of knowledge was reducible to the other.

[9] Writers in other fields, such as business economics (Boisot, 1995), and economic and innovation theory (Foray and Lundvall, 1996), have also explored this issue.

[10] Throughout the 1990s, there were a series of attempts in management and organisational science to develop conceptual frameworks that tried to address this issue. The driving idea behind the search for such frameworks, as Spender has observed (1998, p. 235), is that if firms are to be treated as engines of knowledge creation, firms 'need an epistemological framework that permits them to learn and to be surprised'.

CHAPTER 4

PROBLEMS AROUND THE ROLE OF KNOWLEDGE IN THE ECONOMY

INTRODUCTION

We begin to lay the conceptual groundwork for an alternative view to the social and management theorists' conventional wisdom about the new role of knowledge in the knowledge economy in this chapter. We first argue that the main reason that the social and management theorists offer different explanations about the type of knowledge required in the knowledge economy is because they engage with different expressions of the same epistemological framework, rather than because they have adopted different epistemological frameworks from one another. We illustrate this claim by: (i) locating their respective ideas about knowledge in relation to the philosophical notion of the 'two worlds' view of knowledge (Bakhurst, 1991); and (ii) identifying the ways in which these legacies pre-disposed these writers to overlook certain issues about knowledge, and about the role of knowledge in the economy, that are central to their own theses. In the case of the former, we present an alternative interpretation of Polanyi's ideas about theoretical and tacit knowledge that conceives of them as interdependent dimensions of knowledge rather than as separate and different types of knowledge. In doing so, we start to introduce a *mediated* (a term that we explain in Chapter 6) as opposed to a binary conception of knowledge into our discussion of the new role of knowledge in the economy. In the case of the latter, we argue that the social and management theorists both overlooked the contribution of epistemic cultures to the production and utilisation of scientific knowledge as well as knowledge in other professionals' fields. We use this line of argument to further substantiate the claim made in the introduction that, if we are to understand the new role of knowledge in the economy and the learning challenge posed by that development, then we need to understand the ways in which culture is constitutive of economic and human development.

The 'Two Worlds' View of Knowledge

Introduction
Our contention is that the main reason the social and management theorists presented different views about the role of knowledge in the economy is because of the legacy of dualistic thinking about knowledge in their work. The philosophical origin of the 'two worlds' dualism lies in the work of Descartes, whose ideas about epistemology rested on the separation of the mind from the world. The Cartesian dualism, following Bakhurst (1991, p. 111), can be characterised in terms of: the 'mental world', that is, the idea that individuals have direct access to this world through their

39

thoughts, emotions, beliefs, intentions and interpretations; and the 'material world', which consists of natural, physical and social structures that exist independently of thought[1]. It is beyond the scope of this chapter to address the philosophical history and complexity of this dualism. Suffice it to say that it has set the parameters of the debate in philosophy over the centuries, in regard not only to how to establish grounds for the objectivity of knowledge but also to why the notion of foundational truth should be set aside (Rorty, 1979). Modern discussions about the two worlds of knowledge is generally presented as a debate between 'scientific realists' and 'postmodernists' (Ward, 1996), for this reason, we start by outlining the key tenets of these positions below.

The 'scientific realist' conception of knowledge. The ideas originally expressed in empiricist and rationalist philosophies of knowledge are generally acknowledged to have provided the philosophical foundation for the concept of 'scientific realism'[2] (Toulmin, 2001; Ward, 1996, p. xvi). In ideal typical terms, scientific realists accept: that science is capable of providing objective knowledge of the second of Bakhurst's two worlds – the natural and material world – because science provides knowledge of largely theory-independent phenomena; and that such knowledge is possible, even in those cases in which the phenomena under investigation are not immediately observable (Toulmin, 2001; Ward, 1996). This position is based on three assumptions: firstly that an absolute reality exists beyond human consciousness, and that it can be understood but not altered through human action; secondly that this reality can be apprehended, and thus become more widely known and understood within society, if the proper scientific method is used to identify it and make it intelligible; and lastly that the 'scientific realist' conception of knowledge pre-supposes certain unique modes of constituting and organising reality and truth. These modes, according to Ward (1994, p. 1), are based on '...the imposition of particular ontological, epistemological and methodological prescriptions, divisions and delimitations of reality and truth'.

Ward, following Foucault (1970), argues that these ways of organising and limiting reality and truth can be referred to as 'epistemes'. 'Epistemes' serve two main functions by providing a set of relations that help to organise and to classify knowledge. From this it follows that 'epistemes' also impose moral and symbolic boundaries among individuals and social groups. These boundaries, in turn, create divisions between both correct and incorrect ways of thinking, and right and wrong procedures and practices.

The distinction between belief and truth, as Ward (1996, p. 2) points out, is one of the most important ways that science established its claim to producing objective knowledge of the world. Knowledge that is objective and hence true is assumed to have certain defining characteristics, which can be summarised as follows.

Objective knowledge is:
- governed by cognitive norms that are based on a commitment to the empirical investigation of specific hypotheses, and that are open to criticism, evaluation and reformulation by members of the scientific community (Shapin, 1994);

- produced in a special environment – a laboratory – and through the application of scientific methodology, which serves as a means of imposing 'discipline' on investigations and the investigation process (Toulmin, 2001, p. 6)[3];
- conducted in accordance with the appropriate 'epistemological decorum' to combat the possibility that the senses, on their own, could be misled by visual distortions or other sensory apparitions, while the use of specialist equipment allowed scientists to organise and regiment their senses more effectively to examine and record natural events (Shapin & Schaffer, 1985, p. 37)[4].

The communities of philosophers and scientists that have, since the rise of experimental science in the seventeenth century, held that science produces 'true generalisations' about the world, also maintain that its predictive capacities are established once scientific generalisations are expressed in mathematical terms and thus that their predictions are capable of being transmitted from one context to another (Toulmin, 2001, pp. 44–5). This process of codification has provided science with a resource that other forms of knowledge lacked. First, hypotheses could be tested by other scientists and were only comprehensible to the specialist scientific communities who knew how to manipulate the abstract symbols in which they were now expressed, even if the findings were highly contested within the scientific community and subject to subsequent revision or even rejection (Toulmin, 2001, pp. 44–5). Second, the 'Euclidean assumptions' (Toulmin, 2001, p. 6) of science – in other words, the idea that all scientific theories had a logical structure and that changes in scientific theories were primarily a matter of the replacement of one logical structure by another one – allowed philosophers to use the predictive capacity of science to distinguish it from other forms of knowledge. The net effect of these assumptions was to perpetuate the idea of the 'givenness' of the world, a term whose meaning we will clarify in Chapter 8, in the scientific and lay communities, and also the notion that the development of knowledge was an intrinsically rational process in the Natural and Physical Sciences (Ward, 1996).

The 'postmodern' conception of knowledge. Over the last thirty years the idea that science is able to provide totally objective knowledge of the natural and social world has been consistently challenged in the Human and Social Sciences. The main inspiration for the critique of science has come from the postmodern school of thought[5]. A unifying theme in the multifaceted postmodern philosophies is the claim that all knowledge, regardless of its ontological status, is a product of interpretation.

Nietzsche is generally seen as the founding father of postmodernism, because he inaugurated the view that truth had a rhetorical character and thus concluded that all philosophical and scientific efforts to establish transcendental, extra-human or objective knowledge were in vain (Ward, 1996, p. 19). In response to positivism, which was the dominant scientific realist tradition of his time, and which sought to ground knowledge in pure facts, Nietzsche (1976a, p. 267) argued that, 'Facts are precisely what there is not, only interpretations'. Moreover, Nietzsche also argued that all attempts in science to ground knowledge in empirical methods were fundamentally misconceived. He contested the notion that the senses could be disciplined through practising 'epistemological decorum' in such a way that accurate representations of reality were possible. The concepts of science and philosophy were, from Nietzsche's perspective, merely products of faith that allowed people to endure life.

Nietzsche's strategy for subverting the boundary conventions of 'scientific realism' has been adopted by many postmodernists in their continued attack on two of its most cherished components – the notions of foundational truth and the rational subject. A number of diverse approaches have been spawned under the postmodern umbrella, for example, Baudrillard's 'hyper-reality' (1988), Derrida's 'de-constructionism' (1976), Haraway's 'engendered knowledge' (1989) and Lyotard's 'performativity' (1984). These schools have:

– firmly rejected the idea that science is capable of producing any 'foundational' knowledge;
– argued for an anti-foundationalism based on an 'incredulity towards meta-narratives' because there is no definitive basis for establishing the truth about particular sets of circumstances or events of the world (Lyotard, 1984);
– maintained that the various discourses that support modernity by emphasising spiritual and material progress through the progressive application of science within everyday life have lost their legitimacy and credibility and, as a consequence, philosophy should now concern itself with the 'performativity' (Lyotard, 1984, pp. 46–7) of knowledge – performativity being its contribution to changing the world rather than its ability to provide knowledge about the world.

From this perspective, the descriptive and explanatory language of science is fraught with problems of interpretation, translation, reception and referentiality and, as a consequence, scientific representations can never constitute anything more than contingent and context-dependent approximations of reality. In contrast to scientific realism, postmodernism 'levels or symmetricalises' all forms of discourse and truth claims: a move that requires that all knowledge forms be treated as equally valid (Ward, 1996, p. 38). Stated another way, postmodernism introduces a pluralist conception of knowledge that stresses the similarities that exist between the forms of theoretical knowledge produced in the Natural and Social Sciences, and the 'everyday' knowledge produced locally in different 'community' settings.

Scientific Realism, Postmodernism and the Knowledge Economy

Introduction
Having introduced the tenets of scientific realism and postmodernism, we now move on to trace their legacy in the social and management theorists' respective accounts of the role of theoretical and tacit knowledge in the economy, before identifying how this legacy pre-disposed them to overlook issues about knowledge that are central to their respective theses about the knowledge economy.

The legacy of scientific realism in the social theorists' concept of knowledge. It has been widely accepted that Bell's views about the primacy of scientific/theoretical knowledge rest on an unquestioned assumption about the nature of scientific knowledge and scientific inquiry (Muller, 2001; Schiller, 1997; and Stehr, 1994). Hence Bell accepts as unproblematic the premises that had been associated with science and scientific activity since the nineteenth century, namely: that the pursuit of knowledge is both rational and legitimate, and is governed solely by its own rules and procedures; that it embraces the consensus that had existed within the scientific community about the 'linear discovery' nature of scientific knowledge and scientific discovery (Ziman, 1984, p. 7); and, thus, that it views knowledge as 'linear, cumulative, and quantitative for there are specific rules for the process of growth and differentiation' (Bell, 1973, p. 31).

As a consequence, Bell presents the scientific production of knowledge as though it is a series of ideal outcomes, located in universities and research institutes where scientists work, for which translation into different and varied technological forms is relatively unproblematic. The power and legitimacy that demarcate theoretical knowledge are, for Bell (1973) not affected by time and place, not least because, given that theoretical knowledge is independent of any contingent conditions, it can be 'translated into many different and varied circumstances' (Stehr, 1994, p. 67). Hence, it is a short step from this position, which assumes the givenness of reality and the legitimacy of scientific knowledge, to the idea that theoretical knowledge constitutes the 'axial principle' of economic development.

It is more difficult to identify the legacy of scientific realism in the work of Castells because, unlike Bell, he does not engage in any epistemological discussion about the status of knowledge. Castells only touches tangentially upon epistemological issues, claiming 'no compelling reason' to improve on Bell's own definition of knowledge. Furthermore, as we have seen, Castells went so far as to consolidate his debt to Bell by adopting a definition of 'information' that was more or less congruent with Bell's use of the term. Castells ends up, by default, sharing a similar philosophical position with Bell about the character of knowledge, since he too conceptualises knowledge in accordance with a fairly strong version of 'scientific realism', albeit implicitly (Muller, 2001, pp. 276–7). One overt manifestation of this implicit adoption of scientific realism is that Castells, like Bell, treats knowledge and information as though they are malleable, serve utilitarian functions in society and their meaning is quite transparent.

The legacy of scientific realism manifests itself in Stehr's work in a rather different way. Stehr viewed knowledge work, as we saw, in technical rational terms: this form of work involved experts either applying extant knowledge or generating new knowledge to address current problems. Technical rationalism is, as Schön (1987, p. 3) pointed out, the methodological manifestation of scientific realism: it is predicated on the idea that the process of codification provided experts with abstract forms of knowledge that could be applied objectively to solve problems in a range of different contexts. Hence, although Stehr's (1994, p. 95) argument about knowledge work is expressed in terminology that reflects his commitment to seeing the possession of knowledge as constituting a 'capacity for social action' – in other words, applied according to human purposes – he conceives of the process of the application of knowledge primarily in technical and intra-professional terms.

Implications of this scientific–realist legacy. Social theorists, such as Bell, Castells, Stehr and others, who have taken an epochal attitude to their times, have been particularly pre-occupied with the idea of the conquest of life by science (Osborne, 1998, p. 44). Our claim is that this emphasis on the intrinsic rationality of scientific research and development has led Bell, Castells and Stehr: (i) to disregard a number of issues about the character of knowledge and the application of knowledge, which are central to their own theses as well as to the argument of this book; and (ii) to assume that science is the primary 'engine' that impels technological and social change. As a consequence, they unconsciously adopt a 'design strategy' (Dennett, 1987) notion of social transformation to explain the emergence of the knowledge economy/society.

Bell's disregard is in conceiving of post-industrial societies primarily in economic terms as defined by, and measured in, the increased knowledge component of a nation's Gross National Product. Thus he renders knowledge as an independent variable that can be used, providing the appropriate intellectual technology is in place, to make rational and objective decisions that will spur economic growth. In making this argument, Bell operates with the classic social–scientific conception of the economic and cultural as separate spheres of human activity. Although this position surfaces in *The Coming of Post-industrial Society* (1973), it is much more explicit in his subsequent book *Cultural Contradictions of Capitalism* (1979). Here Bell (1979, p. 15) argues that the, 'principles of the economic realm and those of the culture now lead people in contrary directions'. The former pre-suppose acquiring the forms of cognitive thinking and discipline that facilitate objective decision-making, while the latter pre-suppose a hedonistic existence concerned with self-gratification. This particular interpretation of culture as a separate sphere of human activity overlooks its constitutive role in economic activity, in R&D and in the creation of the scientific mind. We shall return to the implications of this observation later in this chapter and explicitly from Chapter 6 onwards.

The pervasive influence of information systems theory within the artificial intelligence/information technology communities leads Castells, as Webster (1997a, p. 120) points out, to follow two tendencies that have existed in artificial intelligence and information systems theories since their inception in the 1950s. These are: to conflate knowledge and information; and to proceed as though the work that has to be undertaken to transfer data from a computer to the human mind, or from one human mind to another, is relatively unproblematic. Thus Castells operates implicitly with what Reddy (1979) has dubbed a 'conduit metaphor' of communication and cognition. From this perspective, the process of transfer is a technical matter of, in the case of the former, manipulating data encoded in symbolic form and, in the case of the latter, assimilating the representations that underpin the forms of knowledge that are being invoked. In making these assumptions about communication and cognition, Castells glosses over the long-standing philosophical position that the concept of knowledge pre-supposes the idea of a 'knower'. This means – as Seely Brown and Duguid, (2001, pp. 119–20) have presciently observed – that knowledge, and by extension information, are always embedded in a conceptual framework, even if it is not immediately apparent, and that such frameworks provide the implicit (i.e. unarticulated) or explicit (articulated) normative context for assessing knowledge and/or information in relation to the task in hand. What is also missing in Castells' account of the role of knowledge in the economy is any sense of the cultural constitution of knowledge/information and, as a corollary, that unless we have learned the normative basis of knowledge then we may struggle to 'apply' knowledge and/or information in any purposeful way.

Stehr also presents the forms of communication associated with knowledge work as though they are a technical matter of applying pre-given knowledge to solve accepted social and/or political problems. The problem with this position, as Schön (1987, p. 5) identified in his critique of the assumptions of technical rationalism as a set of operating principles for professional practice, is that it completely disregards that problems are 'never in the book'. Schön's case-study discussion, with a range of professionals who are experiencing difficulties within their practice, highlights that problems have to be 'worked up' (1987, p. 5); in other words, features of professional practice that are deemed to be salient have to be identified and shared with other colleagues to enable people to develop a shared understanding of the problem-in-hand. Consequently, solving problems entails developing a sensitivity towards the context from which they emanate and deploying extant knowledge creatively (a process that we shall describe as *recontextualisation* in Chapter 7) to address the problem in hand, rather than assuming – as Stehr is inclined to – that knowledge is a decontextualised resource that experts apply logically to resolve problems[6].

In the case of knowledge economies, Bell, Castells and Stehr gauge the process of modernisation by: firstly pointing to the new structural features of those economies – for example, for Bell, the increased spending on R&D, for Castells the increases in productivity made possible by the informational mode of production, and for Stehr the spread of knowledge work; and secondly to the final output of knowledge inputs – for example, all three writers draw attention to the growth of new products and services within the economy. This focus on the technological output of knowledge set a frame of reference that subsequent 'modernisation' theorists such as Beck, Giddens, Lash and Urry have followed. They too have concentrated either on the transformative effects of knowledge and information on different aspects of social and cultural life (Lash & Urry, 1994) or on personal life and identity (Giddens, 1990) or on the 'risks' (Beck, 1992) that the unfettered application of science to solve economic, social and political problems within society has generated.

It is perfectly reasonable to maintain, up to a point, that the process and consequences of modernisation can be gauged by looking at the transformative impact of science and technology on advanced industrial societies (Noble, 1986). Nevertheless, this pre-occupation with the 'design stance' and the expanding presence of expert systems and knowledge processes in contemporary societies reinforces the sharp distinction that Bell, Castells and Stehr make between the cultural and economic spheres of human activity. Thus, they pay scant attention either to the widely acknowledged cultural constitution of science and technology (Ziman, 2000) or to the social practices that facilitate the production and application of scientific and technological knowledge (Knorr Cetina, 1997; 1999). This constitutive feature of culture and practice has always been at the heart of the production and application of knowledge. What is distinctively different about knowledge economies/ societies compared with previous types of economies/societies is that forms of knowledge other than science are assuming increasing importance economically, socially and politically. Before we substantiate this claim, we will consider the legacy of postmodernism in the management theorists' account of knowledge.

The legacy of postmodernism in management theorists' account of knowledge. The influence of a postmodern sensibility manifests itself in very different ways in the work of Lundvall, Gibbons *et al.*, and Nonaka and Takeuchi. In fact, Lundvall's (1996) argument about the importance of tacit knowledge in economic development could almost be seen as an attempt to redress the imbalance between social theorists' affirmation of the role of theoretical knowledge in the economy and the role of other forms of knowledge, rather than total rejection of the role of the former. We only begin to see how a pluralistic sensibility manifests itself when we consider Lundvall's observations about the relation between tacit and codified knowledge. Lundvall claims that it would be, 'misleading to characterise know-how as practical rather than theoretical', because, as Polanyi demonstrated, finding the solution to complex issues is based on the interplay between 'intuition' and 'pattern recognition' (Johnson, Lorenz & Lundvall, 2002, p. 250). Moreover, Lundvall maintains that the development of this interplay is influenced by the way in which context facilitates experience-based learning, and that this suggests that there may be a, '..."know-how" dimension to our use of even basic forms of "know-why"...' (p. 251).

Nevertheless although he affirms a relation between codified and tacit knowledge, Lundvall ends up equating them in his taxonomy of knowledge. He defines them in accordance with different criteria, offers them equal weighting and maintains that firms employ different strategies to promote each form of knowledge – codified knowledge that has underpinned innovations is publicised in journals or at conferences, while tacit knowledge that has facilitated the innovation is nurtured in networks – rather than retaining his original position about their interrelation with one another (Johnson, Lorenz & Lundvall, 2002, p. 251).

We can detect a much more pronounced postmodern influence in Gibbons *et al*'s work, from the polemic tone that permeates their observation that the emergence of Mode 2 knowledge fundamentally calls into question the whole edifice of scientific realism (Gibbons *et al.*, 1994). They justify their argument that the foundational principles of science are withering away by claiming that Mode 2 knowledge, unlike science, is:

> ...incomplete – no longer in the conventional sense that it will eventually be superseded by superior science (for Popperians) or by a new scientific paradigm (for Kuhnians), but also in the sense that it is sharply contested (and no longer within the controlled environment of scientific peers but in the wider agora); and second, this shift involves re-negotiating and re-interpreting these boundaries.

> (Nowotny *et al.*, 2002, p. 199)

Moreover, in making their case, Gibbons and colleagues imply that Mode 2 knowledge will, ultimately, 'replace' (Muller, 2000, pp. 46–8)[7] science as the dominant mode of knowledge production. They base this claim on the following two arguments. The first is that the emergence of a new market-based economic rationality is now acting as a 'principal filter' to ensure that public and private sources of funding for research are equally concerned with identifying tangible economic benefits. This concern with the performativity of research results in constant pressure from funders to involve a wide range of stakeholder communities in the production and verification of Mode 2 knowledge. This continued weakening of the insulation of science from society constitutes, for Gibbons *et al.* incontrovertible evidence of a trend that they contend will perpetuate a demand for an extension of Mode 2 knowledge. Their second argument is that the increasing development of knowledge in its context of application, for example workplaces, is making the tacit knowledge held by members of the different scientific and workplace communities the bedrock of Mode 2. This consolidates a much more pluralistic conception of knowledge and calls for new standards against which knowledge can be assessed. One consequence is the growth of interdisciplinary research teams, who are increasingly called on to use their tacit knowledge both to identify the problems that require solutions and also to ascertain how far the resulting Mode 2 knowledge constitutes a solution to those problems.

At first sight the legacy of a postmodern sensibility is not immediately apparent in the work of Nonaka and Takeuchi: not only do they view their theory of 'knowledge conversion' as an attempt to overcome the separation of mind and world, they also eschew any explicit references to postmodernism in their writings. Scholars familiar with their work may be surprised to discover that their work is interpreted here as evincing a postmodern sensibility and as remaining trapped in the dualism. We highlight the postmodern inflection in Nonaka and Takeuchi's work below.

One of the clearest is their disavowal of the scientific–realist assumption that scientific methods are the main means whereby new knowledge is produced. In contrast, they maintain that they are following Polanyi and accepting that the reservoir of, 'subjective, bodily, and tacit aspects of knowledge' that individuals hold is an inescapable element in the production of knowledge (Nonaka & Takeuchi, 1995, p. 60). They state that:

> To know something is to create its image or pattern by tacitly integrating particulars. In order to understand the pattern as a meaningful whole, it is necessary to integrate one's body with the particulars.

New knowledge is, according to Nonaka and Takeuchi, produced not by disciplining the senses through practising epistemological decorum but by communicating bodily acquired tacit understandings through the production of 'mental models'. This emphasis on the primacy of embodied perception, which is a key tenet of postmodernism (Callinicos, 1989), in shaping emotional responses to experiences of the world leads Nonaka and Takeuchi to: first, argue that people form tacit pictures or patterns that capture and represent the significance of their experiences

47

of the workplace; and second, emphasise the role of 'metaphors' in assisting the verbalisation of tacit understandings and in the formation of new concepts, for example, metaphorical representations of new production processes. Hence, Nonaka and Takeuchi employ a postmodern trope – without specifically referring to postmodern texts – and assume that people's awareness of the world, including their indirect awareness, can be equated with representations (i.e. metaphors) of their experience. Hence Nonaka and Takeuchi maintain that new products and services can be created through sharing with others the mental representations they produce as a result of personal experience of the world.

Implications of this postmodern legacy. The common manifestation of the influence of a postmodern sensibility in Lundvall, Gibbons *et al.* and Nonaka and Takeuchi's work is the way in which all these writers equate tacit and theoretical knowledge, and justify this position through reference to Polanyi. This process of equation constitutes a misinterpretation of Polanyi's position on the relation between theoretical and tacit knowledge. It is our contention that, as a consequence, the aforementioned writers miss the value of his insights about tacit knowledge for their argument about its role in the knowledge economy. Thus, they perpetuate unintentionally the legacy of the two worlds of knowledge in their work, while claiming that they are operating with a radically different epistemological framework compared with the social theorists.

When Polanyi originally invoked the notion of tacit knowledge, his concern was to present the case for a holistic understanding of scientific knowledge, rather than to introduce another category of knowledge (Thorpe, 1999). Put simply, his argument was that the way in which scientists used and developed knowledge could not be explained only through reference to its propositional basis. Hence, most discussions of Polanyi's work within management theory and other related fields (i.e. organisational theory) tend to end with his famous phrase, 'We can know more than we can tell...' (Polanyi, 1966, p. 4). For Polanyi (1966, p. 4), this was paradoxically only the beginning, as he observed, 'I shall consider human knowledge by starting from [this] fact.'

This is partly because Polanyi was concerned with the relationship between the articulatable and inarticulatable elements of knowledge. He concluded that tacit knowledge is not an informal, inchoate or obscure form of knowledge, whose nature calls for it to be made explicit in order to be understood or useful in practice; his formulation was much more subtle (Thorpe, 1999, p. 24). Polanyi wanted to acknowledge that science, along with all forms of knowledge, always has a tacit dimension. He further argued that if:

> ...the declared aim of modern science is to establish a strictly detached, objective knowledge... [and if] tacit thought forms an indispensable part of all human knowledge, then the ideal of eliminating all personal elements of knowledge would, in effect, aim at the destruction of knowledge.

> (Polanyi, 1966, p. 20)

Thus, the idea of skilful performance in the world of science, just as in art or any other field, for Polanyi, is not achieved solely through following explicitly formulated rules based on propositional knowledge. It also requires that a number of other factors are taken into account in practice that are left out in the formulation of explicit rules (Polanyi, 1958, p. 49).

First, Polanyi is, as Seely Brown and Duguid (2001, pp. 203–4) observe, maintaining that scientific knowledge has two interdependent dimensions. By overlooking this aspect of Polanyi's argument, Lundvall, Gibbons *et al.*, and Nonaka and Takeuchi sever, albeit in slightly different ways, the relation between theoretical and tacit knowledge, and between embodied action and mind, that exists in Polanyi's original conception of these two forms of knowledge and human action. Critically, as a result, they miss the implications of that relation for professional perception and action. By glossing over the disciplinary root of the tacit knowledge developed by transdisciplinary research teams, Gibbons *et al.* fail to give due recognition to its role in enabling scientists and technologists to form tacit judgements that other professionals would not be capable of making. Equally, by playing down the relation between engineers' theoretical and workplace knowledge and action, Nonaka and Takeuchi fail to acknowledge that it is the interplay between these forms of knowledge and action that constitutes the key resource in the production of new knowledge. In contrast, Lundvall does acknowledge that there is a relation between theoretical and tacit knowledge, though he leaves us with the impression that it is the result of a 'natural' rather than a constitutive process. (We shall return to this point later.)

Second, although Polanyi emphasises that scientists' theoretical knowledge is developed through formal study and that their tacit knowledge is developed through 'indwelling' – that is, their immersion or enculturation in a set of theoretical pre-suppositions and physical skills related to their disciplinary field – he accepts that as scientists gradually 'interiorise' these separate processes they form a relation between the practical and the theoretical (Thorpe, 1999, p. 25). Thus, indwelling is, for Polanyi (1966, p. 13), a tacit transmission of culture, which both transcends and consumes the individual, so that the meaning of scientific concepts, practices and interpretations is established through the way practical actions impact on the body or the senses. This process of indwelling consists of a mix of social and psychological dimensions: the enculturation processes described above; and the gestalt perceptions that scientists have whilst they are being immersed in different scientific cultures.

There is therefore a slight tension in Polanyi's argument about the relation between disciplinary and tacit knowledge, because the social and psychological appear to be contributory, yet separate, factors in the development of mind, perception and action. Despite emphasising the interdependent relation between theoretical and tacit knowledge, what is unclear is the philosophical basis of that relationship. In light of this, it is perhaps hardly surprising that Lundvall, Gibbons *et al.*, and Nonaka and Takeuchi treat theoretical and tacit knowledge as separate forms of knowledge, and procedural and embodied action as separate forms of action. Nevertheless, in letting go of Polanyi's position about the interdependence between tacit and theoretical knowledge, all these writers fail to detect what is distinctive about their own observations about the new role of knowledge in the economy. It is less a debate about which form of knowledge is the most important resource, and more an issue about the way in which the use of knowledge as the critical resource for economic activity is making the relationship between theoretical and tacit knowledge much more explicit than in the past. One manifestation of this process is the debate, as we have seen, as to whether theoretical or tacit knowledge is the most important form of intra-professional knowledge work. Another manifestation, as we will see later in this chapter and in Chapter 9, is the role of theoretical and tacit knowledge in interprofessional knowledge work.

Knowledge, Culture and the Economy

Introduction

We now consider a number of issues that we set aside earlier in the discussion. The first issue is the enabling relation of culture to economic activity in general; the second is the constitutive role of epistemic cultures within a knowledge work (hereafter epistemic activity); and finally we will address the relation between theoretical and tacit knowledge.

'Epistemic' cultures and scientific knowledge.   The enabling relationship between culture and knowledge production, which has been a longstanding concern in science studies, has recently come to the fore in the debate about the knowledge economy (Latour, 2000, p. 108). This is partly because of the work of one researcher in science studies – Knorr Cetina (1997, 1999) – who has identified an aspect of the knowledge economy/society debate that has hitherto been neglected by many social and, for that matter, management theorists. In particular, Knorr Cetina has drawn attention to the contribution that knowledge (or, in her terms, 'epistemic') cultures make to knowledge economies/societies.

The cornerstone of Knorr Cetina's thought-provoking argument is that if we only use quantitative evidence about the increase in knowledge-based products and services, and in expert systems, as the primary indicators for understanding the emergence of knowledge economies/societies, then we fail to detect that:

> The expanding role of expert systems does not only result in the massive presence of technological and informational products of knowledge processes. It means that knowledge [that is 'epistemic' cultures] have spilled and woven their tissue into society.

> (Knorr Cetina, 1997, p. 8)

The concept of an 'epistemic' culture, according to Knorr Cetina, refers to:

> Those amalgams of arrangements and mechanism – bonded through affinity, necessity, and historical co-incidence – which, in a given field, make up how we know what we know. Epistemic cultures are cultures that create and warrant knowledge, and the premier knowledge institution throughout the world is, still, science.

She pursues this theme about the enabling relationship between culture and knowledge production by arguing that:

> A knowledge society [knowledge economy] is not simply a society [economy] of more experts, more technological gadgets, more specialist interpretations[8] ... [it is also] a society [and economy] permeated with knowledge cultures, the whole set of structures and mechanisms that serve knowledge and unfold with its articulation.

What emerges from this line of thinking, according to Knorr Cetina (1999, p. 8), is that if the case for the knowledge economy is presented solely in terms of the increase in expert systems or knowledge-intensive products and services, then the crucial role that 'epistemic cultures' make to the production and application of knowledge is overlooked.

The first way Knorr Cetina demonstrates the power of her thesis is to highlight the crucial role that epistemic cultures play in science with regard to the manipulation, deciphering, inspection and interpretation of the outcomes of the research, even though they take fundamentally different forms in different scientific fields. Knorr Cetina does so by comparing how two scientific fields – high-energy physics (HEP) and molecular biology – organise their strategies for acquiring knowledge. She points out that the main challenge for physicists working in HEP laboratories, which are usually spatially and temporally distributed, is to create new knowledge by interpreting the, 'electronically produced negative images of the world' (1999, p. 46), that is, 'the shimmering appearance of bygone events'. This process pre-supposes the existence of two cultural conditions: a culture of 'management by consent' based on communitarian principles of collective responsibility and shared criteria for decision-making, and 'ordering frameworks' based on shared theoretical knowledge, models, simulations and statistical procedures that guide the process of discovery and the establishment of the 'truth-like character of the results' (Knorr Cetina, 1999, p. 179).

In contrast, molecular biology flourishes in more conventional laboratory conditions because experiments in this field are conducted in environments where researchers work in accordance with a set of protocols issued by the head of the laboratory. The primary aim is to generate the acquisition of experimental knowledge about known molecular structures. Molecular biologists achieve this through responding to a problem by competing with one another and trying different variations of their laboratory procedures with the expectation that it will result in the discovery of new evidence.

The second way is to argue that, insofar as it is the practices associated with different epistemic cultures that allow science to play the role in the knowledge economy that Bell, Castells and Stehr claim, it may be the case that:

> ...some of the structural forms one finds in epistemic cultures will become or have already become of wider relevance in a knowledge society [knowledge economy]. For example, the laboratory is such a structural form, and practices of management by consent are associated with it. Other structural forms

are, on a micro-level, object-centred relationships... which I claim characterise knowledge societies more than person centred relationships, since they also characterise expert settings.

(Knorr Cetina, 1999, p. 242)

The integral feature of the knowledge-generating process in science, which Knott Cetina claims is a useful identifier of the ways in which epistemic cultures have spilt over more widely within society, is 'object-centred relations' (1999, p. 242). Knorr Cetina clarifies this notion and the way in which such relationships have manifested themselves in other fields of professional expertise through reference to Rheinberger's (1992, p. 310) ideas about the role of 'experimental systems' in science. The defining characteristics of experimental systems, according to Rheinberger, are: the 'scientific objects of investigation', for example HEPs' sign-mediated data, which are at the centre of the research process (Knorr Cetina, 1997, p. 10); and the 'technological objects' such as computers that scientists use in laboratories to create new knowledge. The outcome of the research process, in Rheinberger's (1992, p. 310) terms the 'epistemic object', is materially defined through the interplay between the question-generating aspect of the research process and the use of technological objects to stabilise that process and to provide answers to the research questions.

'Epistemic' cultures and professional knowledge cultures.   Epistemic objects are not, according to Knorr Cetina (1997, pp. 4–5), the sole province of science, because other professionals in fields other than science also formulate questions and use sophisticated software programmes as resources to help them to answer those questions. Thus, it follows for Knorr Cetina (2001, p. 183), as it did for Nonaka and Takeuchi, that forms of work other than science could be characterised by processes of inquiry that '...rarely come to a natural end [because] everything worth knowing about an object has been established...'. Such forms of work would, like science, develop their own epistemic culture that has an 'open, question-generating and complex...' character. This would clearly differentiate them from either the closed and taken-for-granted character redolent of routinised forms of work, or aspects of work that are gradually re-made through some form of individual agentive activity.

Knorr Cetina illustrates the way that her argument reveals unanalysed aspects of the role of knowledge in professional fields other than science through reference to the operation of global financial markets. She identifies the distinctive forms of epistemic cultures and epistemic activity that financial traders have generated, and the ways in which those activities develop by continually branching out. One aspect of tradings' epistemic culture that facilitates the continual branching out is, according to Knorr Cetina and Bruegger (2002, p. 5), that traders are continually required to '...define the market not only in the sense of trying to read and understand it, but also in the sense of 'making' or articulating it, by testing it, moving it, and manipulating it'. This forces traders to be constantly engaged in a struggle to understand the operation of financial markets through a process of collecting and discounting relevant information. Thus from Knorr Cetina's perspective, financial markets (and by extension other forms of work based on the collection and discounting of information) are knowledge objects for traders. This is because markets are complex entities and as a result traders have to continually question their own interpretation about what is happening. The knowledge that they need to do so consists, like Polanyi's scientists, of a combination of theoretical knowledge about the constitution of, and performance of, different types of financial markets as well as the tacit understanding they develop as they watch the daily, weekly, yearly performance of such markets. In contrast to scientists, the challenge for traders is that they have to create trust-based relationships with their so that clients will accept traders' advice as regards how to plan their investments by minimising or knowingly accepting financial risk.

The implications of Knorr Cetina's thesis about the spilling over of epistemic cultures and the role of epistemic objects in the professions has been extensively explored by Jensen, Lahn and Nerland (2010) in a comparative analysis of the accountancy, education, engineering, and nursing professions. Presented at its broadest, they have demonstrated the role of epistemic cultures and objects in those professions. The former legitimate professionals' use of epistemic objects as both a 'tool and an object of inquiry in a given knowledge practice', because they provide the community and criteria to judge the merits of new forms of knowledge and practice (Jensen, Lahn & Nerland, 2010). Taking the case of software engineers, Nerland & Jensen (2010) direct our attention to how epistemic objects can be used instrumentally and exploratively and, thus, also to the interplay between the confirming and experimental dimensions in engineers' engagement with knowledge. Specifically, they reveal the different epistemic practices engineers engage in. When resolving fairly routine problems, engineers use the Internet to find solutions by reading other engineers' blogs about similar problems, reading manuals and FAQs, and consulting the knowledge bases that firms have made available about their software systems. In contrast, when engineers have to work for customers who have 'hybrid server parks', they face a very different kind of challenge. Engineers have to make sure that their decisions and actions have taken account of the different software systems that have been combined in the server park. This requires a more creative approach to the use of the Internet, for example, that can range from posting questions and asking for help from other colleagues through to modelling solutions and requesting feedback from engineering peer groups.

Jensen, Lahn and Nerland help us to distinguish between professionals' confirmatory and lateral branching practices. In the case of the former, professionals use extant knowledge in a fairly straightforward way as a resource to solve routine problems and, in the process, maintain the quality of a company's software system. In the case of the latter, the process of consultation with the wider engineering community about novel problems reveals the way in which engineers' investigations facilitate their own learning as well as learning within the wide engineering community: engineers use the process of online consultation to develop their own understanding as regards how to resolve the problem in hand and the wider engineering community uses the posting of results to develop their capability.

Despite generating some fascinating insights into the contribution of epistemic cultures and objects to the development of intra-professional practice, Jensen, Lahn and Nerland, like Knorr Cetina, are inclined to gloss over the process of reasoning and deliberation that underpins the investigative process. This is partly because both writers employ cybernetic metaphors, for example, 'apply', 'circulate', 'combine' (see *inter alia* Knorr Cetina, 2007; Jensen, Lahn & Nerland, 2010) to describe the way in which professionals use knowledge and communicate their use of knowledge to other members of their respective professional communities. As a consequence, both writers conflate the relation between theoretical and tacit knowledge in the process of reasoning. We pursue this issue below.

'Epistemic' cultures, and theoretical and tacit knowledge. To shed light on the way in which the increased use of knowledge as a resource in the economy has been making the relationship between theoretical and tacit knowledge much more explicit than in the past, we turn to Zuboff's (1988) classic account of the consequences of the introduction of information and communication technology for knowledge and skill in workplaces. Zuboff's *In the Age of the Smart Machine* (1988) analyses the way in which organisational context, managerial intent and work structures influence both the deployment of information and communication technology (ICT) and the development of knowledge and skill in workplaces (Orlinkowski, 1992). Although it was written twenty years ago, her argument about the effects of the replacement of machine technology by ICT on human skill is relevant to: firstly our use of Knorr Cetina's argument that epistemic cultures are emerging in fields other than science; and secondly our argument about the mediated relation between theoretical and tacit knowledge[9].

Zuboff introduced the concepts 'action-centred skill' and 'intellective skill' to encapsulate the nature of the different types of knowledge and skill required for working with machine technology compared with working with ICT. The former refers to an 'experiential' mode of skill formation that had been typically associated with industrial workers prior to the introduction of IT. Zuboff identified four key aspects of such action-centred skill. It was: (i) dependent upon 'sentience' (that is, the use of information that could be derived from physical clues); (ii) developed through 'action-dependence' (in other words, developed through physical activity); (iii) only meaningful in 'context-dependent' situations (those specific situations where the work occurred); (iv) dependent on being 'personalised' (that is, a linkage existed between the knower and the known, which is 'felt' by the knower). In a nutshell, her argument is that the process of developing 'action-centred skill' (Zuboff, 1988, p. 73) does not necessarily require any theoretical knowledge, because the knowledge and understanding that we derive from manipulating materials or observing the physical performance of machines is largely implicit or tacit.

In contrast, Zuboff employed the term 'intellective skills' to refer to the mode of thinking that is required when working in computer-mediated environments.

Intellective skill involves the interpretation of symbolic data, as Zuboff observed (1988, p. 76): 'in a symbolic medium, meaning is not a given value, rather, it must be constructed'. Thus, where activities involve the use of a symbolic medium (for example, interaction with a computer screen and interpretation of the data it provides), far greater emphasis is placed on the forms of theoretical knowledge that underpin the abstract data. This is because the introduction of IT provides a resource to monitor work processes through the use of symbols; thus work is more opaque, with the result that information about the work process and decision-making is more ambiguous, because:

> ...electronic texts do not have an author in the conventional sense. It may be produced from many individual acts of 'authorship' (for example, account officers enter their own data, managers send messages, customers provide data through automated teller machines), or it may result from impersonal and autonomous processes (for example, microprocessors register data from the production process, optical scanners read and input data).

(Zuboff, 1988, p. 180)

The shift in the quality of knowledge required for working in computer-mediated environments is, however, rather more complex than it may first seem. It is not simply the replacement of one type of knowledge – tacit, sentient knowledge – by another codified or explicit knowledge. Zuboff (1988, p. 192) acknowledges that tacit knowledge continues to play a role in intellective skill development. This is because informated environments pre-suppose that workers, at all levels, have a shared sense of the meaning of textual information and its implications for action, rather than responding sentiently to verbal commands or visual clues. Thus working in informated environments pre-supposes the development of:

> ...a tacit knowledge that facilitates the recognition of decision alternatives and frees the mind for the kind of insight that could result in innovation and improvement. Such tacit recognition depends upon first being able to explicitly construct the significance of patterns and relationships in the data.

(Zuboff, 1988, p. 92)

Thus, it is only possible for us to understand what someone is thinking about by being able to attribute their discourse, or the text to which it refers, to a wider frame of reference. Constructing the significance of patterns and relationships in data:

> ...cannot be achieved without a level of intellective skill development that allows the worker to solve the problem of reference, engage in reasoning that is both inductive and deductive and apply a conceptual framework to the information at hand. Meaning must be constructed explicitly in order for it to become implicit later.

(Zuboff, 1988, p. 192)

Thus, it follows from Zuboff's analysis that work in informated (knowledge-based) environments has a tacit dimension as much as work in automated environments. In drawing our attention to this issue, however, Zuboff introduces a sapient rather than a sentient conception of tacit knowledge. In order to interpret the data that appears on computer screens, workers needed to understand the assumptions about the work process that have been encoded in the software, and the way in which that process of encoding influences the interpretation of data. Only then can they, on the one hand, develop a tacit interpretation of that data because their theoretical understanding provides them with a frame of reference to ascertain the implications of the patterns emerging on the computer screen; and, on the other hand, use their conceptual understanding as a basis to share those understandings and their implication for action with one another. We shall return to the implications of a sentient definition of tacit knowledge for our argument about the learning challenge of the knowledge economy in the next section.

Implications of epistemic cultures and intellective skill for the knowledge economy/ society. Knorr Cetina's concepts of epistemic culture and activity are interesting in a number of respects in relation to our understanding of the new role of knowledge in the economy. First, her concepts allow us to further consolidate our argument that culture has always played a constitutive role in the scientific–realist as much as the postmodern account of the production and application of knowledge. From Knorr Cetina's perspective, it is the epistemic practices that generate diverse aggregation of patterns and dynamics in existing scientific, new modes of knowledge production (i.e. Mode 2), and in professional fields other than science and technology, which enable new knowledge to be produced.

Secondly, Knorr Cetina's concepts can be used to provide us with a very nuanced account of the way in which forms of theoretical knowledge other than science have woven themselves into the texture of society and therefore are contributing to the transition to a knowledge society. This development might appear, at first sight, to have some affinities with the more pluralistic conception of knowledge ushered in by postmodern writers. Where Knorr Cetina differs from postmodern-influenced management theorists is that she does not accept their premise that knowledge claims ultimately rest on forms of political power and hence equate to forms of knowledge. Knorr Cetina's roots in 'social constructionism' mean that, although she does not assume that science is separate from society, governed by its own norms, values and methods of inquiry, or that it constitutes the major source of enlightenment, she nevertheless accepts that science is still the 'premier knowledge-producing institution' (1999, p. 1). Moreover, because Knorr Cetina accepts that science holds this position, she is able to broaden the definition of the concept of epistemic culture.

Epistemology is normally used in the Human, Social and Natural Sciences, as the last chapter noted, to refer to the study of the philosophical foundations on which knowledge in different disciplines stands. However, by revealing the ways in which some of the knowledge-generating practices – for example, the accumulation, verification and distribution of knowledge that have underpinned the traditional notion of epistemology – have become a constitutive feature of professions other than science, Knorr Cetina introduces a new expression of the concept of epistemic. This new expression loosens the strong teleological and foundational connotations associated with the development of disciplinary knowledge, yet retains many of the features of knowledge-generation that have traditionally been associated with science – for example, a concern for the development of practice based on the spread of research-based methods of inquiry and research-based partnerships. These forms of activity have become more commonplace in professional fields other than science as organisations form 'alliances' and/or 'partnerships' to spread R&D costs amongst themselves or to secure forms of 'intellectual capital' that are essential for successfully realising an R&D project (Lundvall, 2000).

Knorr Cetina firstly allows us to see that those professional practices that have an explicit, even if it is a multi-faceted, knowledge base and are part of a well-defined professional field, have a stronger epistemic root than those practices that are not characterised by such features and, moreover, that this root constitutes a key resource for their continuing development.

Secondly, she offers us a way to shed light on the link between knowledge, the development of practice and ipso facto the creation of new products and services. The hallmark of epistemic cultures is an 'epistementality', based on the establishment of rules of trust, exclusivity and loyalty, while the hallmark of epistemic practice is the question-generating process. Both are, according to Knorr Cetina (2006, p. 37), integral conditions for the 'lateral branching out' of practice. By this Knorr Cetina means that, because many fields of professional practice, like science, are characterised by a question-generating process, the forms of knowledge as much as the ways of working associated with a particular field are continually developed. Sometimes this results in the creation of new knowledge that is not immediately used as a source of economic development within a field or firm (Miettinen, 2005). On other occasions, the creation of new forms of knowledge results in new working practices (Gibbons *et al.*, 1994).

What is less developed in Knorr Cetina's account of epistemic cultures and practices is the way that professionals, for example financial traders, learn – in her terms – to 'disembed embedded knowledge' and so to explain the likely movement in the market in a language that is intelligible to other professionals who do not necessarily share a common frame of reference. This is in part, as we have noted, because Knorr Cetina, like Jensen, Lahn and Nerland, employs cybernetic metaphors – such as 'circulation' and 'processing' to convey the nature of intra- and interprofessional communication (Guile, 2009). Yet this requirement for one group of professionals to make their assumptions, judgements and recommended course of action intelligible to other professionals has been an increasing feature of knowledge economies/societies since the 1980s (Bauman, 1987). It is partly a result of what Hage and Powers (1992, p. 4) refer to as the 'complexification' of work and work roles in advanced industrial societies. By this they mean, de-layering has resulted in intra-professional activity being less insular and out-sourcing has resulted in the growth of interprofessional activity. Both developments have resulted in professionals being called upon to explain their reasoning processes and their implications for action to other professionals and lay people. This development raises a question that is central to, but that never surfaces in educational policies for the knowledge economy/society; how do professionals learn to develop this type of capability? We shall return to this question shortly.

Before doing so, it is necessary to turn our attention to the way in which Zuboff broadened the concept of tacit knowledge in a way that complements the broadening of the concept of epistemic knowledge. Zuboff characterises action-centred skill as a sentient form of tacit knowledge whose genesis was purely experiential, and intellective skill as a sapient form of tacit knowledge whose genesis pre-supposes a conceptually structured mind. The latter form of tacit knowledge is, as Zuboff makes clear, influenced by the relationship between disciplinary background, the experience of visualising, articulating and collaboratively agreeing the meaning of text and inferring what follows from it (Guile, 2006). This sapient conception of tacit knowledge is a product of the way in which we co-mingle our theoretical concepts and practical experiences when forming judgements and determining courses of action.

In doing so, Zuboff provides a way to make the implicit social entailment of Polanyi's concept of tacit knowledge explicit. Her work reveals that, although tacit knowledge is still in Polanyi's terms a 'personal' form of knowledge, personal does not mean that it is the result of either a purely embodied experience or some act of direct perception, that is, divined without recourse to the use of language to make sense of material or symbolic experience. Rather, personal means being able either: to articulate the reasons that inform subsequent understandings and actions, and that constitute the basis of communicating them to others; or to operate in accordance with a sense of reason even though the actual reasons for action are not necessarily being explicitly articulated to oneself or others.

This interpretation of the personal introduces the intriguing idea that we act through recourse to a 'mediated' (Derry, 2008) rather than a dualistic mind, that is, a mind that is constituted through an interplay between the social and the personal. In fact, a careful reading of Nonaka and Takeuchi indicates, as Eraut (2004, p. 263) has pointed out (and it can be argued that his insight applies equally to Lundvall, Gibbons *et al.*), that the popular conception of tacit knowledge as an inchoate form of knowledge is a complete misunderstanding of the form of tacit knowledge required in the economy. The form of tacit knowledge that Nonaka and Takeuchi are claiming is critically important in the knowledge economy is the ability to generate hypotheses and persuade others about the validity of possible courses of action to enact those hypotheses.

What is gradually becoming clearer, therefore, is that there can be a tacit dimension to our use of different forms of knowledge. One way to clarify this issue is to follow Jonsen and Toulmin (1988) and distinguish between 'theoretical' and 'practical' reasoning in science-based and profession-based epistemic activity. By and large, the former is characterised by the use of theoretical concepts, discourses and methods as 'axioms' (Jonsen & Toulmin, 1988, p. 23) – that is, the universal rules that guide the research process and the judgements that scientists make. This process of deliberation in scientific research could, as Polanyi observed, occur explicitly as scientists discuss or argue with one another, or implicitly as individual scientists gradually comprehend the meaning and implications of scientific data. In contrast, profession-based epistemic activity is characterised by the use of 'maxims', that is, paradigmatic cases that define their meaning and the force of their applicability (1988, p. 23). This form of reasoning – as Nerland and Jensen demonstrate – occurs as professionals consider the case in hand, select from among the features of the situation those which they feel are significant, compare them with counter or similar examples, as well as with their own experiences, and use this process of individual and collective deliberation to gain insights into how to proceed. This process of deliberation and judgment is, as Jonsen and Toulmin 1988, pp. 38–9) clarify, similar to and different from theoretical reasoning. It is similar in that it presupposes a conceptually-structured mind that understands a professional practice and how to make judgements in accordance with the standard of that practice. Where practical reasoning is different from theoretical reasoning, however, is that professionals are not engaged in making judgements that are supposed to hold good spatially and temporally, instead they are making judgements to address the problem in hand.

The broadening of the concepts of epistemic and tacit knowledge suggest that we may need to consider the relation between explicit and implicit cognition and action more fully than Polanyi, Knorr Cetina, Jensen, Lahn and Nerland have. We shall return to this issue in Chapter 6.

CONCLUSION

We have presented three interrelated lines of argument in this chapter. The first is that the reason that the social and management theorists offer different explanations about the type of knowledge required in the knowledge economy is because they focused primarily on Descartes' classic distinction between the 'two worlds' view of knowledge. The second is the legacy of the two worlds of knowledge, which pre-disposed these writers to overlook: (i) the mediated relation between theoretical and tacit knowledge; and, (ii) the contribution of epistemic cultures to the production and utilisation of scientific knowledge, as well as knowledge in other professionals' fields. The third is that Knorr Cetina's insights about epistemic cultures and practices and Zuboff's insights about intellective skill introduce a very different sense of the learning challenge in the knowledge economy, compared to the idea of supporting people to adapt to this reality by gaining higher levels of qualification. Instead the focus of our argument is, to paraphrase Cook and Seely Brown (2000, p. 394), knowing how to explicate the assumptions that underpin professional practices and discourses, using the resulting knowledge to develop new practices, products and services, and considering the economic, social and political implications of these acts of development. Thus we are left with the challenge: how to support people to develop such capabilities.

NOTES

[1]   A debate that has prevailed to the present time, see for example Rorty (1979) and McDowell (1996).

[2]   Many writers (Nowotny et al., 2002; Toulmin, 2001; Ward, 1996) have invoked the concept of scientific realism as a way of conceptualising the paradigmatic assumptions of the physical, natural and mathematical sciences. Here, the discussion of the meaning of scientific realism draws primarily on the work of Ward (1996). In particular, it uses the first of the three 'divisions' he introduced to clarify the epistemic boundaries of scientific realism.

[3]   Scientific realists contrasted their approach with the traditional forms of knowledge about the world that had relied on hearsay, personal accounts and introspectionism. The idea of an 'undisciplined' interrogation of events and phenomena gradually became unacceptable within the burgeoning eighteenth-century scientific community, which felt that it was possible to establish the true nature of objects (Shapin, 1994).

[4]   One of the most basic propositions of scientific realism, therefore, is that science (and only science) is capable of producing accurate representations of natural reality. The reason science attained this pre-eminent position is simply because its predictive capacities spoke the 'language of nature' (Rescheler, 1987, p. 4).

[5]   Postmodernism is a profoundly complex and ambiguous theoretical tradition which has been shaped by a diversity of intellectual and cultural currents, with the result that the label 'postmodernism' varies considerably according to context. Nevertheless, out of this maelstrom of divergent influences and tendencies a few widely shared principles have emerged, for example, the rejection of foundational accounts of the development of knowledge. Consequently, we follow writers such as Callinicos (1989) and Ward (1996), who have identified broad tenets of postmodernism rather than attempted to offer definitive statements about this theoretical development.

[6]   Schön published his critique of technological rationality less than five years after Bell had celebrated it, albeit through the slightly different terminology of intellectual technology. The force of Schön's critique for the social theorists' argument about how people use knowledge to address problems, however, has never really been appreciated in social theory.

[7]   Muller has, however, detected some ambivalence in the collective position presented in their work about the implications of Mode 2 knowledge. He argues that, from time to time, Gibbons et al. appear to suggest that Mode 2 knowledge production will, ultimately, *replace* Mode 1 knowledge completely. On other occasions they imply it may only *supplement* Mode 1 (2000, p. 48). This book chooses to emphasise the idea of 'replacement' because it is this perspective that informs Gibbons and colleagues' subsequent work on the implications of Mode 2 more widely within societies (Nowotny et al., 2002).

[8]   There is a parallel between Knorr Cetina's concern with establishing a broader definition of the role of knowledge in 'knowledge societies' and the concern of this book to establish a broader definition of the role of knowledge in the economy. Both are interested in identifying, albeit in different ways, the relationship between knowledge cultures and knowledge-producing activities. For this reason, this argument highlights the parallels between the respective arguments by inserting the references to the knowledge economy into her original text.

[9]   Although Zuboff's argument was formulated in the late 1980s, the substance of her argument is still germane. A recent book has used the concept of 'techno-mathematical literacies' to investigate modern manifestations of Zuboff's notion of intellective skills in the automobile, finance and packaging sectors (Hoyles et al., 2010). The authors have demonstrated that learning to make the meaning of workplace practice explicit, so that it can subsequently become an implicit feature of action, pre-supposes the introduction of new managerial and pedagogic practices that have been specially 'designed' to achieve that goal; and offered further confirmation of Zuboff's hypothesis that it is necessary for management to rethink the existing division of labour in the workplace if they want to engender the development of intellective skill.

CHAPTER 5

HIGHER EDUCATION AND THE TWO WORLDS
OF KNOWLEDGE

INTRODUCTION

We concluded in the last chapter that the legacy of the two worlds of knowledge, in the social and management theorists' account of the new role of knowledge in the economies of advanced industrial societies, resulted in those theorists offering only a partial explanation of their own theses about that new role. In particular, they continued the longstanding tradition of treating theoretical and tacit knowledge as separate forms of knowledge, and as different types of input into the production of knowledge-based products and services. As a consequence, the social and management theorists failed to appreciate that: (i) epistemic cultures are a pre-condition for a knowledge economy/society (i.e. it cannot flourish without them) because they play an important role in facilitating the creation of new knowledge and products and services in all spheres of activity; and (ii) the spread of epistemic cultures is making the interdependent relationship between theoretical and tacit knowledge a more prominent feature of forms of professional activity than in the past.

In light of the above conclusions, we have one aim in this chapter: to consider whether current educational policies support people to create the type of epistemic cultures and practices that characterise the creative use of knowledge in the economy, or in society or to adapt to the assumed reality of the knowledge economy. We do so by focusing on one area of UK educational policy: the forms of professional, vocational and workplace learning (PVWL) that are being developed in higher education. We have invoked this term to refer to under- and postgraduate degree programmes that have been most closely associated with preparing people to make the transition from higher education to work or supporting their continuing development while at work. Sometimes these degrees have an explicit workplace component, for example, a work placement, often they are undertaken by people who are at work, and at other times they are designed to provide an orientation to a professional and/or vocational field.

There is a two-fold reason for choosing this area of the higher education curriculum: firstly that professionally and vocationally orientated and work-based learning degrees have expanded exponentially in higher education over the last two decades (UUK, 2005, p. 35); and secondly that UK policymakers maintain both that a degree is the magic bullet to secure employment in such an economy, and that, '...economic competitiveness and improvements in our quality of life depend on the effective sharing between business and higher education...' (DfES, 2003, p. 5). Given that PVWL in UK higher education is a multi-faceted field, the chapter develops a conceptual framework for analysing changes within higher education and traces the implications of these changes for PVWL. It also explores why, despite the best intentions of universities and professional and vocational bodies, PVWL is unable to support people to address the new conception of the learning challenge of the knowledge economy advanced in this book. In doing so, we maintain that the framework could be used to analyse PVWL in other countries, where higher education has developed in comparable ways (Boud & Soloman, 2001; Jessop *et al.*, 2008; Peters, 2007).

Knowledge, Higher Education and Pedagogy

Introduction

This chapter reflects on the impact of the discourse about the knowledge economy in scholarly and policy texts concerned with learning and teaching in PVWL in UK higher education. It starts by locating this issue in a wider debate about the role of higher education and the knowledge economy, before analysing the ways in which policies have been formulated to modernise the higher education (HE) curriculum by broadening the concept of knowledge it makes available to learners. The chapter then identifies the legacy of the two worlds of knowledge in these attempts to modernise the HE curriculum, invoking the notion of the 'pedagogies of reflection' to describe what is creative and unsatisfactory about this response. It concludes by arguing that the concept of reflection constitutes an inadequate basis for addressing the philosophical legacy of the two worlds of knowledge and its manifestation in the contemporary higher education curriculum.

Higher education and the knowledge economy. There has been a flood of publications since the early 1990s that have attempted to consider the implications of the changing relationship between knowledge and higher education (Barnett, 1997, 1999; Delanty, 2001; Fuller, 1997, 2003; Jessop *et al.*, 2008; Peters, 2007). One of their unifying themes is a recognition that the debate about the knowledge economy/ society is the latest example of the type of 'cognitive shifts' that have occurred in modernity; in other words, the way in which:

> ...changes in knowledge production lead to changes in cultural and social structures... [and the way that] changes in the mode of knowledge bring about the articulation of new cultural models leading to institutional innovations...

> (Delanty, 2001, p. 3)

These writers have inevitably differed in terms of their respective assessment of the nature of universities' responses to, and the implications of, the emergence of a knowledge economy/society for the future of the university. This chapter does not attempt to provide a comprehensive review of these debates; instead it draws attention to their central themes (without passing judgement upon them), to provide a context for assessing universities' response to the knowledge economy.

Arguments about the shift from one era of modernity to another can, at first sight, appear to imply that one conception of knowledge has been replaced by another: for example, that the 'liberal modernity' doctrine of the 'enlightenment' has been supplanted by the 'postmodern' doctrine of 'performativity' (Delanty, 2001, pp. 21–3). Such a conclusion is misleading. Delanty's idea of cognitive shifts is a more nuanced explanation of cultural change. It alerts us to the way in which the ideological forces that influenced and shaped the emergence of different conceptions of knowledge can result in each conception being embodied and perpetuated, often conceivably in opposition to one another, in higher education.

One reason why it is difficult to detect the continuing and frequently conflicting influence of different conceptions of knowledge in higher education is that policy-makers pay little attention to shifts in conceptions of knowledge. Instead they tend, on the one hand, to conceive of knowledge as a 'black box' and thus never define it; and, on the other hand, to present the knowledge enshrined in qualifications as the magic bullet that will impel economic prosperity. Thus educational policies in the UK, EU and elsewhere in the world, have consistently, as we noted in Chapter 1, affirmed that we are in a 'knowledge society', that more and more jobs will be 'knowledge jobs', and that this entails the population accumulating more and higher-level qualifications (Guile, 2006).

One of the results of taking the link between knowledge, learning and economic development for granted is that policymakers adopt a design strategy conception of policy implementation. Where the social theorists assumed that the number of knowledge-based products and services constituted evidence of a knowledge economy/society, policymakers assume that measures such as widening participation, and frameworks to assure the quality of learning and facilitate credit transfer and mobility in the labour market, can be 'designed' to produce the desired set of outcomes. One consequence is, as Moore and Young (2001, p. 445) have presciently observed, that there is not only very little clarity within educational policy about what type of knowledge is required, there is also very little discussion as to how it should be acquired.

To explicate the meaning and implications of the longstanding and contending assumptions about knowledge that are embedded in educational policy for UK higher education, and to draw some tentative conclusions of their implications for the way in which higher education should respond to the knowledge economy elsewhere in the world, it is helpful to elucidate the conceptions of knowledge associated with the different cognitive shifts. Rather than use Delanty's general characterisations of the different eras of knowledge, we have chosen to use an alternative set of terms to characterise the different conception of knowledge that have been embraced in UK higher education. They are the 'traditional', the 'utilitarian' and the 'postmodern'[1], and we have used them to highlight pedagogic problems that educational policies that are predicated on different assumptions about knowledge have posed for learning and teaching in universities. Our rationale for doing so is that these terms denote the tensions in higher education about knowledge more fully than Delanty's epochal terminology.

The idea of the traditional conception of knowledge reflects the debate between scientific realists and humanists, in what Delanty (2001, pp. 21–2) has referred to as 'classical' and 'liberal modernity', about the respective validity of both forms of knowledge and the justifications for their inclusion in the university curriculum.

It thus represents a combination of ideas. First, it endorses the view implicit in liberal modernity that there is a given body of foundational knowledge (i.e. literary and scientific knowledge) that should feature in the curriculum, and which universities have a responsibility to transmit. One of the main manifestations of foundational knowledge is the assumption that what was important was submitting oneself to the discipline of a subject and becoming the type of person this process was supposed to produce (Barnett, 1991). Second, it consolidates the foundational and canonical status attributed by universities to disciplines and to the scientific method. One manifestation is the assumption that disciplines constitute the only foundation for conducting research, because new knowledge is formed from engagement with existing disciplinary traditions (Rothblatt & Wittrock, 1993).

By drawing its strength from the different principles that informed the idea of foundational knowledge, the traditional episteme masks the way in which it embraces the scientific and humanistic knowledge in a seemingly coherent position. It simply elevates the 'best' of both of these two worlds of knowledge into a common canon, that, to borrow Moore and Young's phrase (2001, p. 447), '…it duly celebrates by conceiving of knowledge as an end-in-itself'.

The idea of a 'utilitarian' conception of knowledge reflects the view that surfaced in liberal modernity and was subsequently consolidated in 'organised modernity' (Delanty, 2001, p. 24), namely that education will always be related in some way to society's economic and political needs. Thus, it accepts that economic considerations determine universities' relation to society, and it conceives of knowledge as a means to an end. From this perspective, the role of the university curriculum is generally held to be a contribution to realising the particular 'form of society' desired by policymakers, while the role of research is deemed to be to support the growth of industrialisation.

These fairly utilitarian ideas about knowledge were a constant, if marginal[2], feature of the discourse about the higher education curriculum in the UK up to the late 1980s. What has changed over the last twenty years, however, is the scope and reach of the technical instrumental conception of knowledge in higher education. Prior to the 1980s, the utilitarian and instrumental conception of knowledge was largely confined to those areas of the higher education curriculum concerned with technical and/or professional education (Silver, 1988). Its reach within the higher education curriculum received considerable momentum during the late 1980s through the push by the Conservative Government to extend the 'vocational element' within the mainstream higher education curriculum (Barnett, 1994).

The 'postmodern' conception of knowledge reflects the blurring of the epistemic and moral boundaries that characterised, albeit in slightly different ways, the traditional and utilitarian epistemes, with the result that the postmodern episteme is predicated on an opposite set of assumptions to the aforementioned epistemes. Instead of accepting knowledge as a given; that is, an accurate and verifiable representation of the world, the postmodernist episteme directs attention to the historical and cultural basis of knowledge, and argues that the world and knowledge are always a product of different ideological standpoints.

One of the main tenets of the 'postmodern' conception of knowledge is the claim that any curriculum based on the traditional and utilitarian epistemes is relying on essentially arbitrary assumptions about knowledge and culture (Hartley, 1997). The status and epistemological basis of these conceptions of knowledge are no longer tenable, according to the postmodernists, thus their legacies (i.e. structures and hierarchies of knowledge), and the part that they play in reproducing those forms of rationality in higher education, must be challenged (Barnett, 1999). This loss of status is assumed to have occurred because:

> ...if there are no sure foundations and no Archimedean points from which knowledge is generated and assimilated, but instead a plurality of situated knowledges, then the very foundations of discipline-based education are themselves undermined...

(Edwards & Usher, 2000, p. 93)[3]

Another tenet is that the values, interests and perspectives, often referred to as 'voices', associated with the excluded or marginalised groups are equal to the dominant voices of the traditional and utilitarian epistemes in universities (Moore & Young, 2001 p. 190). At one level, this is an updating of a much older debate about the tendency of universities to gloss over the concerns of marginalised and excluded groups. At another level, it has resulted in an argument that any form of knowledge has the potential to be included in the university curriculum.

Pressures to make higher education responsive to the knowledge economy. The distinctions between the traditional, utilitarian and postmodern conceptions of knowledge can be used in a number of ways to shed light on the implications of the competing pressures to modernise higher education. The first way is to identify the changes that have occurred as regards the purpose of the undergraduate and postgraduate curriculum. The second way is to identify the pedagogic dilemma that has emerged as a result of these changes to university degrees.

One of the pressures following the 1997 Dearing Review of higher education in the UK has been to retain many of the values that gave the traditional conception of knowledge its enduring strength, whilst simultaneously modernising university degrees by making their content more transparent for students and employers. The clearest example of the former is provided by the UK's Quality Assurance Agency's (QAA) Subject Review process, which offers some support for the continuation of the canonical status of the knowledge provided by disciplines (Bridges, 2002, p. 51). The Dearing Review's concern (NCIHE, 1997) with establishing the standards to be achieved for all degrees has been rigorously reinforced by the QAA in a number of ways (Bridges, 2002, p. 51). First, it has insisted that degrees define the 'subject knowledge' (i.e. course content) to be taught. Second, it has laid down the choice of subject headings to frame curricula and benchmarks for courses. These acts of reinforcement were, however, accompanied by the stipulation that all courses – academic and vocational – should be expressed in terms of 'learning outcomes' (i.e. what students should be able to do). Such statements were assumed to serve as a proxy measure for employers to help them to gauge students' transferable knowledge and skill (Ecclestone, 2004). The net effect of these developments was to insist that even the teaching of subject knowledge had to achieve clear utilitarian goals.

Accompanying this pressure to maintain many of the values associated with the traditional conception of knowledge has been a determined push by New Labour to extend the utilitarian or instrumental orientation of higher education. The initial foundation for this development was laid in the late 1980s and early 1990s when the Conservative Government sponsored the introduction of a number of measures to 'vocationalise' the higher education curriculum. One measure was the introduction of work-based learning degrees that had been explicitly designed to reflect employers' needs (Fulton, 1996). Another measure was a series of attempts to make mainstream undergraduate and postgraduate degree programmes more responsive to employers' demands (Barnett, 1994). One of the most notable developments was the Enterprise in Higher Education Initiative (EHE), which provided funds for university departments to develop students' 'transferable skills' (subsequently 'key skills'[4]), which many employers and employer organisations deemed were an essential pre-requisite for working in the global economy (CBI, 1991). A further measure was the establishment of various mechanisms to recognise or accredit different forms of what can be referred to as 'experiential' (or tacit) learning or non-traditional learning, which had not previously been recognised within the disciplines as part of degree courses (Bridges, 2002). These mechanisms are normally referred to as the accreditation of prior learning (APL) or prior experiential learning (APEL). They were designed to accredit within degree programmes either knowledge gained from non-formal programmes of study or the everyday or tacit knowledge acquired through professional and/or technical work or forms of prior learning, to give advanced standing in relation to university entry requirements.

The particular form of utilitarianism that has provided the dominant rhetoric for systemic change in response to the knowledge economy since the Dearing Review has been the re-appraisal of the role of disciplines as a means to develop key skills (Moore & Young, 2001, p. 448). In an attempt to broaden the outcomes of degrees so that they developed the qualities policymakers assumed were required for working in the knowledge economy, the Dearing Review (NCIHE, 1997, p. 14) introduced the idea of 'programme specifications'. A tendency that has been institutionalised across the EU through what are colloquially referred to as the 'Bologna' process and 'Dublin' descriptors (Mills, 2004). The effect of these specifications was two-fold: to maintain the longstanding role of disciplines to transmit knowledge by ensuring that universities spelt out the 'subject knowledge' students would acquire through studying for a degree; and to reconceptualise the role of disciplines so that they served a more utilitarian purpose. Universities were required to identify how degrees developed key skills and the qualities of flexibility that are required for working in the knowledge economy, which the Dearing Review stated from now on were 'necessary outcomes of all higher education programmes' (NCIHE, 1997, p. 14). Hence, by accepting the Dearing recommendations in full, New Labour, in effect, consolidated the instrumental orientation of degree programmes within all areas of the higher education curriculum. Higher educational policy since 1997 has been predicated on an explicit link between subject knowledge, key skills and graduate employability, and universities have been required to formulate learning and teaching policies to reflect this new orientation (Mason, 2002).

In contrast to the explicit push to extend the utilitarian purpose of higher education, there have been less overt and more covert measures to promote the postmodern conception of knowledge in higher education. Certainly, aspects of the postmodern argument about the heterogeneity and the performativity of knowledge have become firmly embedded in higher education policy over the last decade (Peters, 2007). One example of the gradual acceptance of the heterogeneity of knowledge is the gradual erosion of the canonical status of disciplinary frameworks for degrees and the growing acceptance of modular frameworks. These frameworks are perceived by policymakers and university vice chancellors to offer a way to extend choice to learners, by allowing them to combine modules from different disciplines to support their future employability, rather than following subject-based courses that have been determined by academics (Gokulsing & de Costa, 1997). One consequence of this broadening with regard to what counts as knowledge in higher education is that some commentators have suggested that universities should abandon the concern for:

...Knowledge with a capital "K"... [and] think of universities as engaged in knowledge processes in different knowledge settings, exploiting knowledge possibilities...

(Barnett, 1999, p. 21)

Consequences of the pressures and the resulting pedagogic dilemma. The cumulative effect of the pressures described above has created three distinct tensions in university degrees. The first tension arises as a result of the clash between the firm emphasis from the QAA on specifying the subject knowledge that is to be taught and assessed within university degrees, and its equally firm emphasis on ensuring that degrees are relevant for the world of work. The former perpetuates the traditional conception of knowledge: that all knowledge is based on forms of generalisation that were rooted in the homogeneous and well-bounded disciplinary traditions within higher education and, moreover, which are normally presented to students in the form of an abstract representation of the world. In contrast, the latter is forcing universities to re-appraise this conception of knowledge, and to encourage lecturers to provide opportunities for students to 'connect' the subject knowledge they acquire to the world of work. One consequence of this tension about the purpose of degree programmes is that universities have been expected for some time to embrace into a coherent pedagogic position two conflicting ideas about the purpose of learning. The continuing, albeit weakened, influence of the traditional conception of knowledge reinforces the idea that in order to learn subject knowledge we have to grasp the meaning of abstract representations, and to know how to use them in ways that are traditionally expected in higher education, for example, when writing a dissertation. Meanwhile the constant pressure to demonstrate the relevance of degree programmes has resulted in a broadening of the systems of assessment, for example, collaborative projects, learning logs, portfolios and so forth, to allow students to connect subject knowledge to the type of problem they may encounter, in the future, at work.

The second tension arises as a result of two versions of the 'practicality' of degrees existing side by side in higher education. This tension has surfaced as a result of the clash between the post-Dearing impetus in higher education to conceive of disciplines as providing a way to develop key skills, compared with the longstanding utilitarian concern in universities for the 'practicality of knowledge' (Rothblatt & Wittrock, 1993). Practicality was defined, from 'organised modernity' onwards, in accordance with criteria that reflected the traditionalist and utilitarian conception of knowledge. This resulted in definitions of practical knowledge being framed either in terms of the perceived 'relevance' of a disciplinary field (e.g. bio-chemistry) for the economy, or in terms of the 'contribution' of, for example, the Natural and Social Sciences to desired forms of social modernisation (Rothblatt & Wittrock, 1993). One reason it was possible to derive criteria to define practicality from a combination of the traditional and utilitarian conceptions of knowledge is that they both shared a commitment to the truth of knowledge produced in universities. Hence, what underpinned these slightly different, but broadly complementary, definitions of the practical value of knowledge was an acceptance of the intrinsic value of knowledge that universities provided (Delanty, 2001, p. 32).

In contrast, the particular version of 'practicality' that policymakers are now urging universities to develop is no longer defined in accordance with the above criteria. The Dearing Review introduced a new conception of the practical value of knowledge: the ability of students to 'apply' knowledge. The change it has ushered in can be described as a shift from 'knowledge that can be applied' to the 'application of knowledge'. The report identified three different expressions of the application of knowledge: the ability to communicate information to different audiences; to use 'number' to substantiate a point of view; and to use ICT to present different types of data in a variety of ways.

This new conception of practicality problematises the longstanding assumption in higher education about the intrinsic value of knowledge that universities provided, because it assumes that any form of knowledge is malleable so long as we have developed the skills necessary to apply it in different contexts. As a consequence universities have had to embrace two different ideas about the practicality of knowledge. Degree programmes are expected to assist students to understand the relevance of knowledge to the world of work as well as to enable them to acquire context-free skills (i.e. key skills) in context-specific situations (i.e. lectures, laboratories and work placements). This is a tricky balance because the former is consistent with the concern in universities to provide evidence of a student's current level of attainment, while the latter constitute a proxy measure that employers can use to gauge attainment in the future (Guile, 2001).

The third tension surfaces as a result of the clash between the utilitarian and postmodern versions of the heterogeneity of knowledge in higher education since the late 1980s (Peters, 2007). The former, as represented by scientific and technological specialisms that serviced the economic needs of society, became firmly entrenched alongside the traditional disciplines in the undergraduate and postgraduate curriculum from the period of organised modernity onwards. The latter attaches importance to any forms of knowledge irrespective of whether they are currently included in the higher education curriculum. The growing prominence of the latter position – about heterogeneity of knowledge in certain areas of higher education – has resulted in a call to replace the utilitarian concern to develop learners as reflective practitioners so that they can work in the knowledge economy with a new pedagogic approach. The goal of this 'pedagogy of (dis)location and translation', according to Edwards and Usher (1994, p. 147), is the, '...mapping and translating discourses into one another and constantly renegotiating the meaning and significance of their work across domains'.

These competing and contending pressures on higher education generate a pedagogical dilemma that reflects the legacy of the two worlds of knowledge in the traditional, utilitarian and postmodern conceptions of knowledge. This legacy can be presented in ideal–typical terms: the traditional and utilitarian conceptions are predicated on the existence of a single world while the postmodern conception is predicated on a plurality of worlds. This dilemma, following Prawat (1999a, p. 60), can be defined as a question of 'head fitting' or 'head splitting'. Prawat invoked these terms to reflect the traditional separation of the mind from the world. The former represents the unifying theme that, as we saw in Chapter 4, runs between the rationalist and empiricist philosophies, which constitute the philosophical bedrock of scientific realism, as Prawat succinctly observes:

> Rationalists, turn the eye of the mind inward. Knowledge is valid if it evidences conceptual compatibility – that is, coheres with the structure one is attempting to create. Empiricists turn the eye of the mind outward. Internal configurations of the mind are valid if they correspond with environmentally given external configurations. All reality is... nothing more than a set of 'linguistic constructions'.

> (Prawat, 1999a, p. 61)

The latter, according to Prawat (1999a, p. 63), represents the postmodern claim that, '...there is no way to get outside of language to the real truth of things and that the meaning of a word is in its use not in an image conjured up in the mind'.

Prawat's distinctions between 'head fitting' and 'head splitting' can be used to demonstrate that although the traditional, utilitarian and postmodern conceptions of knowledge are expressed in very different terms from one another, they are, nevertheless, still predicated on the existence of two worlds of knowledge.

The emphasis on the acquisition of subject knowledge represents, in the UK, a post-Dearing expression of the traditional rationalist and empiricist position that it is possible to provide truthful knowledge about the world. From this standpoint, the pedagogic challenge is, following Prawat (1999a, p. 60), to 'fit' the subject knowledge into our minds via our cognitive structures – or 'schemas', as he refers to them – which are assumed to be pre-given, so that we can comprehend the external world. The emphasis on the ability to apply knowledge constitutes the 'other side' of the rationalist and empiricist concern to provide truthful knowledge about the world. It rests on the idea that once we have 'fitted' the skill of applying knowledge into our heads, we have acquired a generic framework that allows us to transfer the knowledge we have acquired and use it to guide our actions in a variety of different contexts. In contrast, the concern to support students to translate discourses into one another, and to renegotiate constantly their meaning and significance across different contexts, has many affinities with the postmodern position that there is no way to get outside of language to the real truth of things. Once this standpoint has been adopted, the pedagogic challenge is, following Prawat, to 'split' the mind into a multitude of 'minds' that can form and respond to linguistic representations.

The 'head fitting' and 'head splitting' conceptions of the relation between mind and world reveal the way in which the pressure to modernise higher education in the UK to respond to the knowledge economy has resulted in the emergence of a modern version of the problem of the two worlds of knowledge. The traditional and utilitarian conceptions of knowledge assume that knowledge has an objective basis, while the postmodern conception assumes that all knowledge is subjective. This leaves us with the challenge of how to relate these different forms of knowledge to one another. Paradoxically, many writers, irrespective of which of the above positions about knowledge they hold, have turned to the concept of reflection as the basis of a pedagogic strategy to address this dilemma.

Overcoming the pedagogic dilemma: The 'pedagogies of reflection'. The concept of reflection has a longstanding history in education that dates back to the work of John Dewey. In the current era, the most well-known attempt to popularise Dewey's ideas about reflection as a basis for overcoming the separation of theory from practice is Donald Schön's work on the 'reflective practitioner' (1987), and this has, as we shall see, been enormously influential in PVWL. Schön was primarily concerned with the practical implications of the theory/practice problem in relation to professional education in American universities. Schön (1987, p. 3) argued that the curriculum manifestation of this problem leaves us floundering between the 'high ground' of theory, where the solution to all problems is through research-based theory and technique, and the 'swampland' of practice where there are messy problems that defy technical solution. Schön argued that this dilemma has two sources. The first source was the legacy of what he (1987, p. 3) refers to as 'technical rationality'; that is, an '...epistemology of practice based on positive philosophical assumptions which was built into the heart of the modern university'.

The cornerstone of this epistemology is the assumption that the scientific research techniques are independent of their context of use and, for this reason, can be applied unproblematically to resolve any social, economic or political problems. The second source of the problem for Schön (1987, p. 3) was that the, '...swampy zones of practice lie beyond its [i.e. technical rationality's] canons', and, as a result, professional education poorly equipped professionals to deal with the actual problems that they confronted at work[5].

The solution to the separation of theory and practice in professional education that Schön (1987, pp. 22–37) proposed was based on the formulation of an alternative epistemology to the scientific realist principles that underpin technical rationalism. He defined this as 'reflection-on-action', arguing that it constituted a pedagogic strategy for assisting professionals to resolve the dilemmas they encounter in practice. His epistemology reflected, what Schön (1987, p. 36) referred to as, a 'constructionist'[6] view of the reality with which professionals deal. The problems of practice, for Schön, are never pre-given as technical-rationalism assumed and thus not susceptible to resolution through the application of the scientific method of inquiry. Professionals have to construct their interpretation of those problems as well as the modes of competence required to resolve those problems, and their solutions are never 'in the book'; they have to be solved through a 'kind of improvisation' and a testing of the chosen strategies (Schön, 1987, p. 5). Hence, the knowledge and skills that professionals use to define and change the situation are inextricably bound up in that situation and not independent of it.

The implication of Schön's epistemological conception was a shift in professional education away from a 'normative curriculum' that was based on the acquisition of theories and the application of research-based modes of inquiry, and towards a curriculum that facilitated the development of 'professional artistry' through a 'reflective practicum' (Schön, 1987, p. 18). Schön argued that a reflective practicum was based on the principle of learning through inquiry that Dewey (1938/86, p. 364) felt was the 'primary or initial subject matter' for any curriculum. The design of the curriculum, for Schön, should therefore support professionals: to recognise and apply standard rules; to reason from generalised rules to problematic cases; and to learn how to improvise in order to respond to uncertain or conflicting situations of practice.

During the 1980s Schön's concept of reflection-in-action proved initially attractive, in the UK, and especially in those areas of the higher education curriculum concerned with addressing the theory/practice divide in, for example, teacher education and medicine (Brockbank & McGill, 1998), and elsewhere in the world (Dall'Alba & Sandberg, 1996). The main attraction of the concept as a pedagogic strategy, as Winter and Maisch (1996) observe, was that it provided a way for professionals to re-appraise the vexed question of the relationship between theory and practice by 'theorising' their practice. By this they meant that reflection constituted the basis for encouraging professionals to use a repertoire of past examples as a set of precedents or metaphors to re-frame current problems and envisage solutions to them. Furthermore, it recognised the open-endedness of professional inquiry because any solutions are provisional rather than permanent, thereby acknowledging that although participation in professional practice generated a different type of learning from academic study, this learning was equally valid.

The concept of reflection originally entered the higher education lexicon, therefore, as a strategy for developing the skills within professional education. The concept was increasingly called upon throughout the 1990s to provide a new pedagogic 'rationale' for higher education, as universities were consistently put under pressure to make their content more relevant to the demands students will face in their future professional lives (Barnett, 1997, p. 91). Moreover, it is still being called upon to assist people enrolled on professional development programmes in higher education (HE) to make 'situated' decisions in accordance with the demands of their professional practice (Bradbury *et al.*, 2009). Despite this broadening of the use of reflection in HE, the concept still retains its original purpose as a pedagogic strategy:

> ...by which experience is brought into consideration and secondly, deriving from the first, the creation of meaning and conceptualisation from experience and the capacity to look at things as other than they appear...

> (Brockbank & McGill, 1998, p. 84)

The idea of bringing experience under control has a number of attractions in the post-Dearing climate in UK higher education. It does not threaten or de-stabilise the traditional concern for preserving the canonical status of disciplines; it resonates with the new instrumental orientation in higher education to make the university curriculum more relevant to the world of work; and it offers a way for students to personalise their learning so that it is consistent with their own standpoints and interests. Thus, reflection is perceived as the basis of a pedagogy that enables students to become conscious of their own approaches to learning, promotes critically reflective learning in students via reflection on their own practice and paves the way for them to negotiate with their tutors how they would like to be taught (Brockbank & McGill, 1998, p. 73). Furthermore, the development of the power of reflection offers a way to provide evidence that they have developed those 'metacognitive' skills (i.e. learning to learn) that writers such as Reich (1991) claim are highly desirable in the knowledge economy.

In addition to the concept of reflection being embraced by writers who are trying to resolve the tension between the traditional and utilitarian orientation in higher education, the concept has become central to a number of writers who have articulated the principles for what might be called a postmodern pedagogy. Barnett (1997, p. 90) argues that higher education should encourage students to become 'self-critical' about their pre-suppositions about knowledge while R. Edwards (2000, p. 115) suggests that universities should assist learners to 'dislocate' themselves from traditional epistemological positions and engage with the plurality of knowledges that are available. In making this case about the value of reflection, the aforementioned writers acknowledge the tension that exists between the utilitarian and postmodern impulses in higher education. On the one hand, Barnett argues that to adapt effectively to – and even to bring about – a world of unknowable change:

> ...requires self-referential capacities of a high order on the part of individuals. What knowledge of the world there is has to be taken on board so as to inform the self about the self, disturbing and challenging as that may be. 'Reflection' thus becomes an educational codeword for this set of self-reflective and self-monitoring challenges.

> (Barnett, 1997, p. 91)

Yet, on the other hand, he acknowledges that students are not being asked to 'move forward' through their own volition, but rather to ensure that they secure their employability in the knowledge economy (Barnett, 1997, p. 91). A slightly different emphasis about the value of reflection as a pedagogic strategy surfaces in R. Edwards (2000, p. 142). He argues that since 'different locations bring forth only certain possibilities for certain discourses', a pedagogy informed by the concept of reflection will prepare learners to question discourses and to offer alternative interpretations of subject knowledge and/or personal experience.

Problems with Schön's concept of reflection. There are, however, a number of problems associated with the systematic take-up of reflection in higher education since the 1990s, the origin of which lies in Schön's version of constructionist epistemology. At first sight, Schön's epistemology is highly seductive. His critique of technical rationality chimes with the post-Dearing utilitarian direction of government policy for higher education and with the critique postmodernist-influenced writers have levelled against disciplinary knowledge. Hence reflection appears to be consistent with the 'modernising' and 'inclusive' attitudes towards knowledge. Furthermore, Schön's concern to develop 'professional artistry' simultaneously chimes with the different aspects of the traditional, utilitarian and postmodern attitudes towards knowledge. It reflects a weak version of the principle of 'spiritual' leadership that became entrenched within universities in the period of liberal modernity, in the sense that: it affirms the value of intelligence and judgement to performance; it suggests a way to engage with the push to make degrees more relevant since it constitutes the basis of a pedagogic strategy to encourage students to identify points of connection between their studies and the world of work; and it reflects the postmodern sensibility that the claim that there is a hierarchy of professions is deeply divisive because all forms of work are characterised by their own form of artistry.

From our perspective, writers who uncritically accept Schön's concept of reflection unintentionally perpetuate the two worlds of knowledge distinction that is the source of the main problem about knowledge in the knowledge economy. We can demonstrate this claim in a number of ways. Firstly Schön's solution to the problems he identified with technical rationality was merely to:

...turn the relationship between competence and professional knowledge upside down. We should start not by asking how to make better use of research-based knowledge but by asking what we can learn from a careful examination of artistry.

(Schön, 1987, p. 13)

He used his distinction between the 'objectivist' basis of technical rationality and the 'constructionist' basis of the reflective practicum merely to argue for the latter to be privileged over the former in the design of professional education courses. In doing so, Schön (1987, p. 36) maintains the traditional two worlds position and conceives both of the mind as separate from the world, and of theory as separate from practice. Moreover, his emphasis on reflective action displaces the dualism between theory and practice into the realm of the personal. Citing Dewey, Schön (1987, p. 16) argues that we come to know the world through our initiation into the traditions of professional practice; the process of initiation acting as the 'means by which the powers of learners are released and directed'.

The difficulty with this solution is that it leaves us connected to the world through the realm of reflection, which in Schön's case is primarily concerned with the immediate manifestations of practice, rather than asking questions about the constitution of practice. In advocating a solution to technical rationality based on our experience of practice, Schön ends up, paradoxically, embracing the traditional stance that experience is our only source of knowledge of the world: a stance that his intellectual forefather Dewey had opposed in developing his own philosophy (Bernstein, 1971, p. 203). In his attempt to instrumentalise Dewey's ideas about reflection, Schön glosses over Dewey's acceptance that there is a relation between 'universals' (his term for theoretical concepts) and practice, and formulated his ideas about reflection and inquiry to demonstrate the nature of that relationship (Dewey, 1938/86, p. 177). Universals for Dewey, as Garrison (2006, p. 6) observes, '...allow us to impart meaning to particulars...', because all inquiries are undertaken with background knowledge and this knowledge inevitably has some bearing on the questions asked, the methods used, etc. As a consequence of overlooking this relation between theory and practice, Schön inadvertently confirms the conventional scientific–realist wisdom that practice is grounded in the realm of human experience, that theory is an abstraction from the world and that reflection consists of the systematisation of practice. Hence he is unable to offer us a way to comprehend the relation between theory and practice or the significance of that relation for challenging the existing constitution of professional practice.

Any attempt in higher education to base a pedagogic strategy on a Schönian conception of reflection, through the use of notions such as 'reflective dialogue', 'critical self-reflection' and 'dis-locating pedagogies' are, therefore, inevitably characterised by a residual dualism, because writers are proceeding from an assumption that the mind and world, and theory and practice, are separate from and unrelated to one another. Thus, even though many of the observations that Brockbank and McGill, Barnett and Edwards make about learning are relevant to the challenge higher education faces in responding to the knowledge economy, they still end up perpetuating – rather than offering learners a way to go beyond – the two worlds of knowledge.

Furthermore, we can also see the legacy of the two worlds of knowledge in Schön's concept of reflection through reference to what has recently been described as, the 'representational paradigm' (Brandom, 2000a). This paradigm poses the relation of mind to world as one in which knowledge caused by sense experience is made meaningful by the constructions put upon it (Derry, 2003, p. 43). As a consequence, there is a further residual dualism informing the work of those writers who have formulated pedagogic approaches based on, or as a critique of, Schön's ideas about reflection. The clearest manifestation of this residual dualism is the idea that surfaces in the work of Brockbank and McGill, Barnett and Edwards, that learning involves placing a construction on an experience. For Brockbank and

McGill (1998, p. 62), the critical issue that underpins and informs reflective dialogue is our ability to 'name' a situation so that we are able to talk about it. For Barnett (1997, p. 103) critical self-reflection entails, '...reflecting on one's own understanding', while R. Edwards (2000, p. 140) maintains that the hallmark of dislocation is the ability to translate one textual representation into another.

The unifying theme that embodies the above pedagogic suggestions is the representational idea that we respond to sensory impressions or linguistic utterances by making a mental representation and then sharing that construction. One of the difficulties with this assumption is, as Brandom (2000a, p. 48) argues, that, '...even non-inferential reports must be inferentially articulated'. Thus Brandom suggests that acts of inference are best thought of as social practices concerned with making the significance of an action and/or utterance that emerged in one context intelligible to others who inhabit another context. This line of reasoning introduces the provocative notion that the world is laden with meaning and value that can be used to provide a cultural and historical underpinning to our judgements and actions, and thus help make them intelligible to others. Thus it follows that if we are to avoid the legacy of the two worlds of knowledge in the debate about the knowledge economy – and the pitfalls of the 'pedagogies of reflection' in the educational response to that debate – it is necessary to consider whether there is a conception of the relation between mind and world that acknowledges the cultural and historical constitution of concepts, practices and reasons, and a pedagogy consistent with that conception. This will take us, as we will see after our discussion of Dewey in the next chapter, to Cultural–Historical Activity Theory (CHAT).

CONCLUSION

We have argued that the legacy of the two worlds of knowledge results in a parallel between the social and management theorists' explanation of the knowledge economy and in UK policymakers' response to the knowledge economy. The former present one-sided explanations of the knowledge economy while the latter, even though they recognised that the knowledge economy posed a qualitatively new challenge for education, have assumed that the solution is to extend the existing types of knowledge and skill to a greater proportion of the population.

We noted that in their attempt to articulate the basis of a pedagogy to support learners to address the challenge of the knowledge economy, many writers who have written about learning and teaching in higher education or PVWL have – irrespective as to whether they have embraced a traditional, utilitarian or postmodern position as regards knowledge – turned to Schön's ideas about reflection as a pedagogic strategy to facilitate student learning. We have demonstrated that the resulting 'pedagogies of reflection' constitute an inadequate basis for overcoming the dilemmas that they purportedly address. They are deficient because they have failed to recognise that the root cause of the pedagogic problems is the legacy of the two worlds of knowledge in traditional, utilitarian and postmodern conceptions of knowledge that currently reverberate within policy and practice in higher education in general and PVWL in specific. We thus concluded that the challenge for PVWL is to help students to think differently about the assumed differences between the two worlds of knowledge. To address this challenge it is necessary, as we shall see in the next chapter, to identify a holistic conception of mind and world, and theory and practice, and to demonstrate how such a conception offers a different starting point for considering what it means to learn.

NOTES

[1] These conceptions of knowledge are partly influenced by the knowledge distinctions formulated by Moore and Young to clarify the different conceptions of knowledge that inform the current debates about the 14–19 curriculum (2001). They are also partly influenced by our interpretation of Delanty's (2001) argument about the cognitive shifts that have occurred in industrial societies.

[2] The publication of the Robbins Report in 1963 gave considerable impetus to this conception of knowledge by arguing in favour of an extension of technological education in universities to respond to the demands of the post-war economy. The report did not, however, elevate the instrumental orientation into a principle for all of higher education.

[3] It is easier to reference the assumptions of the postmodern episteme than the traditional and utilitarian epistemes, because the former is grounded in current debates in social theory whereas the latter have been derived from a much more eclectic set of sources.

[4] The terms 'enterprise' and 'transferable' skills were employed at the time. They have subsequently been replaced with the term 'key skills'. For the sake of consistency, we have chosen to use the latter term throughout the chapter.

[5] Thus, in the same period that Bell (1973, p. 423) was affirming the virtues of a technical rational model of university education to prepare professionals to address the challenges faced by advanced industrial societies, Schön was articulating a trenchant critique of that model.

[6] Schön uses the term 'constructionist' in a rather idiosyncratic way to refer to the idea that professionals mentally formulate the problems they work on. He does not relate his use to the social scientific discussions about constructionism.

CHAPTER 6

THINKING DIFFERENTLY ABOUT THE TWO
WORLDS VIEW OF KNOWLEDGE

INTRODUCTION

The concept of reflection, as we saw in the last chapter, was turned to variously by a number of writers from different epistemological standpoints, in an attempt to overcome the legacy of the two worlds of knowledge in higher education. The problem was that the resulting 'pedagogies of reflection' became a strategy either to fit people's minds into a given world that was separate from their activity, or to split their mind into a multitude of 'minds' in an attempt to capture the diversity of their experience.

In light of this paradoxical outcome, we adopt a historical approach. We return to John Dewey's original ideas about reflection to assess whether they themselves offer a better resource than in their subsequent development by Schön and in the 'pedagogies of reflection', to address the philosophical and pedagogical problems that this book claims afflict the educational response to the knowledge economy. We pursue our historical strategy by using our account of Dewey to reconsider the work of Schön, and other writers who have used the concept of reflection. We conclude that Dewey's concept and the theory of 'trans-action' with which it is associated do not constitute a conceptual framework for overcoming the two worlds of knowledge and its legacy in the educational debate about the knowledge economy. We then introduce the work of another intellectual figure who was a contemporary of Dewey – Lev Semënovich Vygotsky – and highlight how his theory of cultural mediation provides a more promising starting point for not only formulating a conceptual framework, but also for addressing other issues that the emergence of the knowledge economy poses more generally for advanced industrial societies.

Dewey's Naturalistic Theory of Experience and Learning

Introduction

Dewey is one of several figures, including William James and Charles Sanders Peirce, who belonged to the American school of philosophy known as pragmatism (Bernstein, 1971). This school rejected the assumption that had prevailed since the Enlightenment – and that underpins scientific realism – that philosophy and science could reveal absolute truths about the world. Nevertheless, James, Peirce and Dewey were concerned to establish what it was possible for philosophy and science to discover about the world, if they were relieved of their traditional responsibilities to lay bare the grounds of true belief (Prawat, 1999a, p. 62).

One of the main sources of inspiration for Dewey (1925/53 pp. 141–2) in pursuing this goal, in the early phase of his career, was Hegel's 'transcendental idealism'. Dewey felt that the, '…logic rather than the metaphysics of this [Hegel's] system, that is, the function of thought in the structure of the object, the evidence in thinking that thought and the object lie within the same experience' (Mead, cited in Garrison, 2006, p. 1), offered him a way to synthesise his interests in overcoming the separation of subject, object, matter, spirit, the divine and human in philosophy, and to formulate a philosophy and method of inquiry to analyse their relation to one another.

As Dewey developed his concern to understand the practical aspects of life, he turned away from Hegel's philosophical emphasis on intellectual comprehension and towards 'scientific analogies for illumination' with regard to the importance of experience as a source of understanding our relation to the world. The net effect was that Darwin supplanted Hegel as his main source of intellectual guidance (Bernstein, 1971, p. 172). Darwin's influence on Dewey led him to 'naturalise' the powerful influence of Hegel's transcendental idealism as regards the 'purpose of' and 'organic unity of life'[1], and recast the relation between mind and world through practical interaction in biological rather than transcendental terms (Garrison, 2006, p. 10).

Reflective thought and new knowledge. Dewey formulated his approach to problem solving and knowledge creation in terms of the organism–environment relationship, where an equilibrium is maintained by the integrated unity of the organism and environment. Thus he conceived of people adapting to their environment as they form habits, that is, routine ways of doing things (Garrison, 2002, p. 65). Although these routines facilitate continuity in thought and action there are, nevertheless, occasions when well-established habits are insufficient, and when a problem, an uncertainty or even a crisis emerges that cannot be resolved within existing social conventions or cultural frameworks. What is required to respond to these occasions, according to Dewey (1938/86, p. 201), is a form of thought that can bring about the sense of hesitation and delay essential to creative thinking.

Dewey's solution to this problem (1938/86, p. 113) was to develop his concept of 'reflective thought'[2]. The origin of his concept lies, as Rorty (1986, p. xii) notes, in Dewey's desire to extend his attachment to the method of inquiry associated with the Natural Sciences into other fields. Although Dewey did not accept that science discovered absolute truths about the world, he did accept that the seventeenth-century scientists had not only made a major breakthrough in discovering the layout of the solar system and laws of motion but also in formulating a new method of scientific inquiry. As a consequence, Dewey was concerned to try out this method in areas where it had not previously been applied by, 'generalising the experimental side of natural science into a logical method which is applicable to the interpretation and treatment of social phenomena' (Dewey, 1938/86, p. 11).

Dewey emphasised the potential of the scientific method as a resource for analysing the social world by distinguishing between the 'empirical' and the 'experimental' stances towards the world:

> The term experience may thus be interpreted either with reference to the empirical or to the experimental attitude of mind. Experience is not a rigid and closed thing; it is vital, and hence growing. When dominated by the past, by custom and routine, it is often opposed to the reasonable, the thoughtful. But experience also includes the reflection that sets us free from the limiting influence of sense, appetite, and tradition. Experience may welcome and assimilate all that the most exact and penetrating thought discovers. Indeed, the business of education might be defined as just such an emancipation and enlargement of experience.
>
> (Dewey, 1938/86, p. 277)

From the Deweyan standpoint, the empirical attitude of mind refers to a tendency to observe regularly occurring or coinciding things or phenomena and draw conclusions from them; thus, Dewey claims, it is very useful in coming to terms with everyday situations[3]. In contrast, the experimental attitude of mind refers to the capacity to use the natural scientific method and scientific theories to formulate new ideas or conceptions, so as not to be dominated by the past[4]. Scientific method and theories are central to reflective thought, according to Dewey, because they assist us in questioning the givenness of the world. Moreover, in contradistinction to the popular notion that Dewey was primarily concerned with learning-by-doing (in other words, engaging in empirical inquiry without recourse to theoretical concepts), Garrison explains that theoretical concepts – in Dewey's terms 'universals' – were always central to the process of questioning because Dewey defined thinking as:

> '...knowledge of universal elements; that is, of ideas as such, or of relations,' and he went on to note that 'the universal element which is always the object of thought is an ideal' that has no 'definite place or time'; hence, therefore, it is 'general or universal in nature'.
>
> (Dewey, 1887, cited in Garrison, 2006, p. 5)

It is legitimate to talk about universals, according to Dewey, as long as they are conceived of as the 'norms of action', which 'self-developing entities' (such as the mind) depend on to evolve, rather than external representations of the social and natural world that the mind has to assimilate (Garrison, 2006, pp. 27 and 15). This led Dewey to conceive of the purpose of theories (concepts, universals and so on) as allowing us to 'impart meaning to particulars and to develop it further'; and to maintain that they are central to, 'any inquiry irrespective as to whether the inquirer knows it or not', because theories help us to identify and form relations between natural and social phenomena (Garrison, 2006, p. 8).

Dewey conceptualises the process of reflective thought as a circular series of five steps. The first three steps are concerned with defining and engaging with a problem and can be summarised as follows (Miettinen, 2000; Rodgers, 2002):

– the formation of a tentative conception of the difficulty, and definition of the problem that has to be addressed;

- the identification of the material and social conditions of the situation that are generating the problem by using a universal to provide the criteria for relevancy and irrelevancy of hypotheses and conceptual structures;
- formulation of a hypothesis, a guiding idea or alternative conceptualisation to gain a better understanding of the situation we are confronting.

The fourth and fifth steps are concerned with testing the hypothesis to establish a link between the data that emerges in relation to the universal that underpinned the hypothesis.

Dewey's (1910/86, p. 242) stages of reflection are characterised therefore by a double move that goes 'to and from a meaning'. We start with facts, that is, data whose meaning has been established by prior analysis through inference, and we begin to develop a new meaning that unifies the original and the additional facts that emerge as we explore the implications of the hypothesis – in other words, the idea governing the reflective inquiry (Garrison, 2006, p. 21). The crucial link in this process is, referred to by Burke (1994, p. 224) as, the 'hermeneutical helix', that is, the way in which inference and implication coil around one another. The process of inference allows us to connect data that we have selected out of the situation under investigation, and that may lead to a new universal meaning emerging, while the process of implication entails considering this data in relation to other ideas, and both processes support us to identify new concepts and/or facts.

Thus reflection, for Dewey (1887, p. 200), as Garrison (2006, p. 9) observes, allows us to grasp that, 'what is actually known is always a combination of the universal and the particular, of law and fact; in other words, an individual'. It constitutes the means to provide a provisional sense of truth based on the functional and practical significance of an idea, rather than a way to apprehend the pre-given structures of nature (Miettinen, 2000, p. 69).

The implications of Dewey's concept of reflection. Dewey's concept of reflective thought offers a considerable advance on the way that reflection is conceptualised by Schön and in the pedagogies of reflection, because he accepted that while judgements are always internally related to a field of activity, such fields are constituted substantively and procedurally. By rejecting the principles of technical rationality and focusing on the circumstances of practice, Schön played down the role of universals as a 'body of general principles' that serve as 'working tools' (Dewey, 1910/86, pp. 253 and 280) as a resource for professionals to work experimentally to solve the problems that they have identified.

This focus on the circumstances of practice led Schön to overlook the possibility that professionals use: the norms that underpin the theories that are an integral part of their professional field, to orientate their attention to problematic features of practice; and the norms that underpin experimental inquiry, to engage in the process of analysing and synthesising salient facts or features of that problem in ways that other professionals in their field would accept as justified and valid. In contrast, writers associated with the pedagogies of reflection primarily treat reflection as an empirical device to enable individuals to verify what they have learnt from experience in two senses: to enable experience to be accredited within a qualification; or as a resource to deepen our understanding of, or to criticise, learning and/or professional practice. Hence, reflection becomes in both cases a method for connecting theory to practice, rather than a transactional process that unifies theory and practice.

Nevertheless, we are about to see that the Deweyan solution to the two worlds of knowledge is less convincing than it seems, for a number of reasons. The first reason is that his position rests on an assumption, as Garrison (2001, p. 282) acknowledges, that our relation to reality is 'anoetic', so that we become conscious of events through our sensations rather than through our thoughts. Thus Dewey conceives of our relation to the world in naturalistic terms. That relation emerges through the functional coordination of three things: (i) a natural biological being; (ii) a natural object or event that is used to refer to; (iii) another natural object or event. Mental action emerges, for Dewey, in the transaction – without any break in continuity that could cause a dualism between mental and physical, internal or external. As a consequence, Dewey leaves us with, '...a trans-action wherein nothing is necessarily within anything. Neither do we need world picture, image and so forth...' (Garrison, 2001, p. 294).

One problem is that Dewey's theory of 'trans-action' leads him, as we can see from the above description, to treat the social world as though it is an extension of the natural world. As a consequence, he never considers the extent to which we live in a natural world that has already been 'conceptualised' (McDowell, 1996) or 'humanised' (Ilyenkov, 1977a), and therefore that that world, let alone the social world we encounter in daily experience, is inscribed with human values. Put simply, we have built towns, roads, bridges and so forth, and our lives in these environments are not completely evolutionary – in the Darwinian sense of the term – because they are overlaid and transformed by different values as regards, for example, the relative importance of religion or science as a guiding principle for day-to-day living.

This naturalistic conception of our relation with the world results in a conception of human development that assumes that our understanding of our environment is, 'primarily expanded by the momentum inherent in our daily experiences', rather than the cultural development of our capacity to reason (Kozulin, 1990, p. 79). Thus, Dewey plays down – to borrow Tomasello's (1999, pp. 6–7) arguments about 'nativist' and 'naturalistic' theories of human development – that what is distinctive about human cognition and human life is our forms of 'cultural learning', based on the capacity to imagine ourselves in the 'mental shoes' of other people, so that we:

> ...can learn not just *from* other but *through* other. This understanding of others as intentional beings like the self is crucial in human cultural learning because cultural artefacts and social practices – exemplified prototypically by the use of tools and linguistic symbols – invariably point beyond themselves to other outside entities: tools point to problems they are designed to solve and linguistic symbols point to the communicative situations they are designed to represent.
>
> (Tomasello, 1999, pp. 6–7)

This suggests that mind is, as Miettinen quoting from Lektorsky observes (2001, p. 299), formed and developed through a process of, '...internalising external practical activity *mediated* by cultural tools that we have created and which embody humankind's cultural-historical experiences...'. This is rather than the premise that Dewey believed mind to be a natural biological function, as many Deweyans, such as Garrison (2006) and Hickman (1990), maintain. Thus, it follows that our immersion or enculturation in systems of knowledge allow us to come to understand the, 'intentional significance of tool use or symbolic practice – what its "for", what "we" the users of the tool or symbol, do with it' (Tomasello, 1999, p. 6), rather than being merely a cultural process that complements our biological processes of maturation. From this perspective, instead of transacting with our environment naturalistically, we have a culturally and historically mediated relation with the natural and social world. This relation leads us, according to Tomasello, to continually restructure our understanding of, and our use of, the tools and symbols our cultural traditions make available to us. Thus, they are no longer elements within transactions; cultural tools fundamentally alter our relation with the natural and social worlds because they contribute to the construction of a 'mediated' mind.

Part of the reason that Dewey does not consider our mediated relation to the world is that although he stresses the transactional nature of mind and world, his theory of trans-action rests on a residual dualism: mind and world are unified through transaction rather than constituted culturally and historically through human activity[5]. We pursue the significance of this insight by considering the work of Lev Semënovich Vygotsky – an intellectual contemporary of Dewey's, who also drew on Hegel to grapple with similar issues to Dewey. These writers interpret Hegel, as Miettinen (2001) observes, in fundamentally different ways. The main Hegelian idea that influenced Dewey was the notion of organic unity, which – as we saw when he coupled it with Darwin's notion of evolution – led him to adopt a naturalistic stance towards the relation between people and their environment. By contrast, the main Hegelian influence for Vygotsky is Hegel's ideas about the, 'objectification of activity into cultural artefacts' (Miettinen, 2001, p. 299). This line of influence offers, as we are about to see, a very different starting point to Dewey's theory of transaction for rethinking the relation between knowledge and the world and, in the process, offers a fresh perspective on the debate about the role of knowledge in the knowledge economy.

Vygotsky's Cultural Theory of Learning

Introduction
The cornerstone of Vygotsky's theory of cultural mediation is an attempt to identify the specifically human aspects of behaviour and cognition that differentiate humans from other animals; hence the, 'key words in his psychology are *consciousness* and *culture*' (Kozulin, 1990, p. 4). In the intellectual climate from the 1970s to the turn of the last century, it may seem as though there is not necessarily anything startlingly original with a pre-occupation with consciousness and culture, because many notable anthropologists (Geertz, 1973), philosophers (Rorty, 1979; Dennett, 1987),

psychologists (Gergen, 1994) and sociologists (Archer, 1988) have been grappling with these issues over the last few decades. Vygotsky's originality only becomes apparent when we recognise the way in which he grasped the significance of the constitutive role of the social in things as well as in people.

The theory of cultural mediation. One of the major reasons that Vygotsky formulated his theory of cultural mediation at the turn of the twentieth century was to combat the influence of the American psychological traditions of behaviourism and reflexology and introspectionism on Russian and European psychology. These influences had resulted in a polarisation in Russia between the 'objectivist' and 'subjectivist' schools of psychology (Bakhurst, 1991, p. 63). Vygotsky attempted to overcome three premises: (i) the limitations of the subjectivist claim that mind was only knowable through recourse to introspection and emotions; (ii) the behaviourist claim that the stimulus response model provided the only means for a scientific understanding of human activity; and (iii) to go beyond the work of writers such as Kohler and Lewin, who had developed a limited holism that lacked a cultural–historical understanding of psychological phenomena (Langemeyer & Roth, 2006). Vygotsky (1997a, p. 81) maintained that these schools had, 'mind without behaviour [or] behaviour without mind, that is, understood them as two distinct and separate phenomenon'. Consequently, Vygotsky argued that the challenge for psychology was to grasp the way in which cultural and historical processes and individual mental processes are dialectically related through social practices – that is, patterned forms of social activity such as education and work – and how this contributes to genesis of consciousness (Minick, 1987; Wertsch, 2007).

Vygotsky explored this issue by taking 'psychological tools' (hereafter, cultural tools)[6], for example, language, mnemonic techniques, algebraic symbol systems, writing, works of art, etc. as his generative principle. The distinguishing feature of human behaviour, according to Vygotsky, is that cultural tools mediate between the way we act upon and are acted upon by our cultural environment. This environment:

...is the product of human social life and the very social activity of human beings, and therefore the very act of putting the questions about cultural development of behaviour already leads us directly into the social plane of activity.

(Vygotsky, 1987, pp. 145–6)

The origin of this emphasis upon mediation – the understanding of how culture in the form of practical activity (i.e. modes of reasoning and acting) enters psychological processes and shapes individual behaviour – lies in Vygotsky's debt to the dialectical tradition that runs from Spinoza, via Hegel to Marx (Kozulin, 1998)[7]. In particular, Vygotsky was influenced by Spinoza's concern for the 'exercise of free will', Hegel's emphasis on the 'contribution of reason to human development' (Kozulin, 1998, p. 118) and Marx's philosophical anthropology, which – in contradistinction to Darwin – stressed transformation or humanisation of the natural world through the creation of new environments and new social practices, based on 'collaborative processes of producing and deploying tools' (Stetsenko & Arievitch, 2004, p. 65).

The concept of mediation is considered by Hegel and Marx to be a central characteristic of, respectively, the complex interactive and transformational relation between animals and humans or human activity, and our transformation of the natural through the creation of a social environment. From this perspective, although animals and humans both have natural impulses or desires, they are slightly different from one another: because the activity engendered by desire for animals is extinguished at its satisfaction, whereas we are able to:

> ...conceive of an object or situation as demanding a certain course of action, question the correctness of their conception in the light of previous experience, and project and evaluate alternative procedures.

> (Bakhurst, 1991, p. 64)

Furthermore, our activity in the world 'humanises' the natural environment and, in the process, transforms human nature; thus, we are, 'no longer dependent on immediate natural conditions, but on conditions mediated by human civilisation' (Kozulin, 1998, p. 120). Instead, we develop a greater degree of consciousness through our mediated activity, as we learn to control our behaviour from the outside through appropriating and reformulating 'external symbolic, cultural systems rather than being subjugated in and by them' (Daniels, 2001, p. 15).

Eminent philosophers such as Toulmin (1978) and psychologists such as Bruner (1986) accepted many years ago that Vygotsky's theory of cultural mediation constitutes a rich resource for developing a non-dualistic theory of mind. More recently, eminent evolutionary anthropologists such as Tomasello (1999) and philosophers with an interest in neuroscience such as Clark (1997) have accepted that Vygotsky's theory has profound implications for cognitive science, because he allows us to see how language guides and shapes our behaviour, rather than acting as a medium of information transfer between our pre-given cognitive structures.

We continue both traditions of engagement with Vygotsky's ideas, albeit in a rather different vein. We maintain that the reason Vygotsky's theory of cultural mediation constitutes a different starting point for addressing the learning challenge of the knowledge economy is because: (i) his philosophical pre-suppositions enable us to avoid the problem of dualism that afflicts the discussion of the new role of knowledge in the debate about the knowledge economy; (ii) the concepts that he formulated to explain the distinctive character of human development and freedom – 'higher mental functions' and 'semiotic mediation' – and the distinctive context for human development and freedom – 'zone of proximal development' – can be used to explain the genesis of the notion of a mediated mind from childhood to adulthood; and (iii) that the resulting conception of a mediated mind is central to our understanding of the economic, political and social challenges posed by working and living in a knowledge economy/society[8].

The higher mental functions and the mediating role of signs. The central and revolutionary idea that informs Vygotsky's work is that a transition occurs from direct, innate, natural forms of behaviour to mediated, mental functions that develop in the process of cultural development (Bakhurst, 1991; Kozulin, 1990). This idea was not only revolutionary when originally formulated (because it offered a way to undercut one of the longstanding tendencies in the Human, Natural and Social Sciences to explain psychological phenomena in terms of biological processes) but also in the modern era, when the international clamour of interest amongst policymakers in 'brainism' threatens to displace any consideration of the social constitution of mind (Bakhurst, 2008). The natural forms of behaviour in Vygotsky's (1997b, p. 14) terms – the 'lower mental functions' are biologically programmed, natural behaviours that are immediate responses to stimuli, for example, sucking and rooting reflexes. In contrast, the higher mental functions – voluntary attention, voluntary memory and rational thought – are mental and conscious and volitional because they are socially and culturally created through the use of cultural tools, rather than being preserved in the physical structure of our body (Davydov & Radzikhovskii, 1985, p. 53).

The higher mental functions are not therefore:

> ...simply a continuation of elementary function and are not their mechanical combinations, but a qualitatively new mental formation that develops according to completely special laws and is subject to different patterns...

> (Vygotsky, 1998, p. 34)

Instead they are, for Vygotsky, qualitatively new psychological phenomena that arise over the life span. They constitute the basis of the social formation of consciousness and/or mind (Vygotsky uses these terms synonymously) that emerges through our sustained involvement in cultural development, and they mediate our engagement with the natural and social world, so enabling us to construct a response to those worlds that is wilful and intentional, rather than, 'growing from the elementary functions as if the latter contained them in embryo' (Bakhurst, 2007, p. 53).

The general principle that informs the development of the higher mental functions was referred to by Vygotsky as the, 'general genetic law of cultural development'. Vygotsky defined it as follows:

> Any higher mental function was external [and] social before it was internal. It was once a social relationship between two people... We can formulate the general genetic law of cultural development in the following way. Every function in the child's cultural development appears twice: first on the social level, and later, on the individual level; first between people (intrapsychological), and then inside the child (intrapsychological). This applies equally to all voluntary attention, to logical memory, and to the formation of concepts. All the higher mental functions originate as actual relations between human individuals.

> (Vygotsky, 1978, p. 57)

This 'general formulation' rather than iron law (Miettinen, 2006) of the way in which we internalise forms of material due to our participation in collective activities in society, and how the 'reverse transition' from internal to external forms of thought (i.e. externalisation) results in the creation of cultural artefacts, provides a powerful clue as to why Vygotsky saw cognition as socially organised. Thinking, from his perspective, is influenced by the way we use social concepts – that have been objectified in language and socially structured life activities, and that are underpinned by norms for action – as a resource to facilitate our reasoning and decisions about how to act (Ratner, 2004, p. 403). The development of thinking, as Vygotsky observes:

> ...has a central, key, decisive significance for all other functions and processes. We cannot express more clearly or tersely the leading role of intellectual development in relation to the whole personality of the adolescent and to all of his mental functions other than to say that acquiring the function of forming concepts is the principal and central link in all the changes that occur in the psychology of an adolescent. All the other links in the chain, all other special functions, are intellectualised, reformed, restructured under the influence of these crucial successes that the thinking of the adolescent achieves...

> (Vygotsky, 1998, p. 81)

The gist of his argument is therefore that there is not a natural, pre-cultural or pre-mediated basis to psychological phenomena (i.e. objects of perception, images recalled by memory and so forth), rather they are humanly created, mental phenomena; that is, cultural not natural biological processes. Perception is therefore, for Vygotsky, as Ratner (2004, p. 401) observes, 'intellectual'.

The use of this word in the modern era can be highly deceptive, since it is frequently interpreted as having overly elitist connotations (Lemke, 1999). The term 'intellectual' or 'intellectualisation' in Vygotsky's work, however, denotes something rather different. On the one hand, he meant that since all psychological phenomena rest upon cognitive concepts, what we see is not simply a function of sensory impressions because these impressions are themselves shaped by the knowledge we have developed about things. Thus it follows that an infant's immediate response to being fed or rested is qualitatively different compared with an adult's response to say the warm glow of receiving a present from a member of one's family or a friend. The former is an elementary reaction that lacks cognitive, intellectual, linguistic meaning; whereas the latter is a form of intellectualised perception, because we are able to articulate what we perceive, feel and what follows as a consequence (Ratner, 2004). On the other hand, Vygotsky used the term 'intellectualisation' to refer to the process that occurs as children start to treat their mental activities rationally and to use language to articulate and justify their developing ideas (Meshcheryakov, 2007).

The process of intellectualisation, which is the cornerstone of the development of the higher mental functions, creates a whole new system of behaviour because as we appropriate cultural tools – which represent for Vygotsky humankind's greatest invention – they allow us to:

> ...embody their collective experience (e.g. skill, knowledge, beliefs) in external forms such as material objects (e.g. words, books, pictures, houses), patterns of behaviour organised in time and space (e.g. rituals) and modes of acting,

thinking and communicating in everyday life. Such external (or reified) forms that embody collective social knowledge and experience constitute a unique dimension of existence – human culture, into which each child is born and which he or she has to acquire in order to participate in social life.

(Stetsenko, 2004, p. 505)

Vygotsky's theory of cultural mediation helps us, therefore, to grasp the inter-connectedness of the ongoing phases of human development. As we learn to use previous generations' cultural tools, we are gradually able as a biological species (phylogeny), as a civilisation (social history) and as individuals (ontogeny) to, 'leap from the constraints of the natural environment, defined by the laws of biological evolution – into the realm of cultural–historical development with its infinite degrees of freedom' (Stetsenko, 2004, p. 505).

Initially, Vygotsky pursued the development of the higher mental functions by identifying the way in which we use human created artefacts, such as 'signs' – words, pictorial representations, material reminders – to mediate and thereby gain control of our behavioural processes and, as such, control behaviour from the outside. He crystallised his ideas about the relation of signs and tools, mind and world in a conceptual framework centred around the interaction between the triad of a subject (i.e. a person), object (i.e. the purpose of an activity) and mediating artefacts (i.e. resources to accomplish that purpose) (Vygotsky, 1987, p. 40).

Thus Vygotsky conceived of mediating artefacts, such as signs, functioning as a stimulus for human behaviour:

In artificial memory, mnemotechnical memory... two new connections are established with the help of the psychological tool X (e.g. a knot in a handkerchief, a string on one's fingers, a mnemonic scheme). As is true of the connection A–B (that is stimuli), each of these new connections is based on the natural conditioned response process and is instantiated by the properties of the brain. What is novel, artificial and instrumental about the new connections is the fact... [that an] artificial direction is given to a natural process... by means of an instrument.

(Vygotsky, 1981, p. 138)

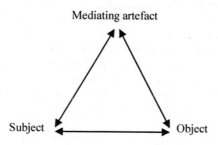

Figure 2. A representation of Vygotsky's mediational triangle.

(*Source*: Vygotsky, 1987)

CHAPTER 6

Using the practice of tying a knot in a handkerchief, Vygotsky demonstrated how this not only serves as a reminder to do something but also create the conditions of our future remembering, as we internalise such techniques through the deployment of mnemonic devices in thought. Although a hackneyed example, the tying of a knot in a handkerchief illustrates that we are not engaging mechanistically or naturalistically with the world. Rather it demonstrates that we are acting for reasons (Derry, 2008, p. 54) and thus we are actively selecting signs to remind ourselves to act in a particular way, to consider how to vary our behaviour in order to accomplish a well-established goal more effectively or to create a new pattern of behaviour to achieve a new goal.

Although Vygotsky accepted the conventional psychological wisdom of his times that thought and speech had different development roots – the former being grounded in problem-solving activities and the latter in communication utterances – we have maintained that they only become meaningful when they converge, and when we can employ them to communicate in virtue of their meaning. Vygotsky (1987, p. 49) coined the term a 'unity of processes' to explain the mediated relation between consciousness (i.e. voluntary attention, logical memory, rational thought) and behaviour (i.e. practical intellect and action) (Lee, 1985, p. 81). His analysis of this unity of processes, through experimental work conducted with colleagues such as Schiff, led Vygotsky to question that signs contained definite meanings as a result of their evolution within the history of a culture and, as a corollary, that learning consisted of grasping such meaning (Davydov & Radzikhovskii, 1985, p. 54). Vygotsky began to appreciate that signs influence us in virtue of their significance and this, in turn, depends on how we understand or interpret them (van der Veer & Valsiner, 1993, p. 65). The trigger for this reconsideration was, as Vygotsky remarked, that:

> In older works, we ignored that the sign had meaning... We proceeded from the principle of the constancy of meaning, we discounted meaning... Whereas our task was to demonstrate what the 'knot' and logical memory have in common now our task is to demonstrate the difference that exists between them.
>
> (Vygotsky, 1987, pp. 130–1)

So instead of assuming that words dropped metaphorically like 'hot cakes' into our mouths, Vygotsky (1987, p. 179) explored how consciousness develops by analysing the function of words – 'word meaning' – in communication (Minick, 1985). Although this new approach reflected, as we shall see below, a more nuanced understanding of mediation, Vygotsky never reformulated his mediational triangle to reflect that new understanding (Langemeyer & Roth, 2006). Despite not doing so, Vygotsky's mediated triangle paved the way for us to understand the constitutive role of language in human consciousness and action.

Semiotic mediation: the relation between theoretical and everyday concepts. This new line in Vygotsky's thinking manifests itself in his work in the emergence of a more explicit focus on the different way words are used in the processes of generalisation, abstraction and concept formation, as well as to facilitate communication and social interaction. Because of his interest in the role that cultural tools play in the formation and development of the higher mental functions, Vygotsky, in contrast to Dewey and other psychologists of the early twentieth century, discriminated carefully between the role that 'scientific' (hereafter, theoretical) and 'everyday' concepts[9] play in this process. He did so by not only pointing out that they are constituted differently from one another, but also that we use these different types of concepts to mediate social practice in very different ways.

Everyday concepts are constructed, according to Vygotsky (1987, p. 168), as we participate in the varied and regularly occurring events of everyday life. We form them either by explicitly choosing and/or taking over a word or phrase to classify: natural phenomena, for example, calling grass 'green stuff'; our experience of an aspect of the social world, for example, calling a group of people irrespective of their sex 'you guys'; or implicitly (i.e. silently and tacitly) coining a phrase to denote something to ourselves such as 'it's one of those'. Thus, although everyday concepts are saturated in our rich personal experience and based on surface characteristics, they nevertheless help us to make connections between natural phenomena and/or human experiences by allowing us to form a 'conception' (i.e. a picture or image) to represent those connections (Davydov, 1990, p. 178). The naming of an object, event or person is, for Vygotsky, no less practical than touching physical or human artefacts, because the very act of naming provides us with a whole new way of dealing with such things. In contrast, theoretical concepts – irrespective as to whether they are a part of the Natural, Physical, Human or Social Sciences – are, for Vygotsky (1987, p. 168), a part of a larger group or 'organised system' of interconnected concepts based on generalisations that can be used to reveal aspects of the world that are otherwise not necessarily apparent to sensory perception. Moreover, because such generalisations are verbally articulated, theoretically embedded and tightly related to other generalisations that are part of a wider system of concepts, Vygotsky maintained that theoretical concepts are best acquired in the course of instruction[10].

The pedagogic challenge is, for Vygotsky (1987, p. 170), to support learners to appreciate all the connections and relations that shape the meaning of a theoretical concept, because it is, 'only when this diversity is synthesised in a word, in an integral image through a multitude of determinations, we develop a concept'. Thus it is, from his perspective, pedagogically fruitless to try to teach concepts in isolation from the system of which they are a part:

> The teacher who attempts to use this approach achieves nothing but a mindless learning of words, an empty verbalism that simulates or imitates the presence of concepts in the child. Under these conditions, the child learns not the concept but the word, and this word is taken over by the child through memory rather than thought.

> (Vygotsky, 1987, p. 170)

Having stressed the differences between the two types of concept, Vygotsky (1987, p. 216) drew attention to the complex relationship that exists between them by invoking the metaphor 'growing down from above' and 'growing up from below'. These metaphors have often been interpreted as meaning – by writers who are sympathetic to the cultural–historical tradition – that Vygotsky adhered to a particularly strong version of the Enlightenment assumption that science constitutes the definitive source of wisdom about human existence in the world (Lemke, 1999; Wells, 1999; Wertsch, 2000). Such assumptions fail to appreciate, as Derry (2008) has cogently demonstrated, the 'Hegelian provenance' of his thinking about the nature of knowledge. Vygotsky did not operate in accordance with Kantian *a priori* assumptions that there were universal criteria by which to judge knowledge, rather he followed Hegel and saw the foundations of knowledge being built up culturally and historically and developed through being subject to criticism and revision.

The metaphors 'grow up' and 'grow down' refer to the different 'measure of generality' (i.e. what is encompassed within a theoretical concept) and 'relations of generality' (i.e. the extent of the connections between such concepts and other similar concepts), rather than to some pre-given foundations and hierarchy of knowledge (Vygotsky, 1987, pp. 227–8). Vygotsky describes the nature of the mediated relation between theoretical and everyday concepts as follows:

> Having already travelled along the path of development from below to above, everyday concepts have blazed the trail for the continued downward growth of scientific concepts; they have created the structures required for the emergence of the lower or more elementary characteristics of the scientific concept. In the same way, having covered a certain portion of the path from above to below, scientific concepts have blazed the trail for the development of everyday concepts. They have prepared the structural formations for the mastery of the higher level of the everyday concept.

(Vygotsky, 1987, p. 219)

He is acknowledging that although everyday and theoretical concepts are formed in different ways from one another, and we usually acquire the former before the latter, the process by which they are learned is profoundly interconnected. We acquire, for example, the everyday concept 'flower' before we acquire the theoretical concepts, 'rose', 'lily', etc. This enables us to use the everyday concept 'flower' to individuate flowers by their characteristic appearance and behaviour and, thus, to operate more effectively in the world than if we were unable to differentiate between natural artefacts and events. However, as we are gradually introduced to the specific names for flowers, we are able to individuate flowers as members of a certain species, the criteria for membership being established by biological theory.

Theoretical concepts therefore have a broader capacity for generalisation compared with everyday concepts, because they are located within a system of interconnected concepts:

> It is completely different for the child who does not know the words rose, violet, or lily than it is for the child who does. Outside a system, the only possible connections between concepts are those that exist between the objects themselves, that is, empirical connections. Within a system, relationships between concepts begin to emerge. These relationships mediate the

concept's relationship to the object through its relationship to other concepts. A different relationship between the concept and object develops. *Supra-empirical connections between concepts become possible.*

(Vygotsky, 1987, p. 234)

Vygotsky is highlighting therefore that speech structures thought, rather than merely represents the way we use the world, and that as we appreciate the different level of, and relations of, generality associated with a theoretical concept:

...there is a sharp restructuring of the relationship between concepts and object and a restructuring of the relationships of generality between concepts.

(Vygotsky, 1987, p. 231)

Vygotsky is maintaining, in other words, that our previous ways of thinking do 'not just drop away' or are 'nullified' as we learn a new concept (1987, p. 231): rather, a much more complex process of learning occurs based on our use of the level of generality contained by a theoretical concept to 'restructure' (1987, p. 231) our use of our existing theoretical and everyday concepts. We use our growing appreciation of the reasons that underpin theoretical concepts – such as mediation, higher mental functions, and cultural tools – to assist us to use those concepts in more encompassing ways in written and/or oral forms of communication. Equally, we use our growing appreciation of the reasons that underpin theoretical concepts, such as, 'rose' and/or 'lily', to animate our use of the everyday concept 'flower' when talking to other people. Furthermore, the rich and diverse nature of everyday experience also allows us to restructure the meaning of a theoretical concept – that is, to appreciate those aspects of experience that it relates to, but which are never fully encapsulated in the concept. These different expressions of conceptual restructuring allow us to see that, on the one hand, we are operating with a mediated mind and, on the other hand, that the process of restructuring repositions us in relation to the natural and/or social world by offering us ways to question its apparent givenness.

The zone of proximal development: the context of explicit mediation. The process of conceptual restructuring is, despite its developmental nature, a fairly 'explicit' form of mediation. It is an intentional process that occurs as we try overtly to grasp a new concept or practice (Wertsch, 2007, p. 180). Vygotsky explores the implications of this process of mediation, and the way in which this repositions us in relation to the natural and social world, through his concept of the 'zone of proximal development' (ZPD)[11]. This concept, as Bruner (1978, p. 4) notes, focuses attention on:

...the dialogue between a more expert teacher and a less expert learner... [to highlight that] Once a concept is explicated in dialogue, the learner is able to reflect on the dialogue, to use its distinctions and connections to reformulate his own thought. Thought, then, is both an individual achievement and a social one.

The common conception of the ZPD in much of the secondary literature that has used that concept rests, as Chaiklin (2003, p. 41) presciently observes, on three assumptions: the 'generality assumption' (i.e. applicable to learning of all kinds of subject matter); the 'assistance assumption' (i.e. learning is dependent on interventions by a more competent other); and the 'potential assumption' (i.e. a property of the learner that permits the best and easiest learning). This conception implies a 'vision of educational perfection', in which insightful teachers help learners to master concepts from a range of disciplinary backgrounds, and has inspired the development of a number of famous pedagogic strategies such as 'scaffolding' and 'reciprocal teaching' to facilitate learning.

The purpose of the ZPD, for Vygotsky, was rather different. It was to explicitly help educators to identify the type of pedagogic intervention that will facilitate movement from one stage of psychological development to another – for example, the type of pedagogic intervention that would assist a child to grasp and reason with a concept such as density, as opposed to pedagogic practices to facilitate the development of discrete aspects of knowledge and/or skill. Hence, the forms of explicit mediation that occur in the ZPD facilitate the development of the psychological functions that have to be formed to support the next stage of development – for example, to reason with mathematical concepts (Chaiklin, 2003, p. 49).

Vygotsky explained this process of explicit mediation through recourse to the concept of imitation. This term is usually associated with behaviourism in psychology and is therefore normally understood to mean an unreflective copying of another person's words or actions. In contrast, Vygotsky used the term to refer to situations in which learners are able to engage with more competent others, around tasks that they cannot yet perform alone because the psychological functions they require are still developing. He pointed out that if:

> ...someone knows arithmetic, but runs into difficulty with the solution of a complex problem, a demonstration will immediately lead to the resolution of the problem. On the other hand, if I do not know higher mathematics, a demonstration of a differential equation will not move my thought in that direction by a single step. To imitate, there must be a possibility for moving from what I can do to what I cannot.

> (Vygotsky, 1998, p. 209)

This movement is possible because, although the maturing psychological functions are insufficiently developed to support fully independent performance:

> ...they have developed sufficiently so that a person can use them to understand how to use the collaborative actions (e.g. leading questions, demonstrations) of others' to help them to grasp the potential implications of the activity.

> (Chaiklin, 2003, p. 52)

The ZPD is therefore, for Vygotsky, a normative concept that reflects the institutionalised demands and expectations associated with a particular tradition of practice – education – rather than a Piagetian description of a phase of biological maturation. From this perspective, instruction should always move ahead of the current level of development because:

> It impels or awakens a whole series of functions that are in a stage of maturation lying in the zone of proximal development. This is the major role of instruction in development. This is what distinguishes the instruction of a child from the training of animals. This is also what distinguishes the instruction of a child which is directed towards his full development from instruction in specialised, technical skills such as typing or riding a bicycle. The formal aspect of each school subject is that in which the influence of instruction on development is realised. Instruction would be completely unnecessary if it merely utilised what had already matured in the development process, if it were not itself a source of development.

> (Vygotsky, 1987, p. 212)

Vygotsky maintained that instruction serves as a source of development, because he wanted to highlight not only the limitations of the subjectivist and behaviourist conceptions of our relation to the world, but also Piagetian conceptions of development and learning that were extremely influential at the turn of the twentieth century – and, for that matter, continue to be so. Drawing on Piaget's famous example of children trying to understand why different objects sink – where they sometimes claimed it was because the object was too small on other occasions they claimed it was because it was too large – Vygotsky (1987, p. 235) highlighted that the problem with the children's answers was that they were based on 'empirical judgements'. He pointed out that, unless we are familiar with the theoretical concepts of density and volume, we will always be forced to speculate as to why some things sink and others do not, or why some things sink faster than others, on the basis of external observable features of the object. Consequently, our judgement will be based on perceived relationships that exist amongst the objects themselves, rather than judgements mediated by theoretical concepts, because:

> The logic of perception does not know contradiction. Within this framework, the child is expressing two equally correct judgements. They are contradictory from the perspective of the adult but not the child. The contradiction exists for the logic of thought but not from that of the child.

> (Vygotsky, 1987, p. 235)

Therefore instruction is important, because although it defines the direction of development, it does not determine mechanistically that direction. As we use a new theoretical concept to re-mediate our everyday concepts, we restructure our thinking about the matter at hand – in this case why things sink or float – and, in the process, we are repositioned to think about and act differently in relation to the natural and social world. What Vygotsky was trying to convey therefore is that the new cultural tool that we have learned in a science lesson, for example, the concept of density, becomes a part of our mental functioning. It is now the means by which we exercise our freedom to choose to question whether we are prepared to continue to take the perceived connections between our impressions about the world for the actual connections that exist between things, or whether we prefer to cling on to our existing conceptions.

Inner speech: the context of implicit mediation.   In addition to the explicit pedagogic and cognitive processes that facilitate conceptual restructuring, Vygotsky also offers us a way to explain why there is a tacit dimension to our mediation of theoretical and everyday concepts. In doing so, he provides us with a way to appreciate that, as we develop the higher mental functions, we come to operate with a conceptually structured mind that we can deploy descriptively and discriminatively when writing and speaking or when engaging in practical actions.

Vygotsky explained the tacit dimension of mediation by drawing attention to the role of inner speech as an 'implicit' or volitional feature of mediation (Wertsch, 2007, p. 180)[12]. Inner and outer speech were viewed in psychology at the turn of the twentieth century as being separate and different from one another, and many psychologists continue to view them in this way. The former was usually defined, as Vygotsky (1987, pp. 256–7) observes, as 'verbal memory', 'un-socialised' speech, 'abbreviated speech' or even external speech minus sound, while the latter was defined as 'intentional' or 'articulated' speech[13]. Vygotsky, however, offers us another way of understanding the relation between these two modes of speech, and this opens up a different way of thinking about tacit forms of knowledge.

Vygotsky's concerns for the unity of processes meant that, instead of seeing inner and outer speech in accordance with the above conventional psychological wisdom, we can identify the different functions they serve and their different 'planes' of development: put simply, the former is speech for oneself while the latter is speech for others. Inner speech does not, according to Vygotsky (1987, p. 272), precede external speech in the sense that it is a rehearsal of fully formed ideas, rather inner speech is, '...an internal plane of verbal thinking which mediates the dynamic relationship between thought and word', and is therefore best considered as a 'rough draft' in thought of our emerging ideas (pp. 279–80). In contrast, external speech is the transformation of that emerging thought into word form through the use of a syntax that is differentiated and comprehensible to others. This means that the movement from inner to external speech is not comparable to the direct translation from one language to another because it requires 'a complete *restructuring* of speech' (Vygotsky, 1987, p. 280).

The form of mediation at play here, as Wertsch (2007, p. 184) observes, is not the 'object of conscious reflection' nor 'externally and intentionally introduced'. It is instead an implicit form that occurs in most cases, because as we are increasingly enculturated in different social practices – for example, learning theoretical concepts, participating in sporting activities, visiting museums, etc. – we 'unintentionally build into [our] mental functioning' the capability to restructure our ideas or practices or tacitly vary our use of them.

This form of mediation emerges as we use our inner speech as a rough draft of something that may or may not become verbalised as external speech to help us to make a connection between thinking, the object of thought and practical action. Vygotsky is highlighting therefore that our thoughts, as we strive to unite or to establish a relationship between one thing and another, always fulfil some function and resolve some concern or task. The flow and movement of thought never corresponds directly with the unfolding of thought into speech because although the 'two processes manifest a unity' – they are intimately connected to one another – they do not manifest 'an identity' (1987, p. 280).

Thus it follows, for Vygotsky, that the path from thought to words – and hence the basis of communication – lies through:

> ...the internal mediation of thought first by meaning and then by words. Therefore, thought is never the direct equivalent of word meaning. Meaning mediates thought in its path to verbal expression. The path from thought to word is indirect and internally mediated.

> (Vygotsky, 1987, p. 281)

This observation about inner and implicit mediation shows that Vygotsky was as sensitive to the ephemeral and fleeting nature of mediation as he was to explicit and intentional forms of mediation. He allows us to see that we use our inner speech, which is rarely transparent to other people nor consciously articulated to oneself, as a resource to help us to understand the meaning and functional significance of theoretical concepts, as much as we use our explicit forms of mediation (Wertsch, 2007, p. 180). Our inner speech contributes, on the one hand, to the way in which we exercise our own volition to form our everyday judgements about the objects of thought and their practical implications, as well as to act on that basis – 'performance before competence' – as Cazden (1981) succinctly and presciently observes. On the other hand, it helps us to mull over the measure of generality contained by, and the system of connections associated with, theoretical concept, and to use our growing understanding of those connections to gradually restructure our everyday concepts.

CONCLUSION

We have demonstrated in this chapter the revolutionary philosophical, psychological and pedagogic nature of Vygotsky's theory of cultural mediation. Specifically we have shown why it provides a different starting point for addressing the legacy of the worlds of knowledge in the debate about the knowledge economy, compared not only to the position adopted by the social and management theorists but also with Dewey's theory of transaction and concept of reflection. We saw that although Dewey's naturalisation of the scientific process of inquiry offered a more robust foundation for the concept of reflection to address the learning challenge of the knowledge economy, compared with the approaches described in the previous chapter, it was still predicated on a residual dualism. This happened because Dewey used the concept of 'trans-action' to co-join the natural and social world through our use of human-produced tools. In contrast, Vygotsky used the concept of human activity to explain how we use cultural tools to humanise the natural world and, in the process, create a mediated world and use the cultural–historical inheritance of that mediated world to develop socially and psychologically.

Despite making this claim, it is important to acknowledge that Vygotsky's writings are, as Bakhurst (2007, p. 57) notes, best conceived of as, 'less presentations of "results" and [more] as *injunctions to think of issues in these terms, to see things in this way*'. Thus it follows that whereas Vygotsky's legacy in the case of philosophy, psychology and pedagogy should be seen as a prolegomenon to further work, in the case of the argument we are presenting in this book it offers us a way to think differently about a number of issues that constitute the unexplicated assumptions that underpin the debate about the role of knowledge in the knowledge economy and the learning challenge of such an economy.

The first issue is the assumption that we gain access to the world sentiently through our perceptions, emotions and embodied experiences, which underpins the management theorists' ideas about how we develop tacit knowledge. Vygotsky's argument that we inhabit a humanised world and develop the conceptual capacities we need to operate effectively in that world through a process of explicit and/or implicit conceptual restructuring offers a very different perspective on tacit knowledge. Instead of seeing tacit knowledge as the result of our direct perception of sense data or our embodied engagement of an external world, Vygotsky reveals the mediated basis of tacit knowledge. It arises as we deploy the forms of intellectualised perception that we gradually develop to understand the forms of social practice that comprise the environment we live and work in. We do so, however, implicitly – rather than explicitly through conscious reflection or intentionally generated activity – as we use our higher mental functions to pick out practically salient features of a situation or form a judgement about a new social practice or a new cultural tool. This can happen, as we saw in the section on implicit mediation, without necessarily having to articulate to ourselves, let alone others, why and how we are doing so.

Vygotsky's argument about the intellectual basis of perception and the implicit and explicit process of restructuring – even though it was formulated before Polanyi wrote his treatise on tacit knowledge – offers us a way to see more clearly what Polanyi meant when he claimed that theoretical and tacit knowledge are two expressions of, rather than two categories of, knowledge. In a nutshell, they allow us to understand that there could be a tacit dimension to our use of theoretical concepts as much as there is a tacit dimension to our use of everyday concepts. We need, however, to pause here for a moment to clarify why this is the case, and why it is relevant to the earlier argument about the role of tacit knowledge as a resource in the economy.

We established in Chapter 4 that the type of tacit knowledge that the management theorists deemed most useful as a resource in the knowledge economy was that which results from the co-mingling of theory and practice. The reason this form of knowledge was useful was two-fold: it was relevant to work situations and could, in principle, be shared with other people. From Vygotsky's perspective, this form of personal knowledge arises from the engineers' mediation of concepts and work experience. To take the example of Nonaka and Takeuchi's engineers: their 'tacit' knowledge arose from the interplay between their theoretical knowledge and workplace experience rather than the operation of some pure act of perception. As a consequence, there is a conceptual element informing their tacit perceptions, and the former constitute the basis of those perceptions being shared when they are converted into metaphors (or, in Vygotsky's terms, everyday concepts). Put simply, other engineers can use their understanding of, for example, motor mechanics, to make sense of the insights contained within a metaphor that is presented to them about their work situation. What was always left slightly under-developed in Vygotsky's account of the mediation of theoretical and everyday concepts, as we noted earlier in the chapter, was the basis of our discrimination between the concepts. Thus, it follows that this is equally true for how people in workplaces mediate between concepts and actions. We shall return to the implications of this observation in Chapter 8.

The second issue is that Vygotsky's argument about the pedagogic conditions that we have to establish – the zone of proximal development (ZPD) – to support people to engage with humankind's cultural–historical traditions, offers us a way to conceptualise the continuity rather than the difference between initial and continuing development. The primary purpose of education, for Vygotsky, was to assist children and adolescents to develop their ability to understand, reason with and develop their cultural inheritance, and that goal was best accomplished by working collaboratively with experienced others – normally, but not exclusively, teachers. Although Vygotsky did not consider the implications of the ZPD for adults, we can see from the philosophical and psychological ideas that inform its formulation that he clearly envisioned the development process as occurring in educational settings throughout the life-course rather than as an age- and phase-related process. Hence it follows that the ZPD provides us, in principle, with a conceptual framework for considering adult learning and development.

If we accept Vygotsky's contention that concept formation develops via social interaction in educational settings, then it follows that this is also the case in workplace settings. As a corollary, if pedagogy is a core concern in educational settings, then it should also be a core concern in work settings. Unfortunately, the contribution that pedagogy makes to the facilitation of learning in workplaces is, as we noted in Chapter 1, consistently disregarded by policymakers, even though there has been a growing body of evidence of the important role that pedagogy serves in that context (Billett, 2002; Felstead et al., 2009; Guile, 2007; Roth, 2004). As a consequence, little attention is paid by policymakers, as we also noted in Chapter 1, to the importance of creating cultural contexts in workplaces to support people to engage with existing professional practice.

Before we can pursue the implication of the above provocative thoughts for how we might reconceptualise personal and vocational workplace learning (PVWL) to address the learning challenge of the knowledge economy, it is necessary to consider the way in which a number of prominent post-Vygotskians developed the concept of mediation. These acts of development generated, as we shall see, not only new insights about the concept – which will have a bearing on how we use mediation as a resource to further address the learning challenge of the knowledge economy – but also destabilised, to some extent, Vygotsky's own insights about mediation.

NOTES

[1] There has been, as Garrison (2006) has acknowledged, a considerable debate amongst Deweyan scholars as to the extent to which Dewey was influenced by James to either reject Hegel (Reck, 1984) or turned to Darwin to extend and elaborate the original Hegelian influence (Shook, 2000; Dalton, 2002). It is beyond the scope of this book to engage with the intricate details of this debate: We follow the common ground between these Deweyan scholars and accept that Hegel was a significant influence on the development of his thought.

[2] Dewey gradually developed his ideas about the role of reflection in aiding the process of adaptation throughout his working life through rethinking the relationship between experience and nature. Dewey's ideas about experience, nature and reflection are contained in several books: *Experience and Nature* (1925/81) *How We Think* (1910/86), *Logic: The Theory of Inquiry* (1938/89) and *The Quest for Certainty* (1929/88), which were also subject to various revisions along the way. Rorty (1986, pp. xiii–iv) acknowledges Dewey's struggle to define what was distinctive about his concept of 'reflective thought' compared with other theories, such as behaviourism, that also addressed the relationship between thought and action. Part of Dewey's difficulty was that he did not want the concept of 'reflective thought' treated as a formalistic device for establishing truth. In contrast, Dewey formulated the concept to extend certain methods of thinking that had become more common in the Natural Sciences since the seventeenth century into other areas of inquiry, by acting as a 'middle ground' between a well-defined procedure and a set of recommendations.

[3] The terms 'empirical' and 'experimental' tend to be used in very different ways in modern philosophy and education compared to how Dewey chose to define them. The term 'empirical' is often used as a definition of what Dewey refers to as 'experimental', while the term 'experimental' usually refers to engaging with the world without a set of formalised procedures to guide one's actions.

[4] Even though Dewey underlines the significance of scientific method and scientific concepts, he tends to alternate between using the terms 'concepts', ideas' and 'intellectualisations'. Miettinen (2000, p. 65) suggests that this is because Dewey wanted to stress that concepts are always tentative and that their practical significance had to be established before their status was verified.

[5] This argument is derived from Bakhurst's (1995) critique of Bruner who, in a similar vein to Dewey, retains a residual dualism while stressing the transactional interrelationships between mind and world.

[6] The term 'cultural tools' has replaced the former term in the writings of contemporary Vygotskian scholars to emphasis the cultural dimensions of his theory and to avoid mentalistic interpretations (Daniels, 2001). For this reason, we employ the term 'cultural' in this text.

[7] Vygotsky's formative intellectual development was deeply influenced by his perception of the limitations of the different traditions that characterised Russian psychology, both before and after the revolution, as well as by his intellectual curiosity about new developments in the field of literary theory. To explore this more fully see Bakhurst (1991), Kozulin (1998), Van der Veer and Valsiner (1993) and Wertsch (1985a). Specifically, Vygotsky was, as Kozulin (1998, p. 10) observes, influenced by: Marx's idea about 'human praxis' (i.e. that human activity serves as both a generator of consciousness and a transformer of the environment), though the precise nature of this issue debt has been contested amongst Vygotskian scholars (see Bakhurst, 1991; Packer, 2008); Engels' ideas about 'labour and tools' (i.e. resources we use to transform our relationship with the environment); Spinoza's ideas about 'free will' (i.e. that we have to accept responsibility for making our thoughts

and actions); and Hegel's ideas about the social basis of reason (i.e. that we develop its foundations historically and culturally).

[8] Readers who are interested in following the actual development of Vygotsky's thought are advised to consult Minick (1987), Wertsch (1985b) and Kozulin (1990) and the introductions to all the Collected Editions of his work.

[9] Vygotsky sometimes used the phrase 'spontaneous concept' as an alternative for 'everyday concept'. For the sake of consistency, we have kept to the latter term, whereas we have followed Hedegaard's (2001) argument and substituted the term 'theoretical' concept for 'scientific' concept. In the current era, the former term is not encumbered by the pejorative meaning that in some contexts is associated with the latter term. Moreover, it is consistent with the dual sense of Vygotsky's original meaning of 'scientific'; it is based on a generalisation and is part of a system of knowledge.

[10] The word 'instruction' in Russian denoted a sense of teaching and learning, in other words, an active engagement with the process of learning. In contrast, in Western traditions, instruction is normally conceived pejoratively denoting a passive form of transmission learning (Daniels, 2001, p. 10).

[11] Two definitions of the ZPD have been distinguished in Vygotsky's writings (Daniels, 2001; Wells, 1999). The version that surfaced in his book *Mind in Society* (1978) emphasises the value of the concept as a way of assessing intellectual abilities and levels of development. A second version of the ZPD is found in the revised edition of *Thinking and Speech* (1987, p. 22). The emphasis here is on reasoning with theoretical concepts. Since my intention is to reveal the widest educational value of the concept, my discussion of the ZPD concentrates on the second version.

[12] Although Vygotsky does not specifically relate his discussion of inner and external speech to the mediation of theoretical and everyday concepts in the ZPD, it is my contention that it is possible to construct the contribution they make to this process from his remarks about them.

[13] The ramifications of these assumptions continue to be felt in contemporary psychology and linguistics: writers influenced by Bakhtin tend to affirm the relation between language and thought, while writers influenced by Pinker tend to forcibly deny any relationship between them.

CHAPTER 7

DEVELOPING THE MEDIATED BASIS
OF LEARNING

INTRODUCTION

We showed in the previous chapter that Vygotsky's theory of cultural mediation was revolutionary philosophically, psychologically and pedagogically. His distinction between explicit and implicit mediation, for example, offered us a way to think differently about the separation of theoretical and tacit knowledge that lies at the heart of this debate about knowledge in the knowledge economy. Instead of portraying the human mind as a naturalistic mind that produces separate and different types of knowledge, Vygotsky allowed us to appreciate that the human mind is a conceptually structured capacity that we can exercise discursively, descriptively and practically. Hence, it follows that theoretical understanding can have a tacit dimension and that tacit understanding can have a conceptual dimension. We now consider how the theory of cultural mediation has been subsequently developed in Cultural Historical Activity Theory (CHAT), the theoretical tradition that Vygotsky spawned, and the extent to which these developments offer us resources to rethink the learning challenge of the knowledge economy.

It is generally accepted in CHAT that Vygotsky concentrated throughout most of his career on face-to-face mediation in a formal educational context, and thus operated within a slightly restricted version of his own theoretical framework in two senses: the distinctive character of the discursive basis of mediation was played down; and the way in which the macro-sociological context is inextricably bound up in the process of mediation was glossed over (Minick, 1987).

The underplaying of the potential of his own theory has, however, provided the source of inspiration for a number of post-Vygotskians – Wertsch, Leont'ev, Lave and Wenger, and Engeström – to make major contributions to the development of the concept of mediation. They have done so by, on the one hand, actively engaging with Vygotsky's legacy and pursuing the semiotic dimensions (Wertsch, 1991), or the societal dimensions of Vygotsky's legacy (Leont'ev, 1978; Engeström, 1987); and, on the other hand, tangentially engaging with it via the concept of 'social practice' (Lave & Wenger, 1991). For this reason, we now consider the nature of their contributions. We conclude that the post-Vygotskians' development of Vygotsky's theory of cultural mediation offers further insights, which we can use to support personal and vocational workplace learning (PVWL) in addressing the learning challenge of the knowledge economy. We note, however, that for this to happen a number of the tensions that the post-Vygotskians' focus on mediation by activity or semiotic mediation generated for Vygotsky's theory of cultural mediation will have to be addressed.

Mediation as 'Dialogue'

Introduction

From the outset of his career, one of James Wertsch's (1991) primary concerns has been to extend Vygotsky's ideas about semiotic mediation. He does this by linking it to the theory of discourse through the incorporation of insights from other disciplines, especially linguistics, to contribute to the construction of a conception of mind and human agency – the 'sociocultural theory of mediated action' – that appreciates that cultural tools such as language are products and sources of socio-cultural contexts[1]. This is necessary, according to Wertsch and colleagues (1993, p. 343), because Vygotsky, '...advocates a kind of universalism that is antithetical to the arguments for social situatedness, that he was pursuing'. They argue that this has happened because Vygotsky treated language as a generalised semiotic system and assumed that the acquisition of theoretical concepts represents the apex of human attainment. Thus the challenge is, according to Wertsch (1991), to develop Vygotsky's ideas about semiotic mediation. He maintains that this entails using his concept of 'mediated action' (1991) to identify the way in which mediation will vary as a function of cultural, historical and institutional setting.

The role of speech genres in mediating action. Wertsch (1991) argues that Bakhtin's (1981; 1986) concepts of 'dialogicality', 'voice' and 'speech genres' provide a way to develop Vygotsky's ideas about semiotic mediation, because they enable us to understand how our engagement with language enables us to formulate a diversity of interpretations. These in turn, mediate actions in profoundly different ways.

The first way Bakhtin helps in this regard, according to Wertsch, is to point out that in order for communication to occur, the context for communication has to be created interlinguistically. For Bakhtin, the meaning of an utterance is never pre-given: utterances always express a point of view because they are, '...constructed and reflect the voice that produced them and the voices to which they are addressed and consumed' (Wertsch, 1991, p. 51)[2]. Thus, it follows that communication is never a matter of simply transferring an idea from the head of one person to another. It is instead a process in which people occupying different 'positions' in a discourse attempt to influence one another's thoughts and actions. Thus it follows that people are always working towards a joint or collective understanding.

Knowing how to locate an utterance in a context in which it is meaningful is not straightforward, because Bakhtin, as Wertsch (1991, p. 54) notes, acknowledges that dialogic orientation pre-supposes that we can further distinguish between 'social' (e.g. local discourses) and 'national' (e.g. English, French, German) languages. The key issue for Bakhtin is that the production of an utterance in either type of language pre-supposes that we have developed the capability to 'ventriloquate' (Bakhtin, 1981). By this he means the ability to communicate effectively with different grammatical and semantic systems or discourses.

Wertsch uses the concepts of voice and dialogicality to demonstrate the link between speech and context. One way he illustrates this link is in relation to the tendency in the Social Sciences (see the discussion of Castells in Chapter 4) to conceptualise communication in terms of the 'conduit' metaphor (Reddy, 1979)[3]. This metaphor, according to Wertsch, assumes language functions like a conduit transferring thoughts and/or information from one person to another, thereby pre-supposing the commonality of goals between speaker(s) and listener(s). Commonality of goals is not, as Wertsch observes (1991, p. 74) a given feature of social settings, even ostensibly normative settings such as classrooms. For communication to occur, all parties have to appreciate the ways in which the particular mode of language use creates meaning, and the range of meanings created subsequently mediate action.

The second way Bakhtin contributes to our understanding of the way in which language mediates action is, according to Wertsch, by revealing how linguistic conventions characteristic of different types of situations such as 'speech genres' shape unconsciously the pattern of communication. The production of any utterance always entails the invocation of a speech genre because our utterances:

...have definite and relatively stable typical *forms of construction of the whole*... We use them confidently and skilfully in practice, and it is quite possible for us not to even suspect their existence in theory.

(Bakhtin, 1986, p. 76; quoted in Wertsch, 1991)

It is, for Wertsch (1991, p. 84), important to recognise that we never 'speak from nowhere' because this would pre-suppose the untenable idea that words or phrases have a 'literal' meaning. Effective communication pre-supposes the creation of intral-inguistic contexts by directing our utterances towards people in a way that is judged appropriate by those involved in the act of communication. The conditions for speech, and hence communication, are shaped by the speech genres that not only constitute 'linguistic tool kits' (i.e. cultural tools) that denote competent linguistic performance in a specific socio-cultural setting – and, moreover, these genres mediate thought and action in subtle, but distinctive, ways – but also provide the possibility for sets of interdependently related but continually changing speech positions (Wertsch *et al.*, 1995, p. 25). On the one hand, we are 'answerable' for these speech positions; and, on the other hand, they permit us as speakers to use certain forms of 'addressivity', that is, to aim our speech at the positions of others.

This recognition that linguistic tool kits influence communication introduces a very important notion about the power of language as a cultural tool that, according to Wertsch, Vygotsky paid insufficient attention to: namely that language has the power to constrain or empower action. As Wertsch observes:

Each cultural activity (e.g. science, arts, everyday life, religion) poses specific tasks that can be solved only by using the corresponding modes of thinking. For instance, practical thinking or common sense is not sufficient to solve scientific tasks, whereas scientific thinking is of little use when writing a poem or sermon or solving everyday problems.

(Wertsch *et al.*, 1993, p. 351)

Cultural activities constitute, for Wertsch, a series of mutually separate forms of knowledge, each characterised by their own mode of thinking and specific logic that do not mutually inform one another. To position ourselves authoritatively within those fields of activity it is necessary to appropriate the correct speech genre in order to have the sense of what we say grasped by other members of that group. To avoid the impending semiotic determinism of the position he is advancing, Wertsch (1998, pp. 143–7) argues that new representations of the world are produced when we use speech genres creatively. For this to happen, we have to identify the way in which speech genres privilege certain 'patterns' of communication and develop the 'analytical tools' that will allow us to 'free ourselves from undesirable patterns and create new patterns'.

The legacy of mediation by dialogue. Wertsch's focus on dialogue supplements Vygotsky's ideas about semiotic mediation in a number of ways. First, by reminding us that all concepts are always located in speech genres, and that learning any type of concept requires us to become more adept at using speech genres, initially to express our own growing understanding of a concept and subsequently to use the concept to articulate a personal position. Second, by deepening Vygotsky's concern for word meaning by drawing attention to the situated and developmental dimension of understanding, Wertsch highlights that the meaning of, for example, a theoretical concept does not inhere totally in the words associated with that particular concept, nor in the system of judgements that inform the use of a word, but rather it emerges at both the point of contact between the words used and also, to borrow Shotter's (1993, p. 388) phrase, the 'movements' they achieve in other people's thinking and speaking in the conditions of their use. Third, by revealing that as we personalise (i.e. ventriloquate), our use of genres, and use words to represent or give an account of something that is not actually present, we are increasingly able to decrease the references to what 'is' the case – that is, a detailed account of everything that occurred; and increasingly able to work with others to explore what 'might be' (1993, p. 388) – that is, to create the interlinguistic conditions for people to extrapolate and/or speculate as to what might happen next.

Wertsch generated these insights as he distanced himself from what he felt was Vygotsky's attachment to some form of abstract rationality. This distancing occurs, as Derry (2003, pp. 47–8) has presciently observed, because Wertsch reads Vygotsky through a 'Kantian' rather than a 'Hegelian' lens. This leads Wertsch to maintain that Vygotsky viewed theoretical concepts as the apex of human attainment and, as such, to overlook both that the formation of knowledge is based on the generation of representations of the world and also that these systems of knowledge can be regarded as a form of culture in mind – something that we are all capable of constituting through participation in practice. Hence Wertsch argues that local meaning-making (i.e. the formation of everyday concepts) is equally important to the generation of, and also equivalent to, theoretical concepts.

This is a misreading of Vygotsky's position and intentions, because he did not assume, as Derry (2008, p. 52) demonstrates, that the foundations of knowledge were pre-given. In fact, he went to great pains in *The Crisis in Psychology*

(Vygotsky, 1997a) to demonstrate: just how the foundations of psychology were historically and culturally built up and hence constantly susceptible to criticism and revision; that new ideas in disciplinary fields continually emerge through the process of criticism; and that these normative conditions upon which knowledge rests provide the foundation for supra-empirical connections to be made across societies and communities.

Once we understand Vygotsky's position that what gives theoretical concepts their supra-empirical power is their measure of generality and the system within which they are located – and that this is built up historically and culturally – we can see Wertsch's insights about speech positions more as a complement than a criticism of Vygotsky's position. From Vygotsky's perspective, we learn to use a theoretical concept, even though he did not use the term, by ventriloquating our growing understanding of the measure of its generality and inferring what follows from that understanding; and, by using this ability to ventriloquate, we learn to restructure the meaning of our everyday concepts. Thus ventriloquation is an integral feature of the process of conceptual restructuring.

The ability to ventriloquate with speech genres in any situation pre-supposes, as Shotter (1993, p. 384) has noted, the 'development of methods for *warranting* in the course of talk', that is, 'giving good reasons' for what *might be* as opposed to what is – and, in addition, it also pre-supposes that we have learned how to use those methods. In most everyday situations, we try to avoid the need for such warranting by learning to speak, as Shotter (1993, p. 385) further notes, in accordance with 'routine intelligibility' (Garfinkle, 1967). In other words, we convey the meaning of our utterances to others because we are speaking confidently within the accepted idiom of a genre or social group within which we and others are acting.

This focus on the importance of *reasons* to the process of warranting when using concepts, allows us to identify a unifying and a diversifying thread between Wertsch's insights about speech genres and Vygotsky's insights about theoretical and everyday concepts. Although everyday and theoretical concepts are rooted in normatively established and validated ways of thinking and acting – based on implicit (in the case of the former) or explicit (in the case of the latter) articulation of reasons, and expressed discursively – the form of warranting differs in each case. The former is based on using empirically based processes of reasoning to sort objects and/or events by abstracting similarities from their surface appearance, while the latter is based on using the inferential connections that concepts provide to explain issues that are not susceptible to perception.

This distinction between empirical and inferential warranting allows us to shed more light on one of the challenges of the knowledge economy that we discussed in Chapter 4, namely bridging traditions of reasoning in interprofessional communication. Whereas intra-professional communication between specialists, such as Knorr Cetina's molecular biologists and high-energy physicists, occurs as a result of a shared tradition of concepts, objects and warrants, interprofessional communication inevitably lacks a shared tradition. Expressed in Vygotsky and Wertsch's terminology, the learning challenge for interprofessional communities is to develop the capability to ventriloquate with one another's concepts in ways that enable other members of the community to infer what follows, and collectively agree the professional actions that they should take. Vygotsky and Wertsch were not concerned with this issue, therefore their ideas about conceptual restructuring and ventriloquation will require further development before we can use them as resources to facilitate interprofessional reasoning, inferring and acting. We shall return to this issue in Chapter 9.

Mediation as 'Activity'

Introduction
Earlier we saw that the concept of activity was used by Vygotsky to explain the genesis of consciousness or mind, by pursuing the role of semiotic mediation. Leont'ev's change of focus to mediation by activity arose as a result of his concern to move away from a focus on face-to-face interaction based on the use of language, and towards a focus on the societal purpose or 'object' of any activity. Thus it was a short step from Vygotsky's concern for the interdependence between historical and cultural processes and individual mental processes, and the development of social meaning and communication, as far as Leont'ev was concerned, to his concern to articulate what he felt was the general principle that lay behind semiotic mediation, namely the role of organised human activity in the formation of consciousness (Minick, 1985)[4].

The meaning of the term 'object', as used by Leont'ev, could be misleading for readers who are not familiar with the semantic inflections of that word in the Russian language, and differs from that already used in this book in the discussion of Knorr Cetina (i.e. object as material and symbolic entity). Russian has two words, *object* and *predmet*, which are usually translated into English as 'object' (Kaptelinin, 2006, p. 6). The former refers to material things, while the latter refers to the 'target or content of a thought or action' (2006, p. 6). Leont'ev limited his use of the term to the latter, defining object as:

> ...something that opposes (German *gegenstad*), something that resists (Latin *objectum*), something which an action is directed (Russian *predmet*), that is, something to which a human is related, as an object of his or her activity, no matter if this activity is an internal one or an external one (for example, "the object of eating", the "object of labour", or the "object of contemplation").

(Leont'ev, 1981b, p. 49)

Hence Leont'ev initiated in CHAT a focus on the way in which the social constitution of an activity plays a part in mediating our everyday actions (Cole, 1996; Daniels, 2001, Engeström, Miettinen & Punamaki, 1999). This social constitution remains a taken-for-granted feature of Knorr Cetina's analysis of epistemic cultures, and her use of the term object follows the conventional meaning of that term in English. We explore how Leont'ev's and Knorr Cetina's work can mutually reinforce one another in Chapter 9.

The theory of activity and its implications for mediation. The principle of object-relatedness rests on two assumptions (Stetsenko, 2005, p. 75). They are that material objects are, 'turned into facts of mind (i.e. become represented in subjective images) through an active process of humans relating to those objects'; and, that although these images are individually understood and engaged with, they are never a purely individual accomplishment because they are absorptions of the collective experience of people. Thus, the psychological is the product of human practical, cultural and social activity, hence the object of activity always appears to us in two forms:

> ...first, in its independent existence, in which it subordinates and transforms the activity of the subject and, second, as the image of an object, as a product of reflection of the object's properties, which takes places as a result of the activity of the subject.

> (Leont'ev, 1983, p. 170)

The crux of Leont'ev's argument is therefore fairly similar to Vygotsky; both writers accept that human consciousness and the formation of the self originate in actual processes of human activity and develop within transformations of the structures of activity. Where Leont'ev differs sharply from Vygotsky is through according greater priority to the complex dynamics of the activities that we engage in, and that lead to the production of human consciousness. This occurs through a 'two-fold transition' of activity (Stetsenko & Arievitch, 2004, p. 484), as: (i) our everyday practical activities (for example, education) acquire their distinctive form(s) by absorbing and embodying the dynamics and structures of the social world (for example, status differences); and (ii) as we develop our mind and our sense of self as we participate in everyday practical activities. In other words, our personal activities and perceptions are mediated by our internalisation of collective experiences, rather than arising from some individual mentalistic process of creation.

Leont'ev explained the way in which object-orientated activity mediates our experience of the social world through his concept of 'object motive'. He uses this concept to illuminate the historical and social basis of individual action:

> The main thing which distinguished one activity from another, however, is the difference of their object. It is exactly the object of an activity that has given it a determined direction. According to the terminology I have proposed the object of activity as its true motive'.

> (Leont'ev, 1978, p. 62)

This positioning of motives outside the individual, which is totally 'counterintuitive' to the conventional wisdom in psychology, is logical and consistent with Vygotsky's foundational principle about the primacy of 'collaborative processes of material activity' (Stetsenko & Arievitch, 2004, p. 487), led Leont'ev to maintain that it is possible to form a meaningful, social and historical constitution or interpretation of the world in which we live without relying on language, concepts or cultural symbols (Minick, 1987, p. 298).

> Although language appears to be the carrier of meaning, language is not its
> demiurge. Behind linguistic meanings hide socially developed methods of
> action (operations) in the process of which people change and perceive
> objective reality.

(Leont'ev, 1978, p. 85)

The purpose of an activity, for Leont'ev, has primacy over semiotic mediation
because it creates the context for that form of mediation. Leont'ev pursued this
issue by focusing on the ways in which the goal, means and conditions of any
social activity are inherently linked to a given individual or group of individuals.

He did so by distinguishing between the following three pairs of constructs:
'activity' and 'motive'; 'action' and 'goal'; and 'operation' and 'conditions'. At first
sight, the term 'activity' is a little confusing since it has two meanings: one refers
to human activity in general (i.e. the theory of activity); while the other refers to
specific activities (education, work, etc.), which constitute the first level of the
theory. From Leont'ev's perspective, each activity – for example, education or
health – is undertaken by a community (deploying a division of labour and various
means of production) and has its own object (i.e. purpose motive). To realise that
object, we undertake different actions (for example, teaching, diagnosing chronic
conditions) that fulfil individual goals (for example, professional pride and
satisfaction) as well as collective goals (for example, governmental expectations).
Equally, the realisation of any actions entails a number of operations, that is,
habituated behaviours that are only possible when certain conditions pertain – for
example, the teaching of science pre-supposes the existence of a laboratory in
a school, and the X-raying of patients pre-supposes the provision of both an X-ray
machine and a laboratory to process the X-rays.

This concern for the hierarchy of human activity and object-motives introduces
a rather different focus on mediation compared with Vygotsky's concern with the
unity of thinking and speaking, and communication and social action. It led Leont'ev
to focus on two different expressions of object-mediated activity, each reflecting
a strong teleological orientation (Wertsch, 1995, p. 130). One manifestation
emerges in the line of development that exists between activity, actions and
operations, and is primarily a consequence of the prevailing division of labour
(Engeström, 1987, p. 18).

A good way to understand what Leont'ev had in mind by mediation through
practical activity is to turn to his illustration of a member of a hunter–gatherer society.
Leont'ev describes the way in which the division of labour results in some members
of that society acting as 'beaters' and startling animals, and other members acting as
'catchers', who are responsible for killing the animals. From Leont'ev's perspective,
there is a mediated relationship between the activity, the actions and operations. This
relation is based on the beater explicitly or implicitly grasping the connection between
the collective motive, goal and conditions to realise each stage of the activities, actions
and operations that both underpin and give meaning to his role. According to
Leont'ev, as we participate in a range of mediated activities, actions and operations,
we develop an understanding of what we are doing and why we are doing it.

The other aspect of mediation through activity emerges in the counter-movement from actions to activity and is a consequence of our agency. This counter-movement is possible because our actions are never totally determined by the division of labour. There will always be instances when:

> ...a person undertakes to perform some actions under the influence of a certain motive, and then performs them for their own sake because the motive seems to have been displaced to their objective. And that means that the actions are transformed into activity.

(Leont'ev, 1981b, p. 238)

Such acts of creativity, however, pre-suppose that we are able to:

> ...engage in certain, special activity, some special act. This is an act of reflecting the relation of the motive of a given, concrete activity to the motive of a wider activity, that realises a broader, more general life relation that includes the given, concrete activity.

(Leont'ev, 1981b, p. 238)

We do this by establishing conditions that position us 'off-line', that is, away from the flux of our everyday commitments, so as to rethink the actions associated with an existing activity and implement those new actions in such a way that they require the activity of which they are a part to be rethought itself (Engeström, 1987).

The legacy of mediation by activity. Leont'ev's focus on object-mediated activity complements Vygotsky's idea that psychological processes should be conceptualised as phenomena that do not belong to a separate mental realm because they are culturally and historically created. Thus psychological processes, for Leont'ev like Vygotsky, have to be conceptualised as cultural–historical actions, rather than in the traditional psychological sense of a natural mind that is theorised as acting as though it were independent of the social environment. Where Leont'ev's concern for the object of activity differs from Vygotsky's focus on semiotic mediation is that he is able to draw our attention to how the purpose of any activity (e.g. banking or education), which is often taken for granted, is a powerful influence on our engagement with that activity and, as a result, is often an undetected influence on the processes of conceptual restructuring and repositioning. In doing so, Leont'ev offers us a way to shed light on an, up to now, under-discussed feature of Knorr Cetina's argument about epistemic cultures: that they are predicated on a shared object and that the process of lateral branching is a continuation in a new vein of activity of that object. We shall return to the implications of this observation in Chapter 9.

At first sight, Leont'ev's insightful, albeit brief, remarks that changing deep-rooted habits requires a special act of reflection appears to complement Dewey's argument about the value of naturalising the scientific method to facilitate experiential inquiry and change (Koschmann *et al.*, 1998). However, in drawing attention to the need for a special act of reflection, Leont'ev offers us, in addition, a way to go beyond Dewey's ideas about reflection. The basis of this move can be revealed if we make a link between Vygotsky's argument about conceptual restructuring and Leont'ev's concept of the object of activity. The process of restructuring occurs as we learn a new theoretical concept – for example, the concept of density – and are, in principle, repositioned towards the world because our options for acting are expanded. In educational contexts, the justification for learning the concept of density in science is taken for granted. The process of repositioning could be deepened, for example, if we questioned the object of activity that justifies the inclusion of science in the curriculum and the pedagogic strategies used to teach the concept of density. Once we do this, we can see that the mediated relation between conceptual restructuring and repositioning can be a trigger for change, but both are required to achieve substantial change. Leont'ev did not explore this issue, and it was left – as we shall see later in the chapter – to Engeström to identify how to accomplish such change. We now turn our attention to the relation between Leont'ev's ideas about enculturation into the norms and experiences of previous generations for his theory and their contribution to human development.

One of the outcomes of Leont'ev's theory of activity is that it results in a rather one-dimensional account of the role of the object of activity in shaping our actions, because his treatment of the concepts of motive and the object of activity is, '...based on a 1:1:1 correspondence between activities, needs, motives, and objects' (Kaptelinin, 2006, pp. 13–14). We can see the limitations of this assumption when we consider 'poly-motivated activities'; that is, activities that are simultaneously characterised by several motives. Within the context of Leont'ev's hierarchical framework of motives, the sense-making motive (i.e. the why we are supposed to be doing something) is assumed to always determine the course of our actions, thus, significantly diminishing the scope to exercise our agency.

This leaves us with the problem of how we explain the moment-to-moment and long-term development dynamics of activity and human intersubjectivity. In the case of the former, the underlying motive of an activity is, '...not the only factor determining the choices people make in their daily lives' (Kaptelinin, 2006). For example, the legal requirement to obey the Highway Code does not guarantee conformity with the law because people may deviate from it in order to avoid an accident. In the case of the longer-term dynamics, the object of activity often undergoes considerable changes even though the underlying motive remains more or less the same, for example, the design of a new product or service can change radically over the life-cycle of production and this generates the need for new forms of expertise and collaboration (Miettinen, 2005; Hyysalo, 2005).

These examples suggest that Leont'ev's portrayal of the omnipotence of social and material condition, resolving around notions of people acquiring cultural norms and experiences, plays down the 'agentic role of the self in transforming and further developing those norms and experiences' (Stetsenko & Arievitch, 2004, p. 489). Any activity – for example, art or music – is only, as Stetsenko (2006, p. 83) observes, the product and carrier of meaning as it is constantly re-enacted and reconstructed:

> Without human agency words and music are mute, even dead, unless someone again and again re-enacts them, giving them new life (if even in a "mere" perception), thus making them alive for a particular person.

This implies that mediation by activity is more of a 'socio-individual'[5] process, in other words produced through the iterative interpolation of socially established activities and human agentic actions, than Leont'ev is inclined to acknowledge.

This is possibly because tool use, particularly symbolic tools, is a rather embedded feature of Leont'ev's theory. His focus on the operations and action associated with socially established and sanctioned activities such as education also tends to convey the impression that tool use is routinised and habitualised, other than in exceptional cases. This fails to do justice to the different ways in which any activity can not only continually be realised in different action forms or 'recontextualised' (van Oers, 1998, p. 138) through the use of different and/or new cultural tools, but also that the symbolic dimension of tool use is central to human creativity and intersubjectivity.

Acts of recontextualisation can occur, according to van Oers, 'horizontally' or 'vertically' (1998, p. 138). The former refers to the possibility that any activity is susceptible to multiple realisations – for example, sculpture can, depending on artists' aesthetic preferences, be realised by using found objects (i.e. old buckets) as much as newly created objects (i.e. bronze castings), and by using tools such as lathes and furnaces to fabricate them. The latter refers to the idea that new ideas about an activity may generate problems, which serve as the pivot for the creation of a new action pattern or debates about what constitutes the purpose of that socially established activity. For example, one result of artists' criticism of the gallery – the 'white cube' (O'Doherty, 1976) – as a context for art that surfaced in the 1950s resulted in artists identifying new contexts for art (i.e. public spaces), new conceptions of sculpture (i.e. installations) and new resources for sculpture (i.e. film and video).

The above discussion of recontextualisation highlights that activity development in Fine Art, or for that matter any other field, consists of a complex and interrelated process of thinking (i.e. conceptual restructuring) and acting differently (i.e. repositioning), towards the taken-for-granted notions of the object of, and the context for, artistic activity materially and symbolically. This suggests that it will be necessary to give further consideration to the three facets of mediation – restructuring, repositioning and recontextualisation – that we have highlighted in this chapter – for two reasons: to better understand their mediated relation to one another; and to deepen our understanding of how they might help us to address the learning challenge of the knowledge economy.

Before doing do, it is important to consider two other important developments of the concept of mediation. One is the work of Yrjö Engeström and is an explicit attempt to extend and apply the scope of Leont'ev's theory of activity to collective activity. The other development has been spearheaded by Jean Lave, whose work does not emanate from CHAT, but has nevertheless been highly influential in that field.

Mediation as 'Situated Participation'

Introduction

Lave is a cultural anthropologist who formulated a theory of learning that was not based on the prevailing psychological wisdom about what counted as the context for learning (i.e. educational institutions), the content of learning (i.e. propositional knowledge) and the process of learning (i.e. mental assimilation of propositions) for granted. Instead Lave wanted to develop a theory that took explicit account of how people learn *sui generis*. In contrast to Leont'ev, Lave and Wenger employ the concept of social practice rather than activity. Both are normative concepts whose roots lie in Hegelian and Marxist thought (Chaiklin *et al.*, 1999): the latter is, as we saw earlier, primarily concerned with the way in which action on the object of activity can, in principle, result in the transformation of consciousness and activity; the former offers us a language of description for both socially sanctioned and organised forms of practice formed in relation to societal needs, such as education, medicine and practitioners' practice – that is, the actions made in relation to practice (i.e. doctors' or teachers' procedures, devices, etc.) (Chaiklin, 2008)[6].

The concept of social practice has a rich and varied history in philosophy and sociology to denote our enculturation into pre-given forms of activity/practice (Bourdieu, 1977; Giddens, 1984; Turner, 1994). Lave and Wenger, however, use the concept generatively to denote our active engagement with, and transformation of, culturally and historically established forms of activity/practice and practitioners' practice (Arnsneth, 2008). As such they developed a different angle on the co-evolution of material and social practice and the situatedness of semiotic activity, compared, respectively, with Leont'ev and Wertsch, even though Lave did not explicitly formulate this as the goal for her work. In doing so, she generated, as we shall see, a number of insights about mediation that can be used to further elaborate and extend Vygotsky and Leont'ev's work, and that have been widely discussed elsewhere in the Social and Human Sciences (Anderson *et al.*, 1996).

The situated, embodied and relational nature of learning and knowing. The cornerstone of Lave and Wenger's practice theory of learning is one of the oldest models of learning in traditional and industrial societies – apprenticeship. They were attracted to apprenticeship because it offered a way of according '...legitimacy to different knowledges to those that would be associated with the school-based paradigm of learning (Vann & Bowker, 2001, p. 251). Lave and Wenger encapsulated their intentions by invoking the concept of the 'community of practice' as a way to capture the:

> ...set of relations among persons, activities and the world, over time and in relation to other tangential and overlapping communities of practice. A community of practice is an intrinsic condition for the existence of knowledge, not least because it provides the interpretative support necessary for making sense of its heritage.

> (Lave & Wenger, 1991, p. 98)

These ideas about learning are based on two theses – 'process ontology' and 'inseparability'. The former denotes that the idea process is the guiding orientation and fundamental nature of reality, while the latter denotes that individuals and the social mutually constitute one another (Sawyer, 2002, p. 291). Lave and Wenger formulated the notion of 'legitimate peripheral participation' to encapsulate the interrelation between these theses:

> ...learners participate in communities of practitioners and that mastery of knowledge and practice requires newcomers to move towards full ...participation in the sociocultural practices of a community. "Legitimate peripheral participation" provides a way to speak about activities, identities, artefacts, and communities of knowledge and practice.

(Lave & Wenger, 1991, p. 47)

Hence, learning does not consist of the acquisition of a discrete body of knowledge that we subsequently apply, instead we develop the skill to perform by engaging in a working and learning process under the 'attenuated conditions' (Hanks, 1991, p. 14) of legitimate peripheral participation that provides, '...learners with opportunities to make the culture of practice theirs' (Lave & Wenger, 1991, p. 95).

The concept of situated learning is a much more subtle and complex notion than much of its use in the secondary literature often acknowledges (A. Edwards, 2004). Situatedness is not an 'empirical attribute' (i.e. with meaning immediately apparent or through sensory perception) of everyday activity. The meaning of a situation is shaped by the historical constitution of that setting as much as the impact of the immediate forms of social and political power existing within that setting. The concept denotes, therefore, a general theoretical perspective about:

> ...the relational character of knowledge and learning, about the negotiated character of meaning, and about the concerned (engaged, dilemma-driven) nature of learning activity for the people involved.

(Lave & Wenger, 1991, p. 33)

This emphasis on the relational character of knowledge and learning allows us to see that the assumed 'decontextualised' knowledge, which is contained in propositional statements that formal education purportedly transmits to learners, is situated much as the knowledge and skill, and 'embedded in everyday activities' (Lave, 1996, p. 153).

We can only start to get to grips, according to Lave and Wenger (1991, p. 98), with the specific form of our situatedness as we participate in the social practice associated with different types of expert practice in which such knowledge exists. This claim introduces the intriguing idea that participation in social practice is an 'epistemological principle of learning', because it is only by varying or changing our mode of participation that we (i.e. legitimate peripheral participants) come to embody the knowledge and skill associated with a community of practice and learn to use it in more encompassing ways.

In Lave and Wenger's parlance, participation means engaging with the ideas and discourses as much as the practical routines, protocols and tools associated with a community, and epistemology means operating with a working sense of the interpolation of the cognitive and practical[7]. They pursue the pedagogic implications of participation by identifying the conditions in communities of practice that give learners opportunities: firstly to grasp the principles that underpin the 'technologies of practice' associated with specific cultural practices and to develop different ways of organising and coordinating those cultural tools so as to use those cultural tools to, 'connect with the history of the practice, and to participate more directly with its cultural life' (Lave & Wenger, 1991, p. 101). Secondly to engage in 'improvisational development' by enabling newcomers to use the 'learning curriculum', that is, the cultural tools, discourses and technical artefacts to simultaneously develop their own knowledge, skill and identity and that of the community (Lave & Wenger, 1991, p. 97). In a nutshell, their argument is that legitimate peripheral participation and learning curricula are the pre-conditions for the ongoing development of practice and identity, even if this development is sometimes a highly contested process between 'old-timers' and 'newcomers'.

What makes communities of practice distinctively different from educational institutions, according to Lave and Wenger, is that there are no special forms of discourse aimed at assisting apprentices to become accepted members of that community. For newcomers the purpose is not to 'learn *from* talk' as a substitute for legitimate peripheral participation; rather it is to 'learn *to* talk' as a key to legitimate peripheral participation (Lave & Wenger, 1991, p. 109). Thus, from Lave and Wenger's perspective, since language is inextricably bound up with practice, and it is in practice that we learn, language is a powerful mediating resource because it supports acting in the world as much as talking about the world (1991, p. 85). Hence learning, for them, is spatially and temporally distributed among co-participants and mediated by the different perspectives, cultural tools and other members of the participating 'community'.

The legacy of mediation as situated participation. One of the unintended consequences of Lave and Wenger's work has been to broaden the notion of the co-evolution of material practice, social interaction and identity in CHAT (Stetsenko, 2004). Because their notion that participation is an epistemological principle of learning is based on an 'emergent' and 'embodied' conception of the relation between preexisting collective practice and the individual enactment and transformation of such practice (Sawyer, 2002, p. 291), Lave and Wenger simultaneously add to and subtract from Leont'ev's theory of activity. In the case of the former, they add another dimension to Leont'ev's concern for the acquisition of previous generations' cultural norms and experiences by participating in pre-given collaborative processes of social life. The mediated activities that result in the production of cultural tools in communities of practice contribute, for Lave and Wenger, not only to the ongoing genesis of social practices, but also to the intersubjective practice of meaning-making as people play the part of active agents in the development of their own identity and the development of humanity (Billett, 2007). In making this argument, they provide a more iterative analysis than Knorr Cetina of the relation between the development of practice and identity, but are less able to identify how such developments benefit the wider field in which the practice is located. In the case of the latter, Lave and Wenger unintentionally deflect our attention away from the object of activity that underpins the cultural and historical constitution of different communities of practice and leave us with a focus on practitioners' practice.

In their attempt to identify a strong non-dualistic explanatory principle for learning that works across all settings and forms of knowledge, Lave and Wenger maintain that it is necessary to eradicate the dominant 'folk epistemology of dichotomies' that surfaces in the work of Vygotsky as much as in other psychological traditions. By this they mean the dichotomies between 'abstract' and 'concrete' knowledge, 'internalisation' and 'externalisation', and 'mind' and 'world', that they felt had dogged traditional theories of learning, including Vygotsky's theory of cultural mediation. By viewing theoretical and everyday knowledge as equivalent forms of situated practice, Lave and Wenger assume that they have achieved their goal of formulating a non-dualistic theory of both our relation to the world and of learning. This attribution of a residual dualism in Vygotsky's work occurs because, in emphasising that all forms of knowledge are situated, Lave and Wenger – like Wertsch – assume that all arguments in favour of distinguishing between theoretical and everyday concepts inevitably rest on the legacy of a 'Kantian' conception of the nature of theoretical knowledge, namely its assumed abstract character and pre-given and immutable foundations (Derry, 2003). Once we appreciate the Hegelian provenance of Vygotsky's thought, as exemplified earlier in this chapter, we can see that his analytical distinction between theoretical and everyday concepts is based on conceiving of both as social practices. Vygotsky's point is that they are both products of a mediated mind, but they are different types of social practice (i.e. the former is a theoretically based way of understanding the world, and the latter the result of our non-theoretical engagement with the world). Hence although the two types of concepts have different outcomes from one another (i.e. one is about grasping the generali-sation contained in a concept and its relation to other concepts and using it to expand our options for acting in the world, while the other is about grasping the meaning of a term that is not defined by a system of concepts and using it in accordance with that meaning), they are both the products of a conceptually structured mind.

This observation about different types of, and outcomes from, our use of concepts does not undermine the force of Lave and Wenger, or Wertsch's, respective, insights about the situated basis of, and the contribution of ventriloquation to, learning: contexts and activities that facilitate participation and ventriloquation influence how we learn to use theoretical and everyday concepts. Rather, our rebalancing of Lave and Wenger, and Wertsch's critiques of Vygotsky enable us to further consoli-date our argument that concepts are an integral part of social practices, and a practitioner's practice nearly always has a symbolic dimension. The practice of, for example, neurosurgery is influenced by the mediated relation between surgeons' theoretical and physical knowledge of anatomy and their 'craft' knowledge of operating procedures. Moreover, although surgical judgements are 'contextual and in the moment', they are also mediated by how surgeons' prior knowledge and experience 'plays out', in other words, are recontextualised in the current context in relation to the problem in hand (Rose, 2004, p. 155).

This suggests that there is an inferential dimension to participation, irrespective of whether it has a symbolic or material basis, and that this inferential dimension constitutes the basis of our ability to transfer (or in our terms, recontextualise) knowledge and skill from one context to another (Guile, 2007). This issue is not explored, as we saw earlier, in Lave and Wenger's account of apprenticeship. Their great insight was to reveal the collective basis of the formation and exercise of expertise (Goodwin, 1994)[8]. Despite the significance of this insight, Lave and Wenger's concept of apprenticeship struggles to convey the complexity of the different varieties of learning that are emerging as forms of work become more interconnected in the knowledge economy (Hughes *et al.*, 2007). In recognition of this deficiency, Wenger (1998, pp. 10–11) has recast the concept of the community of practice from a single to a constellation of communities, to address the complexity of work in the knowledge economy. The gist of his argument is that the challenge that organisations face is to enhance their competitiveness by, 'discovering gaps between official work processes and the real-world practices behind how things actually get done' (Brown & Gray, quoted in Vann & Bowker, 2001, p. 260). This requires members of communities of practice to learn to work across communities' boundaries within an organisation, rather than working within those boundaries. The impression conveyed by Wenger – and the ever-growing community of management consultants who have attempted to operationalise the concept of community of practice as a strategy to assist corporations to leverage knowledge to create commercial value – is that such communities and knowledge are a 'natural' outcome of collaborative work activity, and the resulting knowledge has to be 'harvested' in order to run a successful organisation (Vann & Bowker, 2001, p. 259).

Leaving to one side the inappropriateness of the agriculture metaphors, which reflect a mind–world dualism in relation to a social practice tradition, what are completely eviscerated from Wenger's and the consultants' new use of the concept of community of practice are the two original conditions that he and Lave identified as facilitating learning in communities of practice: namely the learning curriculum and legitimate peripheral participation. Furthermore, there is little sense of the recontextualisation processes, or changes in the organisation of work, that have to occur before the harvested knowledge can play the part in organisational development that Wenger claims. This latter observation leads us to Yrjö Engeström and his work on knowledge creation and organisational transformation.

Mediation as 'Expansive Learning'

Introduction

Of all the post-Vygotskians discussed in this book, Yrjö Engeström (1987) has made the most determined attempt to relate his work to the CHAT corpus as well as to his interpretation of the learning challenge that we face in knowledge economies/societies: namely to address the tensions that surface in organisations by creating new 'objects' and 'forms' of intra- and/or interprofessional activity. To do so, he formulated the theory of 'expansive learning' (Engeström, 1987). Existing psychological theories of learning, such as cognitivism and constructivism, have, according to Engeström (1987, p. 2) little to offer as regards supporting people to create new objects and activities. This is because they are essentially 'reactive forms of learning' whose roots are in formal education and, as such, are predicated on a given context, a pre-set learning task, and a view of learning that assumes that we 'cope with tasks given to us' (1987, p. 2). What was required were a theory of learning and a pedagogic process to reposition us to rethink the object of, and social organisation of, activity. Engeström first presented his theory in his book *Learning by Expanding* (1987), and has developed it conceptually and method-ologically over the subsequent three decades. The account presented here traces this development by showing how he formulated his unit of analysis – an 'activity system', and his intervention methodological strategy – the 'cycle of expansive learning'[9], to support us to envision and collectively realise new activities.

The concept of an 'activity system'.   The starting point for the former is Vygotsky's original mediational triangle, which focused on face-to-face mediation, primarily in educational settings. The conceptual possibilities of that triangle were expanded by Engeström through incorporating Leont'ev's concept of the object of activity to acknowledge the collective purpose of any activity, for example, banking or educ-ation, and the contribution of joint actions to accomplish either of those activities (Langemeyer & Roth, 2006). In doing so, Engeström replaces Leont'ev's overt psychological focus on individual engagement with the object of activity with a concern for the social establishment of, and engagement with, the object of activity. He accomplishes this move by using Marx's distinction between production, consumption, exchange and distribution to explain the constitution and interconnected purpose of different activities (Engeström, 1987, Ch. 3, p. 25)[10].

The net effect is that the initial triangle is now located:

...in an enlarged context so that we see a triangle, but now it is a set of interconnected triangles... the triangles do not exist in isolation from one another; rather they are constantly being constructed, renewed, and transformed as outcome and cause of life.

(Cole, 1996, p. 141)

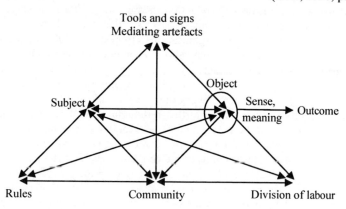

Figure 3. The structure of an activity system.

(*Source*: Engeström, 1987)

Engeström argues that this unit of analysis allows us to grasp the contradictions and complexities in modern working practices, and to appreciate the creative and dynamic potential of work processes and technologies (Engeström and Miettinen, 1999). The top of the figure represents the form of mediated action through which we (i.e. the subject) use cultural tools (i.e. mediating artefacts) to engage with and reproduce an activity. This triangle is located in relation to the components of collective activity – 'community', 'rules' and 'division of labour' – that represent the way in which the processes of production, consumption, exchange and distribution are enacted by individuals and social groups, who share: the same object as one another; norms and sanctions that specify and regulate procedures and interactions amongst them; and the distribution of tasks, powers and responsibilities. The multi-voiced character of those relationships, that is, their different histories, cultural traditions and the sense of ambiguity, surprise and potential for change, is represented through the use of an oval in the model, suggesting the, as yet, 'unknown outcome of the object of activity' (Daniels, 2001, p. 89). In essence, an activity system is the, 'smallest and most simple unit that still preserves the essential unity and integrated quality behind any human activity' (Engeström, 1987)[11] that we can use as a 'theoretical lens' (Russell, 2001) to:

> ...grasp the entire structure of an activity (most commonly workplaces in Engeström's research) – on its own or in its interactions with other activities – and the history of its practices and their changes and developments.

> (Roth, 2004, p. 4)

Over the years, Engeström has expanded his unit of analysis in order to take account of the continuous historical process of the diversification and complexification of work within advanced industrial societies. The first step was to focus on the networks that emerged between organisations as they lost their self-containment, that is, specialist and separate modes of the division of labour, and began to exchange and share objects, means of production, people and so forth (Roth & Lee, 2007). This gave rise to a broader unit of analysis that focused initially on 'joint or networked' activity between organisations (Engeström, 2007) and an interest in using the concept of 'boundary object(s)', i.e. an artefact that can be shared between participants in these forms of activity to, 'analyse the unfolding of object-orientated cooperative activity of several sectors, focusing on tools and means of construction of boundary objects in concrete work practices' (2007, p. 391).

More recently Engeström has further rethought his unit of analysis in relation to two discussions about the emergence of new modes of production, and the way in which they have started to change the relation between the process of production and consumption in some sections of the economy. The first is Victor and Boynton's (1998) argument that the emergence of a new principle of production – 'co-configuration' – is resulting in the gradual incorporation, in some sectors, of customers into the production process to create 'customer intelligent' products and services – that is, products capable of being adapted to reflect changing consumer preferences (Engeström, 2008, pp. 191–5). In recognition that co-configuration results in different combinations of producers and consumers working together for relatively short periods of time, Engeström (2004, p. 153) has coined the term 'knotworking' to describe the form of expertise required in these fluid work settings. Knots involve combinations of people working together for relatively short periods of time to undertake the tightly 'interconnected actions' (Engeström, 2004, p. 153) required to realise different aspects of the process of production. The second is Benkler's (2006, p. 59) argument that the emergence of a new mode of production – social production – that underpins the Open Source Software movement, is based on 'volunteers coming together to collaborate on complex economic projects' outside of firms: a development that challenges economic assumptions about financing and restricting access to the property rights of new developments (Engeström, 2008, p. 209).

The latter is a more profoundly radical development than the former, nevertheless, both have implications for his Developmental Work Research (DWR) programme. This is an interventionist methodology that was originally formulated to support researchers to work alongside members of a single activity system to rethink the object of their activity. The emergence of these new modes of production means that it is sometimes necessary to analyse the mediated relation between networks of organisations and their customers (Engeström, 2008). This mode of expansion of the unit of analysis, in effect, introduces a new learning challenge, 'to construct and acquire distributed agency' (Engeström, 2008, p. 225) by supporting all members of alliances and networks involved in the co-configuration process and/or social production, to generate the forms of expertise required to operate effectively in multi-partner and multi-directional activities. Engeström has been concerned for some time in identifying how to develop these new modes of expertise. The gist of his argument is that it pre-supposes researchers and partner organisations using his interventionist research methodology to facilitate 'de-institutionalised' (Engeström, 2004, p. 163) working arrangements, which are characterised by the continuous negotiation of competencies, tasks and responsibilities between producers, customers and the product/service, rather than the continuation of insular, linear and institutionally focused modes of expertise and activity.

The concept of the 'cycle of expansive learning'. The basic premise of Engeström's DWR methodology is derived from Ilyenkov's (1977a) recasting of Hegel's concept of contradictions from, 'being responsible for changes in thought to being the impetus for change in human activity' (Langemeyer & Roth, 2006, p. 37). Following Ilyenkov, Engeström maintains that contradictions surface as a result of the inherent tension between the use (i.e. human needs) and exchange value (i.e. economic price) of any product or service, and he maintains that if we are to address such tensions (frequently used as a substitute for contradiction) between these two different types of value, then we need a special type of cultural tool to assist us to identify and resolve those tensions.

The primary sources that Engeström draws upon to formulate the 'central instrument' to support people in overcoming tensions are: firstly Bateson's (1973) claim that the most demanding learning challenge is to address the 'double binds', that is, the self-defeating habits that trap us from transforming activities characterised by accumulating tensions; secondly Leont'ev's insight that we require a special act of reflection to scrutinise critically the object of activity so that it does not inhibit change; thirdly Davydov's (1990) argument about the role of 'germ cells' (i.e. core ideas that encapsulate the principle behind the organisation of an activity and interchangeably referred to as kernel concepts) in facilitating thinking in theoretically informed ways; and finally Wartofsky's (1973) argument that we require a special type of cultural tool, in his terms a 'tertiary artefact', to support us to envision new activities. Taken in combination, Engeström (1987) uses these four ideas as the conceptual cornerstone for the 'cycle of expansive learning' (CEL). The CEL serves pedagogic and methodological purposes: to foster the mode of theoretical thinking to identify accumulating tensions in activity systems; and to facilitate the formulation of a new concept to guide our actions to overcome those tensions.

The cycle can, in theory, be engaged with at any point. The first two phases – questioning and analysing – encourage us to engage with the situated basis of our activity by identifying contradictions affecting performance and outcomes. The next phase – modelling – is concerned with the formulation of a new concept, kernel notion or idea, to represent a way of moving beyond the constraints of the existing

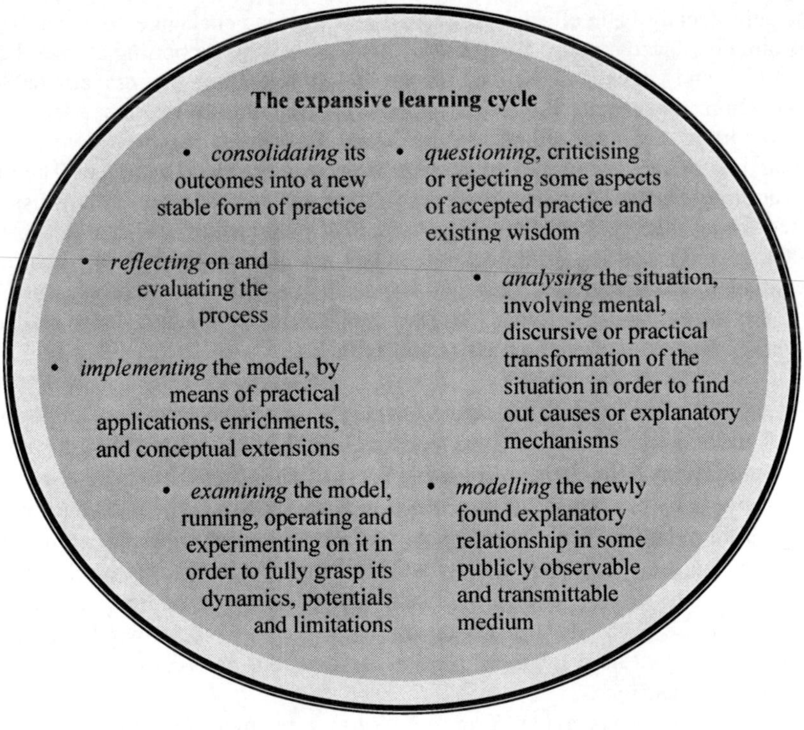

The expansive learning cycle

- *consolidating* its outcomes into a new stable form of practice
- *questioning*, criticising or rejecting some aspects of accepted practice and existing wisdom
- *reflecting* on and evaluating the process
- *analysing* the situation, involving mental, discursive or practical transformation of the situation in order to find out causes or explanatory mechanisms
- *implementing* the model, by means of practical applications, enrichments, and conceptual extensions
- *examining* the model, running, operating and experimenting on it in order to fully grasp its dynamics, potentials and limitations
- *modelling* the newly found explanatory relationship in some publicly observable and transmittable medium

Figure 4. The expansive learning cycle, after Engeström (2004).

(*Source*: Engeström, 1987)

practice. The next two steps – examining and implementing – involve the kernel concept being step-by-step enriched and transformed into a concrete system of multiple and constantly developing changes within an activity system. While the final two phases – reflection and consolidation – support collective deliberation as regards fine tuning the agreed changes to the activity system.

The idea that we need a special tool to facilitate expansive transformation was further refined and developed as Engeström *et al.* (1996), inspired by Wartofsky's (1973) argument that any rethinking of an accepted and embedded social practice is more likely to occur when we have a special 'space' where the normal rules and conventions of activity are waived. Engeström gradually articulated his ideas about the nature of this space by discussing the strength and weaknesses of other attempts, for example, Lewin (1984) and Senge (1990), to use laboratory conditions to facilitate organisational change and development. The result of this process of debate was his concept of a 'Change' and/or 'Boundary Crossing' (hereafter boundary-crossing) laboratory[12]. Boundary-crossing laboratories are based on the twin principles of 'remediation' and 'separation and embeddedness' (Engeström *et al.*, 1996, p. 10). They are established either inside a single activity system, or a network of activity systems, so that researchers can work alongside participants from one or more activity systems. The researchers aim firstly to support them to depict the solutions to the tensions they identify in the division of labour, rules and community(ies) of which they are a member or to which they have strong ties; and secondly to work collaboratively to reconfigure the division of labour, etc. (Tuomi-Gröhn & Engeström, 2003, p. 31).

The process of expansion in these single or multiple contexts is designed in accordance with Engeström's recasting of Vygotsky's (1999) principle of 'dual stimulation'. Participants in the laboratory are initially encouraged to separate themselves from their normal practice by working through the first two stages of the CEL to 'mirror' the multiple implications of a problem or disturbance in their work and then to move onto:

...constructing a more encompassing object and motive for the activity in the form of a new concept, and socially, by recruiting a growing number of participants in the transformation effort.

(Tuomi-Gröhn & Engeström, 2003, p. 31)

The outcome is the creation of a new type of concept that Engeström (2004, p. 230) describes as 'theoretically grasped practice'. By this he means that new kernel concepts are developed through using the concepts of activity system and object of activity to analyse tensions in a single or network of activity systems. The features originally worked up during the application of the first three stages of the cycle to overcome an agreed tension – the 'declared' concept – are then re-mediated as participants use the concept to guide the reconfiguration of work practice to form the 'experienced' (i.e. final) version of the kernel concept and to establish the new object of activity (Engeström, 2001, p. 233). The resulting concept constitutes a 'new instrumentality', that is, a cultural tool that individuals and groups use to guide the process of reconfiguration (Engeström, 2004, p. 233). The most well-known example of this type of concept formation is the 'care agreement' (Engeström, 2001, p. 20), which grew out of doctors, nurses, health administrators, patients and their families working in a boundary-crossing laboratory to tease out how to offer a more holistic and patient-centred service.

The legacy of the concepts of activity system and cycle of expansive learning. Taken in combination, Engeström's unit of analysis – the activity system – and his pedagogic strategy – the CEL – reposition us to, as A. Edwards (2001, p. 153) observes, 'construct new ways of conceptualising what may be familiar objects' and 'change our relationships to them'. In doing so, he generates a number of new insights about the relation between expertise and activity in CHAT and in the knowledge economy.

The first insight is that Engeström's concept of the activity system introduces a broader and more developmental conception of expertise than surfaced in Lave and Wenger's work. Their great contribution, as we have seen, was to demonstrate that professional knowledge is the result of participating in the social practices associated with different communities of practice. Professional knowledge can therefore no longer be explained through the conventional wisdom in psychology that the mind either processes information (Simon, 1979), appropriates and manipulates schema (Sternberg, 1990) or intuitively latches onto things (Dreyfuss & Dreyfuss, 1986). Engeström, however, develops Lave and Wenger's insight about the collective as well as Hutchins' (1995) insight about the 'distributed', that is, stretched between objects and people, basis of expertise. Expertise, from Engeström's perspective, is a systemic-mediated phenomenon; in other words, it is integrated into the dynamics of a single activity system or network of activity systems or the knot(s) that emerge from those systems as people fleetingly come together to negotiate solutions to problems that cut across their domain of expertise. Thus, it has affinities with and differs from Knorr Cetina's notion of expertise. In the case of the former, Engeström and Knorr Cetina both see expertise as constituted by the mediated relation between people, cultural tools and their context of work. In the case of the latter, Knorr Cetina is primarily interested in the lateral branching of extant practice and the further development of homogeneous modes of expertise, whereas Engeström is concerned with the development of expertise that occurs as the object of activity is expanded. From his perspective, this requires the active involvement of a cross-section of the workforce and thus results in the development of heterogeneous forms of expertise.

The second insight is the role of objects and workplace pedagogy in the development of new activities and expertise. Engeström's focus on the expansion of objects can be used to highlight the limitation of another adaptation of Dewey's concept of reflection. Many writers in the field of Organisational Science, from Argyris and Schön (1978) onwards, have claimed that the reflective element of looped learning constitutes a strategy to facilitate change in individual and/or collective activity. Clearly there is a reflective dimension to working with the CEL in a boundary-crossing laboratory to envision a new object of activity. This reflective dimension gains its power, however, from the way in which participants use the CEL to identify the properties, connections and relations that sustain collective activity, and that formulate a new object (i.e. kernel concept) to guide the redesign of that activity, rather than using feedback on the performance of an activity system to identify where to make micro-level changes. We shall return to the significance of relation between objects and reflection for the learning challenge of the knowledge economy in Chapter 10.

The third issue is that the process of concept formation that occurs in the CEL is rather different from Vygotsky's conception of the process of concept formation, as a creative meeting between everyday concepts and theoretical concepts in the zone of proximal development. In contrast, Engeström's more overtly Leont'evian concern for the object that lies behind different activities leads him to consider how we use concepts to transform activity, rather than engage with our cultural–historical heritage. His argument, in a nutshell, is that as we use the CEL we form a new type of theoretical concept – theoretically grasped practice – based on:

...the continuous construction of the anticipated future object (outcome) of the activity through active material and mental *experimentation,* and the equally continuous sensuous or contemplative experiencing and *observation* of the object as it is.

(Engeström, 1987, p. 21)

What is distinctive about a concept such as the care agreement is that it does not fall neatly into either of Vygotsky's categories because it is not a pure disciplinary or everyday concept. Concepts such as the care agreement are underscored by Engeström's conceptual constellation – object of activity, activity system, cycle of expansive learning (CEL), etc., which provide a hidden, but nevertheless unifying, link between theory and practice. As such, they constitute to a significant extent the space of reasons – that we live in a mediated world, that change occurs as a result of using tools to reconfigure activity, and so forth – that underpins the expansion of objects in the boundary-crossing laboratory, and in which the new concept is disclosed and acted on.

Viewed from this perspective, we can see that Engeström's real achievement is to contribute to the reconceptualisation of the relation between theory and practice that we have undertaken in this book. In the case of theory, Engeström's broadens the meaning of a theoretical concept beyond its origins in disciplines by revealing the different ways in which theoretical and practical concerns are interwoven once the locus of knowledge production is no longer restricted to university and disciplinary contexts. Where theoretically grasped practice differs from other new types of theoretical concepts that we encountered earlier, such as the notion of transdis-ciplinarity put forward by Gibbons *et al.* (1994), is that it explicitly pre-supposes changes in the context, use and outcome from an activity, as opposed to the combination of contributions and insights to accomplish an activity more effectively. In the case of practice, Engeström alerts us to the humanised nature of the environment, in other words, that values are embedded in the division of labour, community and rules, and therefore that the formulation of new concepts and practices to implement that concept requires us to ask questions about what otherwise can

123

appear to be a natural state of affairs.

This linked thesis of concept formation and the emergence of new activities represents another expression of mediation to sit alongside the ones that we have encountered – conceptual restructuring, repositioning and recontextualisation – in this and the previous chapter. Rather than use Engeström's term 'expansion', we will use the term 'reconfiguration' hereafter in the book. This will allow us to retain Engeström's insights about the link between concept formation and the emergence of new activities, but to detach it from his DWR programme. The implication of this move will be returned to in Chapter 10.

The notion of reconfiguration continues the extension of Vygotsky's concept of the zone of proximal development (ZPD) that we initiated in the last chapter. Our extension drew attention to ZPD as a way to conceptualise learning from childhood to adulthood: as we learn theoretical concepts, we develop the capacity to engage in new forms of reasoning and acting. Engeström, however, radically extends the scope of our use of the ZPD by pointing out that it can be reformulated to reflect:

> ...the distance between their everyday activities and the historically new form of social activity that can be collectively generated as a solution to the double bind potentially embedded in the everyday actions.

(Engeström, 1987, p. 17)

Hence, the ZPD becomes a way to conceptualise the continuing development of the collective higher mental functions, as represented by the formation of the psychological processes that adults in an activity system have to develop, as much as the symbolic and material practices they have to engage in, to rethink the object of their activity.

There is, however, a tendency in Engeström's work to: on the one hand, underplay the challenge involved in eliminating sources of friction in a single activity system or networks of activity systems; and, on the other hand, to overstate the necessity for, and suitability of, his interventionist methodology as a strategy to support organisations to reconfigure their object of activity. As a consequence, he ends up implying that his DWR methodology is the definitive way of addressing his definition of the learning challenge of the knowledge economy: namely to produce new activities.

In the case of the former, the elimination of sources of friction in a single activity system or networks of activity systems is more complex than Engeström is inclined to indicate. The basic postulate of his approach is that the boundary-crossing laboratory and the CEL constitute, respectively, a sufficient condition for – and pedagogic strategy towards – repositioning a cross-section of a workplace community to work collaboratively and identify contradictions in activity systems, and to change those systems. Certainly, it is easier to see how the use of a single or series of interacting triangles in such conditions helps such communities to comprehend the final outcome of change in an activity system, than it is to see how it sheds light on the 'rhythm of activity' that needs to occur to achieve that change (Langemeyer & Roth, 2006, p. 30).

What remains invisible in this latter process is how, 'people embody their under-standing of the changes that will have to occur in their practice, and develop the potential and capabilities to sustain the change process that they are engaged in implementing' (Langemeyer & Roth, 2006, p. 30), if the new object is to be realised, whether it is added experience or living through that change. This is in part because Engeström's framework bears the mark of its Leont'evian inheritance; thus despite his concern for multi-voicedness in an activity system, he conveys the impression that the subject's motives and intentions for becoming involved with a change activity are from the outset, or come to be, identical with the outcome. This has the effect of conveying that the official reasons within an institution for their participation in Engeström's DWR programme are synonymous with the perspective of the indivi-duals who work there (Langemeyer & Roth, 2006, p. 30). Thus, the role of reason in the boundary-crossing laboratory in either warranting one course of action rather than another to reconfigure an object of activity is an under-developed feature of Engeström's accounts of organisational development and change. As a consequence, the role of reason in supporting people to participate in the process of questioning and envisioning that occurs in a boundary-crossing laboratory is rarely addressed. Yet other research has shown that unless people are supported to explain the reasons that informed decisions in the boundary-crossing laboratory to other colleagues who were not present, then it can be extremely difficult to mobilise support for new ways of working (Edwards *et al.* 2009).

Furthermore, Engeström's tendency to assert that the DWR programme is an unrivalled strategy to accomplish the rethinking of the object of activity overlooks: firstly that there is a rich vein of research in Technology Studies from the develop-ment of the Internet to Open Source Software (von Hippel, 2005), and Art from the 'white cube' to 'installation art' (Bishop, 2007) in the recent era that has developed new objects and activities; and secondly that not all sectors of the global economy are characterised by strongly framed objects of activity and entrenched divisions of labour, rules and communities, and are not therefore as resistant to the creation of new objects and activities as he is inclined to imply. The creative and cultural sector, for example, is increasingly characterised by network-based forms of work, and project teams that only come together for the life of a project and that actively involve stakeholder communities in such networks (Bilton, 2007 Caves, 2000). The formulation and instantiation of new objects of activity in such settings is therefore a regular rather than an exceptional feature of work, and occurs without any explicit reference to Engeström's theory of expansive learning or his interventionist metho-dology. We shall return to the implications of this observation in Chapter 9.

CONCLUSION

In examining the work of a number of post-Vygotskians who have elaborated different aspects of Vygotsky's theory of cultural mediation, we have highlighted the significance of the concepts of the object of activity and expansion, participation and ventriloquation to that development. In the case of the former pair, we have done so in two senses: to grasp how the purpose behind the social constitution of different forms of activity plays a hidden role in mediation; and as the basis for fundamental change or creation of new modes activity. In doing so, we have accepted that the concept of the object of activity is central to the development of ideas about mediation in CHAT and any attempt to use mediation as a cultural tool outside CHAT. In the case of the latter pair, we have highlighted that although words attain their meaning through their use in social practice, this is never a purely situated process: the legacy of their conventional meaning is a continuing, albeit often unappreciated, influence on their usage. We have also identified: (i) three additional facets of mediation – repositioning, recontextualisation and reconfiguration – that can be used to supplement Vygotsky's notion that mediation entails a process of conceptual restructuring; and (ii) two ways, in addition to Knorr Cetina's notion of 'lateral-branching', that practice can develop – Lave and Wenger's evolutionary and Engeström's transformatory (i.e. expansive) notion of the development of practice.

We contend that, taken in combination, the concepts of the object of activity and ventriloquation, the four facets of mediation, and the three ways in which practice develops: (i) constitute the basis for a new conception of learning; and (ii) that this conception is a significant advance on Dewey's concept of reflection or its technicisation in the form of the pedagogies of reflection; and (iii) that this offers us a way to rethink how personal and vocational workplace learning (PVWL) can address the learning challenge of the knowledge economy. Before we demonstrate why and how this is the case, it is necessary to address a number of tensions that the post-Vygotskians concern for mediation by activity or semiotic mediation has generated for Vygotsky's theory of cultural mediation.

NOTES

[1] Wertsch employs the phrase 'mediational means' rather than cultural tools. For the sake of consistency in this book, we use the term 'cultural tools' throughout.

[2] In contrast to the Saussurian linguistic tradition, which views language as referring to objects within the world and has been a dominant influence on thinking worldwide about the relation between language and the world, Bakhtin's theory rests on a non-referential theory of language, Shotter (1993, p. 381). Although it may seem undeniable that words are used referentially, Bakhtin would say that this is only possible because they are used within a form of life already constituted by the speech genre within which such words are used. This point will be returned to in the discussion of Brandom in Chapter 9.

[3] The impetus for the 'conduit' metaphor lies in the work of Shannon and Weaver's (1963) mathematical theory of communication, which, according to Wertsch (1991), stresses that ideas could be expressed unequivocally and communicated unambiguously. The apparent simplicity and generalisability of this metaphor has shaped the wider public perception of the process of communication.

[4] There has been a considerable difference of opinion over the years as regards why Leont'ev – one of Vygotsky's most conscientious colleagues and collaborators – left Moscow and moved to Kharkov to develop his 'theory of activity'. Some writers have stressed that Leont'ev wanted to distance himself from the cultural–historical focus of Vygotsky's work, which was attracting considerable criticism in the Stalinist era (Kozulin, 1998), others have maintained that his theory completed the direction Vygotsky's work was taking prior to his premature death from cancer (Minick, 1987), while still other writers have suggested that their respective focii on mediation by cultural tools or practical activity represented different expressions of engagement with CHAT's core tenets that psychological

processes emerge from collective practical involvements between human beings (Stetsenko, 2004). The presentation of Leont'ev's work in this chapter accepts the affinities between the logic of the second and third interpretations, whilst being respectful of the intense concern many have expressed as regards Leont'ev's motives.

[5] I am indebted to Anna Stetsenko's presentation at the 3rd International Socio-cultural Activity Research Conference, University of California, San Diego, 9 September 2008, for this term.

[6] Jean Lave and Etienne Wenger are, respectively, a cultural anthropologist and cognitive scientist who were contemporaries at the Palo Alto Research Laboratory in the 1980s. The starting point for their collaboration was their mutual interest in the debates about learning at work; they became concerned to 'rescue' a specific form of learning at work – apprenticeship – from the general confusion and uncertainty that surrounded that term (Lave & Wenger, 1991, p. 29).

[7] Unfortunately, this subtle interpolation is often lost from sight in the secondary literature, where many writers operate with a 'folk' version of participation and effectively render the term as meaning little more than 'joining-up' (A. Edwards, 2004). As a consequence, little attention is paid to the conditions that Lave and Wenger identified that facilitate participation in different forms of social practice and thus enable participation to serve as an epistemological principle of learning.

[8] In contrast, one of the great oversights of Lave and Wenger's ideas about apprenticeship is that they present learning and teaching curricula as diametrically opposed to one another, rather than having a relation to one another (see *inter alia* Guile, 2009; Hughes *et al.*, 2007; Young, 2008).

[9] My account of Engeström's theoretical and methodological development has attempted to show their interrelation. Thus it is different from, but a complement to, his own account of the development of different generations of Activity Theory, which focuses on the principles that underpin the different generations (see Daniels, 2008, for the clearest and most up-to-date exposition of this development).

[10] For a fuller account of the way in which Engeström used Marx's ideas about the relation between production, consumption, exchange and distribution to underpin his concept of an activity system see his book *Learning by Expanding* (1987). See Jones (2009) for a critique of Leont'ev and Engeström's use of Marx's category of activity in their respective theories.

[11] Engeström's use of the term 'activity system' can cause confusion. In *Learning by Expanding* (1987) it is presented as a theoretical lens that can be used to analyse workplaces such as schools, hospitals, etc., whereas in later work (2001; 2004) it is regularly used as a descriptor of such workplaces.

[12] The concept of the 'change' and/or 'boundary crossing' laboratory is an attempt to go beyond Lewin (1984) and Senge's (1990) attempts to use a laboratory approach to facilitate organisational change and development (Engeström *et al.*, 1996, p. 13). According to Engeström, the defining difference between the respective approaches is that Lewin and Senge were primarily concerned with analysing 'practice from a distance' (i.e. speculation about the implications of change), whereas his approach is embedded in the practice of the activity system in an attempt to change that practice.

CHAPTER 8

THINKING DIFFERENTLY ABOUT MEDIATION BY ACTIVITY AND SEMIOTIC MEDIATION

INTRODUCTION

Before we can address the challenge that we set ourselves at the end of the last chapter, to consider the conceptual relation between the four facets of mediation (restructuring, repositioning, recontextualisation and reconfiguration) and the three ways that activity can develop (evolve, laterally branch and transform), it is necessary to consider the implications of the post-Vygotskians' legacy: mediation by activity and semiotic mediation. We do so by turning to the work of three philosophers – Evald Ilyenkov, John McDowell and Robert Brandom. We firstly use a number of epistemological and ontological premises that Ilyenkov, a little-known figure outside of CHAT, articulated to explicate one of the under-developed philosophical tenets – humanisation – which, as we saw in Chapter 6, underpinned Vygotsky's theory of cultural mediation. We use this discussion to further clarify the *rapprochement* we identified in the last chapter between the post-Vygotskians concern for activity and semiotics, by restoring Vygotsky's concern for reason to discussions about mediation. We then develop the implications of this argument further by turning to McDowell and Brandom: two contemporary philosophers who emanate from the philosophy of mind. We use a number of their epistemological and ontological premises about the role of reason in human action to understand why the normative context that McDowell and Brandom refer to – the 'space of reasons' – constitutes both the conditions for the unity of mind and world, and a unified view on mediation by activity and semiotic mediation. We conclude by arguing that the concept of reason has, even if it has slipped from view, always been central to the process of learning, and that addressing the learning challenge of the knowledge economy involves understanding the implications of reason for the four facets of mediation and the three ways that activity can develop.

A Mediated World

Introduction

The post-Vygotskians' exploration of separate lines of mediation generated, for many years, polarised positions in CHAT. However, in recent years the issue has become more unified, in particular when Ilyenkov's (1977a) concept of 'ideality' has been invoked (Daniels, 2001). This is because Ilyenkov's concept provides a way to understand that the transformation of the natural environment pre-supposes the co-mingling rather than the separation of activity and discourse (Bakhurst, 2008).

The concept of idealisation and its implications for mediation. Conceived at its broadest, the concept of ideality is an attempt to explain the way in which humankind's transformation of nature results in ideal (that is, non-material) phenomena (for example, values, reasons, psychological processes and states) existing in the material world (Bakhurst, 1997). Ilyenkov does so by arguing that when we humanise the physical world through our activity – in Bell's terms a 'game against nature' – we inscribe significance and value into the objects that we build within the environment – and, ultimately into the environment itself – in such a way that it is possible to identify how there can be contact between mind and world. Thus, it follows from Ilyenkov's philosophical premises that, as we transform the natural world through such activities as building roads and bridges and airplanes, we create the conditions for both internal and external migration and tourism, and new social ways of living and relating to one another.

To grasp the implication of Ilyenkov's argument for Vygotsky's theory of cultural mediation, it is helpful to turn to Bakhurst who has written extensively on this issue (1990; 1997; 2007). He points out that the substance of Ilyenkov's contribution is to offer us a way to understand that the context of activity, the forms of activity and the processes of and resources for mediation are *idealised* rather than natural accomplishments. This is because we do not stand:

> ...in relation to a brute, physical world, but to an *interpreted* environment, an environment conceived of as being *of a certain kind*. This being so, our behaviour can never be simply 'called forth' by the world itself. Rather we act in the light of some reading of reality, a reading that renders our behaviour an appropriate response to the perceived situation. On this view, our actions are more like conclusions to arguments than effects of physical causes.

> (Bakhurst, 1990, p. 201)

The distinctive character of human life, for Ilyenkov, stems from the fact that we respond to the structure of the normative conventions that previous generations have established, rather than emanating from the causal influence of the material world upon us. These conventions or social practices, for example, logic, law and morality, which previous generations have been established for specific reasons, constitutes a domain of culturally and historically shaped meaning. Our external environment is therefore no longer a purely natural world based on pre-given 'laws' and 'regularities', it also a nature that has been re-made by human labour in two senses (Ilyenkov, 1977b, pp. 41–2): objects from nature have been brought into the sphere of human culture, for example, wood, landscape, and as such acquire a new existence and meaning[1]; and we become creatures who respond sapiently to the reasons that underpin our social practices, as opposed to animals who respond instinctively to stimuli.

The idea that we idealise the world through our activity and as a result live in an interpreted rather than a natural environment, offers us a clearer sense of Vygotsky's use of the term 'humanisation', and its implications for overcoming the apparent split between mediation by activity and semiotic mediation. In the case of the former, the idealisation argument allows us to appreciate that we develop knowledge and understanding of our relation between the natural and social world as we participate in different forms of social practice. Let us take, for example, the condition of blindness to illustrate the force of this claim. Blindness may be an inherited trait and therefore generally interpreted as a 'brute' condition. From a cultural–historical perspective, the development of Braille is a social practice that enables blind people to read and participate more fully in disciplinary, professional and everyday social practices: hence they are indelibly part of a mediated world rather than inhabiting a natural world. In the case of the latter, it becomes easier to see that activity and discourse have always co-mingled with – rather than been separate from – one another, for example, the humanisation of the landscape by building bridges, roads etc. is an intentional (i.e. underpinned by reasons) and material (i.e. results in new artefacts and social practices) form of human activity. Even though we sometimes focus on activity and semiotic mediation as separate entities, the above conclusions invite us to give further consideration to the role of reason in constituting the link between mind and world, and theory and practice. To do so, we have to consider the link between reasons, concepts and activity.

Reasons, Concepts and Activity

Introduction
The focus on the concept of reason in the work of John McDowell and Robert Brandom has been gradually recognised over the last few years as offering further epistemological and ontological substance to, on the one hand, Ilyenkov's argument that we live in a humanised world and, on the other hand, to Vygotsky's theory of cultural mediation (Bakhurst, 1997, 2007; Guile, 2007; Derry, 2008). We use their work to clarify the relation between concepts, reasons and actions and, in the process, to highlight the benefits of employing a more multi-faceted concept of mediation than has often been the case in CHAT.

Living in an interpreted environment: the concept of the 'space of reasons'.
McDowell's (1996, p. 3) starting point is to challenge the misleading picture of the relation between the mind and world that has characterised much philosophy since Descartes: an impression represented by the twin metaphors of 'inside' our minds (i.e. purely subjective) and 'outside' (presumed to be 'real'). He does so, like Ilyenkov, by focusing on the normative context that underpins the social basis of knowledge. Where he differs from Ilyenkov is by exploring how concepts mediate the relation between them. In the process, McDowell develops a, 'radically new understanding of the nature and limits of knowledge in philosophy' that offers a way to avoid the legacy of the two worlds of knowledge (R. J. Bernstein, 2002, p. 15).

The source of inspiration for McDowell's understanding of the nature and limits of knowledge is Kant's great insight: 'That thoughts without contents are empty, and intuitions without concepts are blind' (R. J. Bernstein, 2002, pp. 10–11)[2].

One of Kant's great achievements, according to McDowell, was to recognise that empirical knowledge results from some form of integration between concepts and intuitions. The enduring difficulty was that Kant never quite resolved how those two distinct features of experience can resist combination, that is, the idea of experience as a causal notion, denoting the way the world impinges upon us; and the idea that it is a normative notion, providing grounds for belief. McDowell follows Kant and talks about concepts and intuitions, but maintains that they have to be understood in relation to, rather than in isolation from, one another (Thompson, 2004).

In an attempt to overcome the interminable oscillation between them and to identify their relation to one another, McDowell turned to Sellars' (1997) concept of the 'space of reasons', which comprises our normative notions, including ethics and epistemology (Putnam, 2002, p. 187). The attraction of Sellars' concept, the 'space of reasons', according to McDowell, (1996, p. xiv) is that it offers us a way to overcome both the total separation of mind and world, and the separation of concepts and intuitions. This possibility exists once it is recognised that the way we are caught up in the natural world already involves the exercise of conceptual capacities. Stated another way, 'experience is already conceptualised' (in Ilyenkov's terms, underpinned partly by the historical reasons and values that constituted the creation of the environment), it is, 'not the result of subsequent clothing in concepts something that is given in non-conceptual form' (Thompson 2004, p. 213).

McDowell uses the concept of the space of reasons to refute the idea that the limits to thought are provided by an *a priori* 'given' (i.e. the position of scientific realists), or the idea that there are no limits to thought (i.e. the position of postmodernists). In doing so, he relocates his original Kantian source of inspiration within a Hegelian sensibility[3], arguing that the space of reasons allows us to appreciate that knowledge belongs in a normative context:

> In characterising an episode or a state as that of knowing, we are not giving a logical description of that episode or state; we are placing it in the logical space of reasons, of justifying and being able to justify what one says.

> (McDowell, 1996, p. xiv)

This emphasis on the normative context that makes knowledge possible, according to McDowell, exists outside us in the world, that is, the social world we inhabit.

McDowell is suggesting therefore that we approach the assumed split between mind and world from a different starting point to the longstanding idea of operating in a framework in which we distinguish between what is 'out there' – and is presumably independently real, from what is somehow 'in our minds' – which is presumably subjectively real (R. J. Bernstein, 2002, p. 15). By combining the idea that experience represents the impingement of the external world upon the mind with the idea that experiences are states in which our conceptual capacities are already engaged, McDowell argues – in common with Vygotsky – that it is possible to think of the world as exerting a rational influence over us, and to view perception as warranting, rather than just causing, belief (Bakhurst, 1997, p. 45). The basis of this rational influence is the placing of an event in the logical space of reasons and the awareness that the space of reasons offers a normative context for judging such events.

For McDowell (1996, p. 39), when we engage in any judgement of our experience of the world our:

> ...conceptual capacities are not exercised on non-conceptual deliverance of sensibility. Conceptual capacities are already operative in the deliverance of sensibility themselves.

Experience is not, in other words, an apprehension of raw data, rather it is an awareness that *'things are thus and so'* (McDowell, 1996, p. 26), in other words, there are reasons why the world is organised in a particular way. Thus, it follows that we should not confine our ideas about conceptual, meaningful and rational thought to the mind or to social practice and juxtapose them with a natural world that is assumed to lack meaning but somehow imposes itself on human life. In contrast, McDowell (1996, pp. 26–8) urges us to explore the mediated basis of our relation with the natural and social world or, in his terms, the 'unboundedness of the conceptual'; that is, the way in which the conceptual permeates the natural and vice versa. We are not therefore trapped somehow in a conceptual sphere that is unrelated to a world that is presumably 'outside' it; rather, as McDowell (1996, p. 26) observes:

> Thus, the idea of conceptually structured operations of receptivity puts us in a position to speak of experience as openness to the layout of reality. Experience enables the layout of reality itself to exert a rational influence on what a subject thinks.

This observation about the link between receptivity and reality is a key point in McDowell's argument because it constitutes a direct challenge to the enduring idea of nature that strips the world of, 'everything normative, and immures it within the space of law-governed processes' (Larmore, 2002, p. 197). This conception of nature tends to manifest itself in folk notions such as 'we are all subject to the laws of nature' and 'underneath it, we're all animals'. The problem with such notions from McDowell's position (and by extension CHAT) is that these folk notions perpetuate the gap between conceptual thought and everyday experience and, in the process, deny us any way of understanding the relation between human action and the natural and social world.

To understand this relation, it is necessary, according to McDowell, to rethink the concept of nature itself. Following Weber, McDowell points out that nature has been viewed since the rise of modern science as a 'disenchanted' world, that is, a 'realm of law where the kind of intelligibility that is proper to meaning is excluded' (R. J. Bernstein, 2002, p. 16). Unfortunately, this position gives a false impression of nature because that concept has always included the notion of 'human nature', and we end up with a decidedly non-human conception of that notion unless we have a more relational conception of mind and world[4].

To reinsert the concept of meaning into nature in order to conceptualise the materiality of thought, McDowell turns to Aristotle's insight as regards our 'second nature' as rational animals. The idea of second nature is particularly attractive to McDowell because it offers a way to integrate the space of reasons into a concept of nature (R. J. Bernstein, 2002, p. 218). In the Aristotlian argument, human societies rely upon the development of ethical foundations that, in turn, underpin cultural development and thereby support us to develop a sense of rationality that orientates us in our practical lives. This line of thinking opens up the possibility:

> That since ethical character includes, dispositions of the practical intellect, part of what happens when character is formed is that the practical intellect acquires a determinate shape. So practical wisdom is second nature to possessors.

> (McDowell, 1996, p. 84)

Thus, it follows that our interaction with the world enables us to 'open our eyes' and to appreciate the reasons for action or belief that are always there, irrespective of whether they are susceptible to sensory perception. In this sense, McDowell suggests that second nature is both natural and normative: it is a distinctly human accomplishment because it emerges from a developmental process; that process however is shaped as we learn to inhabit the space of reasons (Pippin, 2002, p. 65).

The crucial component of the formation of a cultural identity – second nature – is, for McDowell (1996, pp. 87–8; 123–4), the acquisition of language, through a process of '*Bildung*' (Bubner, 2002, p. 211). McDowell assigns *bildung* a central element in the normal maturation of human beings, because the concept encapsulates the discovery of possibilities and capacities whereby character is shaped, not only in accordance with socially established ideals but also through the development of personality as we engage with, interpret and develop our cultural history. Stated another way, this mediated process constitutes an invaluable conceptual resource to help us make sense of the relations between experience and judgement (Bubner, 2002, p. 214).

The feature of language that matters, for McDowell (1996, p. 126), like Vygotsky, is that it serves as a, 'repository of tradition, a store of historically accumulated wisdom about what is reason for what', and that pre-supposes being, 'initiated into a tradition as it stands'. Where he supplements Vygotsky is by making something explicit that is an implicit feature of Vygotsky's idea about the process of conceptual restructuring that occurs in the ZPD: namely, that as we learn and use language, we are gradually initiated into the space of reasons.

> Being at home in the space of reasons involves not just a collection of propensities to shift one's psychological stance in response to this or that, but the standing potential for a reflective stance at which the question arises whether one ought to find this or that persuasive.

> (McDowell, 1996, p.125)

So although he does not invoke the notions of conceptual restructuring and repositioning, McDowell's (1996, p. 891) position about learning is predicated on an engagement with these ideas. We find new theoretical concepts persuasive by engaging with the network of reasons that underpin them and, in the process, we develop, through education, the capability to recognise that our conceptual space already embraces a world with more to it than is immediately present to the senses.

Reasons, Concepts and Social Practice

Introduction
Despite generating a number of powerful epistemological and ontological insights about the relation between reason and concepts, McDowell leaves us with the impression that *bildung* enables us to 'magically inhabit' the space of reasons (Bubner, 2002, p. 211). This slightly asocial account of *bildung* arises because McDowell under-emphasises the social basis of his concept of the space of reasons, as Brandom (1995, p. 902) forcibly states:

> The complaint I want to make about McDowell's discussion is that he makes nothing of the essential social articulation of that space.

Brandom is not therefore disputing the philosophical drift of McDowell's argument; instead he claims that he is revealing its social entailment.[5] In doing this Brandom enables us to further consolidate the link we have begun to make about the centrality of the concept of the space of reasons to Vygotsky's theory of cultural mediation. He does so, as we are about to see, by highlighting the crucial role of a specific form of social practice to operation within the space of reasons and to cultural mediation more generally.

The 'giving and asking for reasons'. The reason that McDowell implies that we can achieve flawless standings in the space of reasons through our own efforts is, according to Brandom, that he never acknowledges the extent to which we need to engage in particular forms of social practice to accomplish both the type of understanding he describes and the forms of action in which it results. The issue for Brandom (2000a) is that the social articulation of the space of reasons pre-supposes participation in a specific type of social practice – the 'giving and asking for reasons' – because this enables us not only to understand the historical constitution of the space of reasons but also to develop the cultural capability to operate effectively in that space[6]. We do this by learning throughout our life-course to understand either what counts as a warrant for a concept or action, or how to set about formulating new warrants to justify new concepts or actions. Brandom pursues the implication of his argument, like McDowell and Vygotsky, by establishing what is distinctive about human, as opposed to animal, nature.

In the process, he firstly supplements their argument about the development of second nature and the higher mental functions by distinguishing between a *sentient* and *sapient* conception of human action (Brandom, 2000a, pp. 157–9). Secondly, he accomplishes this move by developing an 'inferential' interpretation of Sellars's concept of the space of reasons (Brandom, 2000). This enables Brandom to further consolidate Vygotsky and McDowell's ideas about the conceptual basis of perception. In doing so, Brandom helps us to further clarify why Dewey's assumption that perception is purely a 'natural biological function' (Garrison, 2006, p. 33) is an unhelpful characterisation of that process.

Brandom argues that sentience, which is an exclusively biological phenomenon, is what we share with non-verbal animals such as cats – 'the capacity to be *aware* in the sense of being awake' (2000a, p. 157). Although it results in a form of multi-layered awareness of objects, events and people, a sentient response does not enable us to select and control our behaviour based on our understanding of the meaning of such objects, etc. Instead it equips us to respond instinctively without thought. Sapience, by contrast, 'concerns *understanding* or intelligence rather than irritability or arousal' (2000a, p. 158). We treat something as sapient, in other words, when we explain, 'its behaviour by attributing to it intentional states such as belief and desire as constituting *reasons* for that behaviour'. Thus, it follows for Brandom (2000a, p. 158) that what is distinctive about human beings is that we develop the capacity to act in accordance with, to ignore, or even to challenge reason. Irrespective of which course of action we choose, we are still rational agents because these forms of behaviour are intentional, that is underpinned by reason, and therefore capable of being made intelligible to others. We can do so by discerning what type of inference was made to support one course of action over another, and what type of inference can subsequently be made as regards what follows from that initial action.

The distinguishing feature of human thinking and acting is, according to Brandom (2000, p. 4), responsiveness to reasons, and this pre-supposes an 'inferential' rather than a 'representational' conception of the role of language. The gist of Brandom's argument is that, like McDowell, he is building on the way in which writers such as, Hegel and Sellars, have built upon Kant's account of the role of inferential relations within judgement. Brandom maintains that Hegel 'completed the inversion' that Kant had started of the traditional order of semantic explanation, 'by discussing the making of judgements and the development of concepts entirely in terms of the role they play in inferential activity…' (Brandom, 1994, p. 92). He pursues this line of thinking by engaging with the 'broadly Hegelian features' of Sellars' development of the role of inferentialism in understanding and applying concepts. As Brandom observes:

> One of the most important lessons we learn from Sellars's masterwork, *Empiricism and the Philosophy of Mind* (as from the 'Sense Certainty' section of Hegel's *Phenomenology*) is the inferentialist one that even noninferential reports must be inferentially articulated. Without this requirement we cannot tell the difference between noninferential reporters and automatic machinery such as thermostats and photocells, which also have reliable dispositions to respond differentially to stimuli.

> (Brandom, 2000, p. 48).

Brandom explains the significance of this observation by arguing that when we talk about concepts as being places in the space of reasons, we are talking about, according to Brandom (1995, p. 896), 'things that can in principle be given as reasons, and for which reasons can in principle be asked'. To explain what he means by this suggestion, Brandom distinguishes between concept use and non-conceptual activity, that is, the difference between human and animal behaviour. Brandom does so by asking: what is the difference between a parrot trained to say, 'Rawk, that's red' in the presence of red things, a thermostat that turns the furnace on when the temperature drops to 60 degrees and a human who makes similar responses under similar circumstances? What distinguishes us, according to Brandom, is that in order to understand what follows conceptually and practically from a situation we have to have learned a number of concepts, because:

> ...the content of each concept is articulated by its inferential relations to other concepts. Concepts, then, come in packages.

> (Brandom, 2000a, pp. 15–16)

So to return to the difference between a human and a thermostat, the reasons that we can infer what follows from our observation of the changes in the thermostat are that we have the concepts of colour and temperature. These concepts allow us to identify what would be reasons for the changes, what they would entitle us to do and what would preclude such entitlement.

This observation about the link between reasons and concepts allows us to see how Brandom has deepened both Vygotsky's insight, that the primary purpose of concepts is to support reasoning, and McDowell's insight, that the process of reasoning pre-supposes locating thought and action in the space of reasons. The basis of this act of supplementation is Brandom's recontextualisation (2005, pp. 349–53) of Sellar's 'two-ply' account of observation. The process of observation, for Sellars, pre-supposes that we can respond differentially to a stimulus and use language to make our response intelligible to others (Redding, 2007, p. 13). Drawing on this analytical distinction, Brandom points out that knowing what follows from an utterance, action or an event pre-supposes participation in a specific form of social practice – the 'giving and asking for reasons' – and that this constitutes a form of 'practical know-how', that is, being:

> ...able to tell what they [red or 70 degrees] would be reasons for and what would be reasons for them – is as much a part of their understanding of 'red' and '70 degrees' as are their reliable differential responses. And it is the *inferential articulation* of those responses, the role they play in reasoning, that makes those responsive dispositions to apply *concepts*'.

> (Brandom, 1995, p. 897)

Brandom's idea of practical know-how is rather different from the conventional meaning of that term that we encountered in Chapter 3. There the term, know-how referred to a form of skill that was developed from either a sentient manipulation of objects or experiential action. In contrast, know-how from Brandom's perspective has a conceptual dimension. Concept use irrespective of its context of application, for Brandom, involves moving thought and/or action in the space of reasons by mediating between differentially elicited responses and situating them in a 'network of inferential relations' that are historically and socially constituted (1995, p. 897). To do this we have to be able to distinguish, according to Brandom, between what other people are talking about (the propositional dimension of thought and talk) and what they are saying about the object of their talk and thought (the representational dimension of thought and talk)[7]. This distinction is important because it enables us to avoid embracing a vapid form of cultural relativism that assumes that differences between cultures renders communication incommensurable.

Hence Brandom maintains, along with Vygotsky and McDowell, that concept use has a normative character, in the sense that the employment of concepts in inquiry is governed by norms. What his elaboration and extension of Sellars' 'two-ply' account of concept use adds to the picture is, first, that concept use pre-supposes that we have learned to move thought in the space of reasons by engaging in the social practice of giving and asking for reasons (Brandom, 2005). What remains an implicit feature of his argument is that, although the process of reasoning is a rational pursuit, it will inevitably vary according to the logic associated with the disciplinary, professional or everyday field with which it is associated. Secondly he posits that, even though we use words or concepts without having grasped their meaning fully, our use of them is still dependent on the reasons that underpin those words and concepts. Thirdly, that words and concepts only become meaningful as we use them to restructure our previous understanding, to enlarge the space of reasons in which we operate, to infer what follows from that process of enlargement and to use this new understanding to reposition ourselves in relation to the object of our activity.

These observations shed further light on the discussion about the relation between theoretical and tacit knowledge that we started in Chapter 4 and developed further in Chapter 6. We pointed out that Vygotsky's argument about implicit mediation and conceptual restructuring could be used to help us to appreciate, respectively, why people sometimes struggle to convey what they know and why the theoretical might be embedded in the tacit and *vice versa* (i.e. the unbound-edness of the conceptual). Brandom's argument about the social practice of giving and asking for questions, as we are about to see, enables us to take this discussion another step forward.

To do so, let us return to Zuboff's workers. They were primarily engaged, to use Brandom's language, in mediating symbolic data by picking out what was proposi-tionally relevant, inferring what followed from their developing understanding of the data and, in the process, enlarging the space of reasons in which they and their work colleagues operated. This entailed grasping an interpretation or sugge-sted course of action that often needed further explication, that is, making the reason behind an action or thought explicit. Such acts of discernment were required to facilitate the forms of practical reasoning and communication in which they were engaged, even when dealing with tacit understandings. This practical reasoning, which, as we saw, had an embedded conceptual dimension, was occurring within an existing – albeit gradually developing – space of reasons.

Brandom's insight that the space of reasons pre-supposes the social practice of giving and asking for reasons strengthens McDowell and Vygotsky's respective epistemological and ontological positions, as regards the culturally embedded constitution of experience and perception. From Brandom's perspective, when we acquire some form of knowledge non-inferentially, for example, taking something for granted or being encouraged to believe something to be true reason is still in play. This is the case because to be capable of making a claim about something or even to believe that claim, it requires:

> ...that we *understand* it: that we have at least a rough practical mastery of its inferential role, the know-how to discriminate some things that follow from it and others that don't, and some things that would be evidence for it and others that would not.

(Brandom, 1995, p. 905)

We have to be able, in other words, to identify what is propositionally contentful, to articulate inferentially what does and does not follow from our understanding of such propositions and to consider their implications for our future activity.

The legacy of the concept of reason.   By generating new insights into the socio-genesis of the mind, McDowell and Brandom elaborate and extend the philosophical premise – humanisation – that underpinned Vygotsky's theory of cultural mediation. In the process, they offer further substance to the claim made at the start of the chapter that mediation by activity and semiotic mediation are intrinsically related as opposed to diametrically opposed modes of activity. From their argument about the centrality of reason to human development – that we should think of reality as contained within the conceptual rather than lying outside it – it follows that we should treat, 'appearances as starting points from which we can move about in interior space, the space of reasons, drawing inferences from them in ways that reason can endorse' (Bakhurst, 2007).

Moving thought meant, for Vygotsky, learning to mediate between theoretical and everyday concepts in the ZPD, and to infer what follows for thought and action; for Wertsch, it meant ventriloquating with language; for Leont'ev it meant identifying our relation to the object of activity and understanding how that object gives rise to our goals and motives; and for Engeström it meant expanding the object in order to create a new pattern of activity. What remained rather under-developed in Vygotsky's theory – and for that matter in Wertsch, Leont'ev and Engeström's respective positions – was the context for, and process of, inference. McDowell's insight about the role of reason in human activity offers us a way to comprehend the link between the process of conceptual restructuring and the forming of inferences as to what follows – it requires us to create pedagogic processes to make our theoretical, theoretically grasped practice or practical inferences intelligible to one another in the space of reasons. Equally, Brandom's argument about the giving and asking for reasons is as integral to learning in an educational institution as it is to learning in adult life, because it constitutes the basis of forming inferences from concepts or actions and determining what follows as a result. Clearly the process and outcome of forming inferences varies according to whether we are in an educational or work setting, and working on a pre-given or collectively generated task that involves theoretical or practical reasoning. We shall return to this issue in the next chapter.

The strong emphasis in their work on reason underscoring social practice could appear, at first sight, to imply that McDowell and Brandom are committed to some form of abstract rationality. They accept, in other words: that objects and events

139

can be represented in terms of formal logic and quantifiable categories; the existence of a pre-ordained teleology; and that there is a universal and logo-centric mode of reasoning that can be used to resolve disputes – and, therefore, they deny the existence of, or are impervious to, cultural diversity and hermeneutics. Such a conception, however, would be an unfair depiction of their respective positions[8]. It is more accurate to see McDowell and Brandom as, to borrow Sypnowich's phrase (2000), 'egalitarian perfectionists' who are concerned to retain the valuable elements of the Enlightenment's commitment to reason by rethinking that concept in relation to subsequent developments about epistemology and ontology in philosophy (see *inter alia* Brandom, 2002, 2009; McDowell, 2009a, 2009b).

McDowell and Brandom's fidelity to the notion of a maximally rational person is, like Vygotsky's, not grounded in an *a priori* notion that we are born responsive to reasons, but a recognition that we become so, even though reason is not necessarily a consistent feature of our actions, through enculturation. Hence, their work is characterised by a modest concern for rationality – rather than a full-blown commitment to abstract rationality, pre-determined teleology and formal reasoning – based on an acceptance that our transformation from natural into cultural creatures means that history now plays the role for us that nature plays for non-discursive beings. The notion of history in operation here is not linear and essentialist, rather it is hermeneutic and rests on a reciprocal and recontextual engagement with tradition.

The issue of hermeneutics allows us to further rebalance Brandom and McDowell's somewhat overly rational presentation of the role of reason to our participation in and transformation of social practice. Brandom (2002) and McDowell (2002) both acknowledge the hermeneutical dimension of their thought, by following Gadamer (1989) and accepting that tradition plays a vital part in our understanding of a particular text because it allows us to locate that text in its context of origin. Brandom (2002, p. 110) develops this dimension more fully than McDowell[9], by arguing that we develop culturally and historically by 'retrospectively rationally reconstructing' the traditions – disciplinary, professional, workplace – that we inherit as we strive to distinguish progressive, rather than regressive, elements and are thus, in principle, positioned. Central to this process of the retrospective rational reconstruction of a tradition are the processes of 'navigating' and 'negotiating' (2002, p. 110) between different perspectives from which a text can be interpreted; in other words, taking account of the different interpretations of texts that have arisen in different eras and then deciding which is the more authoritative. This requires us, according to Brandom (2002, p. 109), to develop the capacity to move between 'perspective-relative inferential significances' so that we can move from an implicit to an explicit mode of operating by articulating our thoughts and inferring what follows from them. Moreover, he maintains that this back-and-forth movement pre-supposes 'talking with a tradition' (2002, p. 110) in a dual sense: employing the tradition to retrospectively specify its contents, claims, and the texts it comprises, in order to establish a perspective on its conceptual content; and engaging in an 'immediate reading' by ascribing to oneself the most developed position in that or a related tradition. This necessitates using selected and supplementary materials provided by such traditions to redefine the original concepts and derive, by multi-premise inferences, the claims that follow from this new interpretation (2002, p. 113). Translated into the terminology we have introduced to capture the different expressions of mediation, we use our engagement with different traditions – for example, disciplinary, professional, everyday – to initially reconstruct their purpose and social constitution and to consider their potential relation to one another. Having done so, we are able to restructure our thought, to reposition ourselves in relation to the object of our activity and to recontextualise our new thinking as a resource to engage with other emerging events. In making this case, Brandom alerts us to the importance of the notion of reconstruction for the different expressions of mediation that we have identified. We will pursue the implication of this observation in the next chapter.

One remaining problem with the slightly different, albeit related, position that Brandom and McDowell develop about the link between concepts, reasons and practice are – as Dancy (2006, p. 121) has pointed out about McDowell, but it is equally true for Brandom – based on a 'belief–action' relation. As a consequence, they do not discuss the implications of their ideas about reason for an 'experience–belief' relation. To understand this relation it is necessary, according to Dancy, to develop a broader conception of how we use the concept of reason to explain an action. Dancy initiates this move by distinguishing between the 'reasons why we act' and the 'reasons for which we act', defining the former as the:

> ...considerations in light of what we do. These are the features which we take to tell in favour of acting; they will figure prominently in our deliberations, and they will normally be the ones we specify when asked why we did what we did.

> (Dancy, 2006, p. 123)

The reasons for which we act are, however, rather different because they normally constitute a narrower set of reasons, based on an act of selection from the wider 'why' reasons. The following example helps us to clarify Dancy's point. A shy person may not go to a party because she/he will meet new people. So the reason for which she/he uses to decide not to attend the party is meeting lots of unfamiliar people, whereas the deeper reason why she/he actually stayed away is shyness.

The distinction between belief–action and action–belief allows us to strike a better balance between forms of explicit mediation when discussing the normative basis of the space of reasons, as well as to take account of the emotional or ambiguous dimension of decision-making or forms of implicit mediation). This introduces the notions of ambiguity and judgement, rather than dishonesty, into the reasoning process and, in the process, allow us to develop a richer and more complex sense of the process of conceptual restructuring and repositioning.

CONCLUSION

We have established in this chapter that a unifying thread runs between Ilyenkov, McDowell and Brandom's respective epistemological and ontological arguments, namely that we live in an interpolated world. By this they mean that although we can distinguish analytically between nature and culture, and research them separately from one another, they are also inextricably connected to one another. From this perspective, it does not make sense to talk about as experience being separate from conception. This is because, to return to McDowell's elegant phrase, 'the unboun-dedness of the conceptual', the distinctive feature of our contact with the world is that our perception has a conceptual dimension.

This insight provides us with a way to restore the concept of reason, which was central to Vygotsky's theory of cultural mediation, but vanished or was underplayed in the post-Vygotskians' concern for mediation by activity or semiotic mediation. It forces us to recognise that, on the one hand, all human activity is underpinned by reasons, even though the reasons for their constitution is not stated; and, on the other hand, to understand an activity it is necessary to engage with the reasons (i.e. space of reasons) that lie behind its public manifestations, and to transform an activity it is necessary to persuade people to rethink the reasons for an activity.

The common thread between the process of understanding (i.e. the restructuring of thought) and transforming (i.e. repositioning oneself to develop a new mode of activity) is the social practice of giving and asking for reasons. This practice is, however, more multi-faceted than Brandom and McDowell acknowledge. One way to highlight the implication of this issue is to return to Toulmin and Jonsen's distinction between theoretical and practical reasoning that we introduced in Chapter 4. We used the former term to refer to a process of inferring in theoretically informed activities what is or is not the case from 'axioms' (i.e. universal rules), and the latter to refer to a process of inferring in professional practice what is the case from 'maxims' (i.e. the heuristic use of theoretical and everyday concepts). Clearly both are underpinned by the space of reasons; the difference is that the former's space is constituted by disciplinary considerations, whereas the latter's is constituted by the co-mingling of disciplinary, professional/vocational and workplace considerations.

Invoking this distinction takes us back to the central concern of this book: the learning challenge of the knowledge economy. That challenge has been consis-tently presented by policymakers, as we saw in Chapter 1, as the attainment of higher levels of qualifications to support us to adapt to the new role of knowledge in the economy. We stated at the outset that this conception of the learning challenge was not only based on the legacy of Cartesian notions of the relation between mind and world and, as a corollary, the idea that there are two worlds of knowledge, but also the neglect of pedagogy in the process of learning. We have demonstrated throughout the book the limitations of policymakers' analysis of, and prescription for, the learning challenge of the knowledge economy.

We have presented an alternative starting point, based on our elaboration and extension of Vygotsky's theory of cultural mediation, to understand and respond to the learning challenge posed by the new role of knowledge within the economy: that it is transgressive and is increasingly cutting across disciplinary and professional traditions and areas of work. This starting point for addressing this challenge, as we have shown in this chapter, appears to be rather traditional because it places the concept of reason at the heart of the process of learning, irrespective as to whether we are referring to learning in educational or workplace contexts, or a combination of both modes of learning. The twist that we have given to our use of reason is, on the one hand, to reveal that it is a developing and contestable concept, rather than an ahistorical and uncontestable one; and, on the other hand, to demonstrate that we are now in a position where we can conceive of learning as a process of understanding our mediated relation to the world, and thinking and acting to remediate that relation. To understand the process of remediation more fully, it is necessary to consider the relation between the four expressions of mediation – restructuring, repositioning, recontextualisation and re-configuration – and the three expressions of the development of activity that were identified in the previous two chapters.

NOTES

[1] The process of humanisation can equally have malignant consequences, for example, the environmental 'risks' (Beck, 1987) generated by our scientific and technological activity.

[2] Kant expressed the problem in the following way: 'Without sensibility no object would be given to us, without understanding no object would be thought. Thoughts without content are empty, intuitions without concepts are blind' (Kant, 1929). Bernstein (2002, p. 22) points out that Kant's views about concepts and intuitions are open to quite different interpretations because, in the *Critique of Pure Reason* and the *Prolegomena*, he slips between either arguing that knowledge has a conceptual basis (i.e. based on reasons) or arguing that there is an independent world that constitutes the empirical basis of knowledge.

[3] McDowell (1996, p. iv) states that he sees *Mind and World* as a 'prolegomenon' to a reading of Hegel's *Phenomenology*. The extent to which McDowell and Brandom, whom we discuss later, have understood Hegel correctly is hotly disputed by some (see Rockmore, 2000; Westphael, 2006) and affirmed by other philosophers (Redding, 2007). The position adopted in this book follows Redding, that McDowell and Brandom are operating within the Hegelian tradition of finding unity between philosophies that are usually taken to be antithetical while respecting their critics' view that they have yet fully to accomplish this project.

[4] In making this argument, (McDowell, 1996, p, 77) is not trying to reject the achievements of modern science, nor limit our understanding to the disenchanted conception of nature because there is no place for human agency in that conception. He is interested in bringing a responsiveness to meaning back into the 'operation of our naturalistic sentient capacities' and recognises that this is not possible while 'meaning cannot be captured in naturalistic terms, so long as meaning is glossed in terms of the realm of law'.

[5] This claim is rejected by McDowell. Brandom, according to McDowell, has not taken sufficient account of his argument about the role of experience in warranting a belief. Brandom in response maintains that his ideas about inferentialism incorporate empirical content and therefore their respective positions are not so different from one another (see Warrander (2008, Ch. 8) for a very clear account of the debate about this issue between McDowell and Brandom).

[6] Redding (2007) and Wander (2008) acknowledge that McDowell and Brandom develop their respective engagement with Sellars' concept of the 'space of reasons' and Hegel's interest in the sociality of reason in rather different ways. It is beyond the scope of this book to explore the implications of this issue. Instead I have worked with the spirit of engagement that both writers see that exists between their respective interest in Sellars and Hegel.

[7] Brandom does not use the term 'proposition' in the Kantian way that informs the thinking of many scientific realists, that is, to convey the impression that we consciously formulate a set of statements or ideas about the world that correspond to a world of which we have knowledge. In contrast, his use

CHAPTER 8

of the term is informed by a Hegelian argument that meaning arises inferentially within a system. Hence propositions are formed and tested within the space of concepts and space of reasons.

[8] Brandom (1995) and McDowell (1995) have acknowledged the affinities and differences between their respective positions on a number of occasions, as have other writers (Bakhurst, 2007, Derry, 2003).

[9] Bubner (2002, p. 214) points out that although McDowell enhances his thesis in *Mind and World* through his discussion of language and meaning, he does not really develop this 'hermeneutic turn', an observation that McDowell (2002, p. 297) accepts in his reply to Bubner.

CHAPTER 9

LEARNING AS REMEDIATION

INTRODUCTION

In the last three chapters we have shown why our conceptual reframing of Vygotsky's theory of cultural mediation offers us a different starting point for thinking about the legacy of the two worlds of knowledge, which has afflicted the debate about the new role of knowledge in the economy, as well as the educational response to the emergence of a knowledge economy. Specifically, Vygotsky's theory enables us to appreciate the difference and the relation between mind and world, and theory and practice; and therefore to avoid both the split between theoretical and tacit knowledge, and the consequent vain search for pedagogies of reflection to assist us to connect them in some meaningful way. In the course of these chapters, we have identified: firstly, a number of facets of mediation – restructuring, repositioning, recontextualisation and reconfiguration – that were either a relatively under-developed feature of Vygotsky's work or that arose from the work of the post-Vygotskians, or that shed light on hitherto under-appreciated aspects of the process of learning; secondly, that the concept of reason has always been central to these facets of mediation, even though it has often remained an implicit or unacknowledged feature; and thirdly, a relation between the expressions of mediation and the three ways – evolve, laterally branch out and transform – that we can develop activities/ social practice. Taken together, what emerged was a compelling case that learning is a process of remediation, in other words, understanding the conceptualised nature of the world and using that understanding as a resource to develop ourselves and the world.

Because the relation between reason, the expressions of mediated learning and the modes of developing activity emerged from our critical re-appraisal of Vygotsky and the post-Vygotskians, what was left rather under-developed was their collective implication for our understanding of what it means to learn, both in general and in a knowledge economy/society. We now address this issue, in order to be able to see clearly why Vygotsky's theory of cultural mediation, and its subsequent development as described in this book, provide a conceptual framework for addressing our redefinition of the learning challenge of the knowledge economy.

Mediation and Learning

Introduction
Our starting point is an extremely interesting recent discussion of mediation by Michael Roth (2007). Roth's article charts the historical and philosophical lineage

145

of this concept from Hegel and Marx through to its contemporary usage in CHAT. He observes that:

> In some scholarly contributions (e.g. on the XMCA list [the CHAT web list]) it appears as if everything, every process in human culture, is mediated either by materials, tools or by language. If, however, everything is mediated and if the notion of mediation explains everything, then the notion no longer makes distinctions, and therefore, it explains nothing.

(Roth, 2007, p. 655)

Roth develops the implication of this observation by arguing that the concept needs to be rescued from its current usage because '...a concept or category that explains everything in fact explains nothing, because it does not articulate difference' (2007, p. 658). He proposes to do so by reintroducing the specificity associated with Hegel's and Marx's original formulation and development of the concept; who, he maintains, employed the adjective expressing the opposite of mediation – 'immediate' – in their writing. To this end, Roth argues in favour of making a distinction between situations where mediation can be, 'explicitly linked to the development of consciousness and to the resolution of contradictions' (2007, p. 661) and situations characterised by '...non-conscious, and therefore non-mediated performances' (2007, p. 663).

The argument that we have developed throughout this book both concurs with and differs from Roth's position on mediation. In the case of the former, we have continually argued that it is important to distinguish between different facets of mediation in terms of their purpose, process and outcome and their implications for our understanding of what it means to learn, and we pursue the implications of this position throughout the remainder of the chapter. Thus we would agree with Roth that the distinction between mediate and immediate is valid. From our use of McDowell and Brandom, the former are the results of inferential judgements, that is, 'from the application of concepts that we have made', while the latter are the result of 'noninferentially elicited perceptual judgements or observations' (Brandom, 2002, p. 224). In the case of the latter, where we differ from Roth is that, by following McDowell and accepting the logic of his argument about the unboundedness of the conceptual, we do not accept Roth's stark contrast between mediation and immediacy, which rests on the idea that either there is or is not an intervening 'member, medium or agent' (2007, p. 663) in the environment and that the environment itself is therefore unmediated.

The position adopted here, which we will revisit and further develop throughout this chapter, is that we do not 'merely inhabit an environment', rather we are always 'orientated towards the world' (McDowell, 2007b, p. 338). At first sight, McDowell's distinction may appear somewhat opaque. What he means is that reason is always in play, in the forms of habituated and tacit human operations, and in forms of embodied coping, that occur in conceptualised environments (i.e. those underpinned by norms), even when it is not consciously articulated. This line of argument introduces a slightly different sense of the immediate from the one that Roth adopts: immediate means, for us, an operation where although there is no obvious intervening member, medium or agent, the activity we are engaged in is still only possible because of the 'mindedness' of our embodied perception which we have developed culturally and historically in relation to the conceptualised environments we are orientated towards. We highlight the implications of this argument concept-ually for what it means to learn in general as we explore the difference and the relation between the expressions of mediated learning and modes of development of activity throughout the chapter.

Restructuring, reasoning and acting. Our exploration could start, in principle, with any of the facets of mediation. We have chosen to start with Vygotsky's notion of conceptual restructuring, because it is central to his account of the development of the higher mental functions, and hence why we are cultural rather than natural creatures. As such, it has been the cornerstone of the development of CHAT, even if many theorists have engaged with the implications of Vygotsky's argument in a variety of ways. To recap Vygotsky's argument briefly: we overcome the limitations of sensory perception by using the greater measure and relation of generality associated with theoretical concepts to restructure our understanding and use of the associative connections that generally characterise the way in which we and others deploy everyday concepts. We do so through engaging in the volitional activity of forming 'judgement[s] or deduction[s]' about the merits of their general-isations, and the range of insights and connections to other theories that they offer us (Vygotsky, 1987, p. 233).

This emphasis on the process of deduction and judgement reminds us that concepts do not emerge in the mind 'like peas in a sack [and] do not lie alongside one another or on top of one another with no relations of generality' (Vygotsky, 1987, p. 224). Instead learning a theoretical concept entails grasping the general-isation that lies at the heart of that concept and its relation to other concepts. This essence is for Vygotsky an:

...enrichment of the reality that it represents, in the enrichment of what is given in immediate sensual perception and contemplation. However, this enrichment of the immediate perception of reality by generalisation can only occur if complex connections, dependencies, and relationships are established between the objects represented in concepts and the rest of reality. By its very nature, each concept presupposes the presence of certain systems of concepts. Outside such a system, it cannot exist.

(Vygotsky, 1987, p. 224)

The way in which we grasp the generalisation contained within a theoretical concept and the relations of generality between all concepts, was outlined by Vygotsky (1987 p. 226) schematically and metaphorically through reference to the notion of the 'longitude' and 'latitude' of concepts. The gist of his argument was that we use the relationship of generality within any given theoretical concept to: (i) locate it vertically in relation to other theoretical concepts; and (ii) to locate it horizontally to understand aspects of the world. Having learned how to do this, we are able to make transitions from one concept to another.

CHAPTER 9

This metaphoric invocation of the terms 'latitude' and 'longitude' can have the unfortunate effect of conveying the impression that Vygotsky assumed that, providing we follow teacher-determined learning actions in the Zone of Proximal Development (ZPD), it is possible to learn all the known applications and even extensions of a theoretical concept – and, as a corollary, that theoretical concepts always have to be learned in educational contexts. It is as though the relationships of generality are coiled up inside the kernel like a spring, constituting 'rails' along which our thoughts can run, and waiting to be released as we move through each successive stage of the cycle of learning actions.

To avoid this emphasis on generality and connections being interpreted as endorsing a deterministic account of the development of theoretical thinking, and an instrumental view of pedagogy, we tempered Vygotsky's passion for the explanatory power of conceptual systems with a concern for the dialogic dimension of understanding. We did so by following Wertsch, and acknowledging that theoretical concepts are always embedded in disciplinary and discursive practices and are learnt through participation in different pedagogic and linguistic practices, as we gradually develop our understanding of them and our ability to use them, through a process of ventriloquation.

The process of restructuring introduces a complex and intriguing idea about learning: namely that our existing concepts 'acquire whole series of new relationships' with any new concept that we learn (Vygotsky, 1987, p. 229). Consequently, our understanding of these relationships has implications for how we think and act and lie. These can be conceptualised on a continuum, from accepting that there are reasons for reconsidering our views and concomitantly considering how we could change our social practice, through to contesting the authoritative basis of a particular theoretical concept and considering the implications of that act of contestation for the discipline or professional field from whence the concepts originate.

This range of possibilities exists because our understanding of the generalisation contained in a new theoretical concept is:

...partial because each new stage of generalisation emerges from the generalisation that was generalised in the previous structure of objects. It arises as a generalisation of generalisations, not as a new mode of generalisation of isolated objects. The result of previous efforts of thought which are expressed in generalisations that dominate the previous states do not come to naught. They are included in the new work of thought. They are the prerequisites for it.

(Vygotsky, 1987, p. 229)

Vygotsky's insight about the gradual nature of our understanding of a theoretical concept – which emerged as he revised his earlier view about concept formation and recognised that our existing everyday or theoretical concepts constitute the foundations upon which we construct our understanding of a new theoretical concept – is as important today as it was when he first challenged the highly influential Piagetian tradition of assuming that when we learn a new concept it automatically nullifies or replaces our existing concepts. This is because a 'folk' version of Piaget's ideas about concept formation has been assimilated with

148

the language of cybernetics. As a consequence, policymakers (European Commission, 2000), social theorists (Castells, 2000; Reich, 1991) and educationalists (Edwards & Usher, 2000) are, as we saw in Chapters 1 and 5, inclined to unconsciously or uncritically treat concepts as information that the mind filters and processes to make that information meaningful, that this new information automatically replaces information previously held by the mind, and that a new way of thinking emerges from this process of replacement.

We have developed a counter-argument in this book by maintaining that we grasp and use the generalisation contained within a theoretical concept as we refor-mulate our existing understanding. We do this by learning, to return to the language of McDowell, to 'navigate the space of reasons' that underpin concepts, and by extension action, by being responsive to reasons (McDowell, 1996). It is important to remember that in saying this McDowell is not endorsing a scientific–realist conception of reasoning, that is, assuming that reasoning consists of engaging in a mode of formal, abstract, situation-independent practice, or apprehending the representations that are presented to us through disciplines or professional fields or rule-following in those fields of activity. Rather, being responsive to reasons, for McDowell, includes sensitivity to considerations for connections between concepts, the relative significance of concepts to practice as ways of appreciating aspects of practice that are not immediately detectable through sensory perception, and the contradictions or tensions associated with concepts or the field of which it is a part.

Being responsive to reasons in these different ways also involves, as Brandom enabled us to appreciate, understanding the thoughts of others (and by extension the reason for their actions). We do this by grasping what they are thinking or talking about (the propositional dimension), and what they are thinking or saying about it (the representational dimension). It is only as we develop the capability to do this that we are able to make thought and behaviour intelligible to ourselves and others by moving our and their thinking in the space of reasons. Taken in combination, these insights deepen our understanding of the process of conceptual restructuring: it entails a conscious choice on our behalf to choose to revise or not to revise a previously held belief or an aspect of our goal-orientated activity.

Because our use of any new concept is always mediated by the legacy of our understanding of prior concepts, there is always a sense of provisionality as we learn to operate the space of reasons and use the generalisation contained in a theoretical concept. Our understanding, for example, of the measure of generality contained within a theoretical concept such as mediation influences the range of possible ways for how we use the concept in theoretical or professional discourse. In the case of the former, to convey our developing understanding of a disciplinary field; and, in the case of the latter, as a resource to shed light on an aspect of practice that our normal sensory perceptions have failed to detect. It also shapes the extent to which our existing everyday concepts such as 'learning-by-doing' are restructured as we gradually come to understand the implications of the concept of mediation. Thus we have learnt how to use the concept of mediation in a new and more encompassing way and, in the process, reposition ourselves in relation to the world because we have expanded our options for action.

As we develop our ability to use the social practice of giving and asking for reasons – as either a personal and/or collective pedagogic strategy – to deepen our understanding of theoretical concepts and their implications for action, the provisionality of our use of concepts gradually disappears. For us to understand why and how this happens it is important, as Brandom (2000a, pp. 167–8) notes, to appreciate that we become more confident in our use of the following inferential practices as we appreciate that communication consists of the development of the practical ability to navigate perspectives, rather than to transmit meaning. This practical ability, according to Brandon, entails firstly attributing an, 'inferentially articulated, hence propositionally contentful, commitment' towards a theory or concept, so that we are able to discern the basis of the theory and why this might be true. Secondly, recognising that when we attribute, 'a sort of inferential entitlement to that commitment', we are able to articulate the justification for the theory. Thirdly, also recognising that in accepting the validity of a theory by endorsing the principle of commitment and entitlement, we are able to realise what the commitment entitles us to infer and moreover what follows from that inference.

The argument that we are making here is that we develop our capability to conceptually restructure our thinking, as we actively use the procedures and techniques of theoretical or practical reasoning to mediate the relation between different types of concepts. We saw in Chapters 6 and 7 that our actions and thoughts are not transformed through merely learning the word that embodies the meaning of a theoretical concept such as mediation, nor do we use a kernel concept in some routinised way to identify its diverse developmental forms and manifestations. Our understanding of such concepts is completed and formed as we, working in the ZPD, learn to use concepts as a resource to reason in more compelling ways in our writing, in our conversation, in our inner speech and in our practical activity.

The slightly formalistic account of Brandom's ideas of linguistic reasoning may have the unfortunate effect of playing down the intersubjective aspect of communication and the way in which we establish the meaning of concepts, which can be a contested process; and, as a corollary, how we use our understanding of a new theoretical concept to reposition ourselves in relation to the object of our activity. This potential formalism can be avoided, however, if we recast our use of Brandom's insights about the role of inference in accordance with Wertsch's ideas about 'dialogic engagement'. This allows us to see that we personalise the practice of giving and asking for reasons as we ventriloquate – that is, speak in a personal way within an appropriate idiom – to address different audiences and constituencies and try to convince members of those communities about the significance of the argument we are making and its implication for action. By using Wertsch in this way, we can not only highlight the intersubjective dimension of linguistic reasoning and its relation to conceptual restructuring, but also reveal an implicit feature of the giving and asking for reasons, namely that it entails us having to learn how to be answerable for our speech positions.

Being answerable for our speech positions, as Pinkard (1994, p. 5)[1] points out, pre-supposes the social acceptance of 'authoritative reasons'. This notion enables us to both consider and establish why, for example, the concept of mediation offers us a greater scope for explaining and generating inferences about learning, compared with the notion of reflection. In Wertsch's hand this would be treated purely as an issue of semantic form (in his terms 'idiom'). Whilst there is no doubt that in general terms the correct idiom is important in convincing a community about the efficacy of an argument, it can be a slippery term. All too often when idiom is invoked it either results in the conflation of form and content and/or the glossing over of the iterative relation between them. Yet as we saw in Chapter 7, it is the interplay between idiom and the authoritative nature of the reasons and the actions they warrant that is responsible for persuading disciplinary and/or professional communities to accept or reject something. The notion of warranting pre-supposes that we can give, and that others are prepared to accept, that 'a non-question-begging account' (Pinkard, 1994, p. 5) has been established or reached to explain why certain reasons are the authoritative reasons for accepting the explanation based on disciplinary or professional concepts and evidence, rather than the idea that there are foundational truths that, once learnt, will literally guide our thinking and acting.

Our second expression of mediated learning – repositioning – offers us a way to deepen our appreciation of how we use authoritative reasons, to understand and develop socially sanctioned or practitioners' practice.

Repositioning, reasoning and acting. The mediated relation between conceptual restructuring and repositioning, as we saw in Chapter 6, was promissory rather than a substantive accomplishment on Vygotsky's behalf. Leont'ev enabled us to see why by pointing out that, because Vygotsky was inclined to take the purpose of socially sanctioned activities such as education for granted, he tended to concentrate on analysing our engagement with humankind's distinctive cultural and historical traditions. Specifically, he focused on how this engagement was constitutive of the development of mind by primarily concentrating on educational contexts where the object of activity was pre-given. By forcibly drawing our attention to the wider economic, social or political purposes that all forms of socially sanctioned activity serve – in other words, their object of activity – Leont'ev offered us a way to understand how our psychological processes emerge from our collective practical involvement with socially constituted forms of activity, and how an object is a necessary condition for the development of any activity. This insight offers us, as we are about to see, the basis for grasping the connection between conceptual restructuring and repositioning.

To recap briefly: Leont'ev highlighted the way in which psychological processes emerge from our collective practical engagement with one another and the world of which we are a part, rather than following the traditional philosophical and psychological approach of assuming that mind emerges from a solipsistic internal mental realm. So from Leont'ev's (1983, p. 128) perspective, what we perceive is a result of 'objects out in the world' impacting on the photoceptors of the eye's retina, rather than a product of the internal working of the receptors themselves. From this perspective, we turn objects, for example, the organisation of work, into facts of mind as we actively engage with these objects through our activity and present them to ourselves in the form of a subjective image, rather than through a passive reception of inputs that somehow impress their meaning upon us (Stetsenko, 2005, p. 75). Hence, the psychological is, for Leont'ev, the product of a specific type of practical activity. Expressed in Vygotsky's terms, Leont'ev contends that we understand objects through engaging in a process of conceptual restructuring, rather than a process of accumulating associations or apperceptions. This process of restructuring is based on the way that we gradually understand, to echo Pinkard's phrase, the authoritative reasons that underpin socially sanctioned or practitioners' practice.

Despite generating these profound insights into the material constitution of psychological processes and potentially paving the way for a comprehensive theory of the co-evolution of material production, semiotic activity and human subjectivity, Leont'ev tended to accord primacy to the former. As a consequence, he assumed that the reason for the constitution of an activity is synonymous with our motives for engaging with the everyday manifestation of that activity. He was inclined therefore to pay far less attention to the way that we continue to change as human beings, as we develop and contribute to the ongoing development of different social practices, and so the cognitive and symbolic dimension of activity vanished from the picture. From Leont'ev's perspective: the reason, for example, for the provision of education in society is to inculcate people into socially worthwhile values, customs and habits; and the reason for someone choosing to be a teacher would be to contribute to the accomplishment of that social goal.

This tight coupling of activity, motive and needs resulted in, on the one hand, an over-emphasis on the normative goals of activity and the habitualised nature of the actions and operations to realise that activity; and, on the other hand, a playing down of the contribution of human subjectivity and human agency to the evolution of practice. The net effect is that Leont'ev, in his determination to avoid abstracting us from society and severing our connection to the object of our activity, limits the focus of any reflective activity (i.e. repositioning) to what he assumes are the paradigmatic – and hence socially widespread – manifestations of social practice. In the process, he glosses over our continual re-enactment and reconstruction of social practices that are the result of our collective and self-generated motivation and desire to transform the way in which we live.

We rebalanced this tendency on behalf of Leont'ev to play down our active participation in producing and contributing to the further expansion and growth of social practice, as we saw in Chapter 7, by turning to Lave and Wenger (1991). They, unlike Leont'ev, demonstrate that participation in practice – in his terminology, the movement between activity, actions and operations – could be viewed as an epistemological principle of learning. Thus Lave and Wenger provide us with a language of description to conceptualise how we learn in disciplinary, professional and everyday settings. They do this by identifying the pedagogic conditions and cultural tools – legitimate peripheral participation and the technologies of practice – that are necessary to support the ongoing development of the desired forms of not only knowledgeability (i.e. practice-specific forms of knowledge and skill), but also professional/vocational identity.

Nevertheless, the potential of their insight about the generative basis of practice was tempered by Lave and Wenger (1991), who in their determination to avoid succumbing to what they felt would constitute a mentalist conception of mind, refused to distinguish between (i) different types of practice and their outcomes, for example, disciplinary as opposed to professional, and (ii) different types of tools and their outcomes, for example, theoretical as opposed to everyday concepts. Thus, the net effect is that the role of reason in shaping the constitution and development of different forms of practice is unintentionally played down: old-timers and newcomers may clash over the form of practice, but there are underlying reasons why they do so that remain hidden within Lave and Wenger's formulation. By overly generalising about the epistemic dimension of participation, Lave and Wenger deny themselves, and by extension us, a way to distinguish between the types of resource that different practices – disciplinary, professional, everyday – offer us to reposition ourselves towards the object of our activity, and the different types of outcomes associated with those practices and their resources.

This is in part because the role of mind is an embedded (or denied) dimension of Lave and Wenger's argument that participation is an epistemological principle of learning. Consequently, it is difficult to see the mediated relation between the process of conceptual restructuring and repositioning in their account of learning. Because they do not delineate between these expressions of mediation, Lave and Wenger conflate different aspects of learning and conceive of them only as a process of participation. To clarify the nature of the relation between conceptual restructuring and repositioning and the part that they play in facilitating learning, it is helpful to distinguish between the types of 'doubts' that can surface as regards the constitution of social practice (Pinkard, 1994). The first doubt is the question of whether the reasons that currently underpin the constitution of a social practice – and that are used by practitioners, irrespective of their disciplinary or professional background, to justify the continuation of that practice – are in order and, as such, either do not warrant any kind of change to those practices or only warrant modest remediation of the day-to-day actions intended to realise that object. The second type of doubt is whether the reasons currently taken as authoritative with regard to the purpose of, and the social constitution of, an activity and practitioner's practice should continue to remain authoritative in light of the identification of contradictions, tensions or concerns about either type of practice. In confronting the former type of doubt, we are unlikely to call into question the purpose of, and paradigmatic assumptions about, practices and tools in activity; whereas in the case of the latter type of doubt, we are much more likely to do so.

There are a number of different manifestations of the first type of doubt. One classic manifestation is social contestation. Lave and Wenger demonstrated, as we saw in Chapter 7, that communities of practice constantly evolve as 'old-timers' and 'newcomers' clash over whether the existing rules and procedures of their actual practice should change or remain the same. Equally, writers such as de Certeau (1984) have identified the range of 'strategies and tactics' we constantly formulate to reclaim personal autonomy from the all-pervading forces of management culture in workplaces or politics in everyday life. Another manifestation is addressing doubts about practice through the constructive and creative transformation of social practice. Billett (2007) has highlighted the way in which we exercise our 'personal' agency' by using the 'affordances' that we perceive workplaces to provide, to help us to evolve practice in ways that are meaningful for ourselves. Edwards (2005) has drawn attention to the value of 'relational agency' when trying to change practice, in other words, the ability to persuade other people who may not be a part of the immediate situation to act jointly with you in order to realise the desired change. While Knorr Cetina (2001) has highlighted the way in which professionals in fields such as science and finance are motivated by the 'incompleteness' of their practice and/or the objects of practice, in other words, the fact that there is always scope to improve them, to constantly strive to develop both practice and objects creatively.

Despite generating these powerful insights about, for example, the exercise of 'agentic' and/or 'relational' activity (Billett, 2007) in evolving practice, and the motivating force of professional 'desire' in facilitating practice to branch out (Knorr Cetina, 1997), some features of the aforementioned writers' accounts of changes in practice remain rather hidden. These are, notably: the types of questions that were asked to initiate the process of being repositioned; the pedagogic processes that facilitated the remediation or transformation of practice; and the non-question-begging nature of the reasons that led the individuals and/or communities studied to restructure their existing conceptions about practice, and to accept and implement proposed changes to practice. These questions, pedagogies and articulation of reasons are central to the process of learning that has been occurring amongst individuals and groups in the situations that Billett and others describe. To shed light on how they contribute to the process of learning it is necessary to consider the third mediated expression of learning: namely recontextualisation.

Recontextualisation, reasoning and action. The introduction of cultural tools such as concepts or artefacts that are not within our direct or peripheral field of vision or awareness to solve a problem is often presented as a matter of 'intuition' (Dreyfuss & Dreyfuss, 1986), 'affordance' (Gibson, 1979) or 'blinking' (Gladwell, 2005). These suggestions rest on a quasi-naturalistic account of our relation with the environment that assumes that we can respond to people, artefacts or events that populate our environment without requiring a higher level of cognitive awareness. It is as if, as Derry (2008, p. 506) observes, 'meaning can be conveyed directly by our senses by virtue of a co-evolved relation to the environment'. In contrast, our decisions to incorporate a new cultural tool into our practice is, for Vygotsky (1999) and most post-Vygotskians, mediated by our knowledge of those tools, based on our ability to name them, and exercising our creativity by inferring – or working with others to infer – what might follow from using them in relation to the task-in-hand. We are only able to do this if we have developed the capability to assess their potential relative contribution to whatever the task in hand happens to be, and to consider whether any additional tools may also be required to solve that problem.

The recontextualisation of cultural tools therefore inevitably has a retrospective and prospective dimension. It requires us to have learnt the purpose of different cultural tools, to understand how those tools are embedded in well-established or recently created forms of social practice and speech genres, and to be prepared to consider how they could be used in other situations. This is never as straightforward as it sounds. Disciplinary (Toulmin, 1978) and professional (Goodwin, 1994) practice and discourses tend to be mediated, on some occasions, implicitly by the theoretical concepts and pre-suppositions that are part and parcel of the special and distinctive domain of professional competence; and, on other occasions, 'invisibly' by the ubiquitous classification systems (ways of segmenting things) and their associated standards (procedures for how to do things), which are embedded in 'working infrastructures' that constitute the context for professional activity (Bowker & Star, 2000).

We have seen that the insight that emerged from Lave and Wenger's work is that the ability to 'see' relevant entities – and by extension to understand discourse – is never solely lodged in an individual mind, but rather is influenced by how far we are able to participate within a community of practice and to learn to use their 'technologies of practice'. Whilst undoubtedly true at a general level, this insight does not offer us, as it stands, a way to distinguish between the different types of activity required to recontextualise a cultural tool to assist us to re-mediate a practitioner's practice or to radically rethink the social constitution of practice.

However, if we accept the reformulation of Lave and Wenger's principle, advanced in Chapter 8 – that participation in practice is an epistemological condition for learning as long as we engage in the social practice of giving and asking for reasons – then the first step involved in coming to terms with the world of practice entails learning to locate extant cultural tools (for example, concepts, heuristics etc.) in the space of reasons, which underpins the use of different technologies of practice by retrospective rational reconstruction of the purpose of those cultural tools. The next step is to use this process of reconstruction to infer what follows from our understanding as regards the use of such tools. Only when we have completed these steps are we in a position to disembed the tool from the discourses and practices within which it is embedded, and to recontextualise the tool so that it can serve a new purpose and in the process support the lateral branching of practice. These steps are, as we are about to see, more problematic than is often appreciated by policymakers and from the above description.

To understand why this is the case, it is helpful to return to the notion of horizontal recontextualisation that we encountered in Chapter 7, where we defined it quite broadly as the use of an existing tool in a different context to modify an existing object of activity. We now need to consider the way in which different expressions of the use of existing activities or tools pre-suppose different processes of recontextualisation and generate different outcomes. We start our exploration of this issue with three expressions of horizontal recontextualisation: the use of existing activities and tools to create a new interdisciplinary/professional curriculum and a distinctive form of interprofessional collaboration in fields characterised by practical reasoning. These examples illustrate different manifestations of one aspect of the learning challenge of the knowledge economy described in Chapter 4: namely how to support practice to laterally branch out.

The first example is the creation of a new interdisciplinary/professional curriculum to support people to move into the field of aeronautical engineering, where there is a shortage of skilled maintenance engineers (Evans *et al.*, 2009). Aeronautical engineering consists of a mix of concepts drawn from disciplines such as mathematics and physics that are integral to the development of any under-standing of aeronautics, the legal requirements and standards set by the aeronautic industry and 'work process knowledge' (Boreham *et al.*, 2002). These are the sector-specific technological and organisational issues that transcend particular organisational settings, but whose actual character is site-specific and hence integral to a practi-tioner's practice. This eclectic mix of curricula elements presents curriculum designers and planners with a particular conundrum: to combine concepts, heuristics and artefacts from these diverse fields to create a curriculum that 'connects' them in a way that is meaningful and beneficial to learners (Boreham *et al.*, 2002).

To accomplish this task, the designers and planners had to create, as Evans *et al.* (2009) reveal, a curriculum structure that allowed forms of knowledge contained within disciplinary and work-based discourses to cohere meaningfully alongside one another in an interdisciplinary curriculum. This is not straightforward, as they are underpinned by rather different logics[2]. The nature of the challenge was high-lighted by Evans, by drawing on Young's (2006; 2008) and Barnett's (2006) respective elaboration of some ideas about knowledge in Bernstein's (2000) work on 'knowledge discourses' and 'recontextualisation' practices.

Workplace discourses tend to be 'local, segmented and context-bound' and, as such, do not readily embody specific rules for transferring meaning across sites or occupational sectors, whereas disciplinary knowledge tends to be 'general, explicit and codified' (Young, 2006, p. 148). Hence, in order to create an interdisciplinary/ professional curriculum, these forms of knowledge have to be 'reclassified' and 'pedagogically' recontextualised (Barnett, 2006), albeit in different ways. The former refers to the criteria that are used to selectively restructure disciplinary knowledge or knowledges, with regard to the technological or organisational problems encountered in specialised work settings. The latter refers to attempts to make the selection of disciplinary knowledge more readily teachable and learnable in conceptual modules that sit alongside practical modules, and reflect both the operational demands of workplace activities and the requirements of professional bodies.

The first challenge that curriculum planners and designers faced therefore was to determine which concepts, ideas and heuristics from disciplines, workplace and professional knowledge(s) should be selected for inclusion in an interdisciplinary/ professional curriculum. This is more straightforward for highly codified forms of knowledge, because the codification process provides explicit rules that can be used, as Evans *et al.* and other analyses of the development of interdisciplinary curricula demonstrate (Dyson, 1987; Layton, 1993), to formulate criteria to guide the transfer of knowledge from the context of the subject domain, to another context – that of an interdisciplinary curriculum. The lack of explicit rules underpinning work-based knowledge, however, means that the planners and designers have to not only formulate criteria to determine which aspects of work-based knowledge should be included in the curriculum, but also to harmonise both sets of criteria, so that the sequence in which codified and work-based knowledge is introduced and taught mutually reinforce rather than fracture one another.

The second challenge that lecturers faced was to identify appropriate pedagogic strategies to assist learners to develop academically and professionally. Their solution was described by Evans *et al.* as a combination of 'dialogic inquiry' (Wells, 1999) and 'legitimate peripheral participation' (Lave & Wenger, 1991). The former idea referred to the pedagogic strategies that were used, for example, lectures, case studies, discussions, to assist learners to apprehend the meaning of the general principles that underpinned the elements of physics and mathematics that were being taught; to explain the interface between technological and work process knowledge (practice-based and academic); and to convey the rationale for the legal requirements that have been imposed on the aeronautical industry and account for the way in which they have influenced the process of engineering maintenance (e.g. systems and skills). The latter was employed to provide opportunities for learners to use this eclectic mix of knowledge as a resource to ask questions about the organisation of work within the aeronautic workshops, and to move from undertaking fairly routine to more demanding work tasks to develop the forms of knowledgeability required to service and repair aeronautic engines. Taken in combination, the integration of the pedagogic principles of inquiry and participation positioned the people enrolled on the Foundation Degree (FD) to develop the capability to infer what might follow when they are actually maintaining engines that are a part of an actual plane.

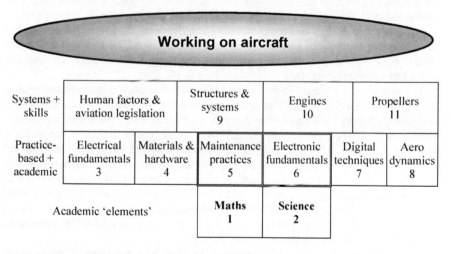

Figure 5. Working on aircraft. (from Evans, K., Guile, D., & Harris, J., forthcoming)

The second example is the interprofessional activity required to remodel two public libraries, to create access for people with disabilities and to strengthen the buildings against earthquakes in a professionally sound way. Hall *et al.* (2003) explain how this process of recontextualisation[3] is accomplished when people from different professions, for example, structural engineers, architects and environmental-conservationists, collaboratively work together. They do this by drawing on Bowker & Star's (2000) notion of 'infrastructure' to refer to the profession-specific ways of classifying phenomena and organising perception; and Star's (1989) notion of 'boundary objects' to refer to the way in which representational devices such as diagrams, gestures, phrases can be used by professional and lay communities with different interests, needs and accountabilities to facilitate communication between them.

Hall and colleagues use these concepts to identify three interconnected recontextualisation challenges that the interprofessional team had to overcome to realise the object of their activity. The first one is to 'assemble, juxtapose and evaluate' one another's cultural tools (i.e. concepts, discourses, material artefacts, etc.). To do so, each person has to find a way to animate, discursively, symbolically and materially, their understanding of the nature of the problem-in-hand to the other members of the team. Hall and colleagues highlight that they accomplish this animation by moving back-and-forth in time, highlighting the current manifestations of the problem, speculating as to the reasons why the problem might have occurred, and suggesting to one another how to resolve the problem. The second challenge is to learn how to respond to different forms of 'disciplinary perception and action'. This potential problem was overcome by recognising that different disciplinary specialists see the same project in different ways and strive to avoid allowing discipline-specific perceptions to trigger disagreements and 'de-stabilize' other members' expertise (2003, p. 297). The third challenge was to ensure that, as people from different disciplines made distinct and complementary contributions, they were linked together to help move the project forward. This was accomplished, as Hall and colleagues (2003, p. 297) observe, by all participants, 'making infrastructure an ongoing historical accomplishment'.

Using a pivotal moment in the interprofessional discussion, Hall and colleagues highlight the way in which the team resolved the problem by simultaneously addressing all three challenges. They describe how the concern that one of the conservationists in the team continually voiced – that the only way to resolve the problem was to modify the existing safety standards, otherwise the integrity of the original architecture would be spoilt – inspired one of the structural architects to revise his ideas about how to deploy the 'seismic resisting elements' (i.e. the materials to strengthen the building) in a library. Instead of continuing to pursue his initial ideas that a number of library walls may have to be replaced with more structurally sound materials, the engineer proposes that resistors could be strapped to the ceilings in such a way to enhance the design of the building.

Hall and colleagues use this example to illustrate how the team members made their respective classification systems and cultural tools transparent to one another. They point out that the structural engineers' inscriptions (i.e. sketches), gestures (i.e. highlighting where the resistors would be placed) and their accompanying comments provided other members of the team with visual and oral clues about his proposed solution. The team members used these clues to gradually infer what follows from someone else's perceptions and judgements for their own interests and attachments. Thus the team gradually recognised that they needed to understand rather than to reject one another's insights. This enabled them to appreciate the logic that lay behind one another's suggestions, for example, to agree upon the least intrusive modification of architectural design, in order to reach a non-question-begging stance regarding the appropriate course of action. The determining feature of this process, according to Hall and colleagues, is that specialists who are actively trying to learn to use another professional's insights or tools to resolve a common problem are only able to do so as they gradually develop 'hybrid and selective forms of perception and action'. These forms of perception enable them to respond to the proposed use of another specialist's cultural tool, by developing 'relations of selective visibility' in terms of understanding the tool's implications for their collective work practice and the kinds of organisational accountabilities they must meet.

There are a number of interesting issues about the link between reason, inference and action in these two expressions of horizontal recontextualisation. The first issue of note is that this link allows us to appreciate the relation between our redefinition of Lave and Wenger's argument that participation in practice is an epistemological principle of learning, and our observations in Chapter 4 about the contribution of practical reasoning in the knowledge economy. Although the two cases employ, respectively, different discursive terms – 'logic' and 'represent-ation' – to convey the challenge of interdisciplinary work, the unifying link between them is a joint concern to make explicit how the problems the two teams confronted were resolved. Translated into the argument we are making and the terminology we are using in this chapter, the process of reclassificatory and pedagogic recontextualisation – as much as the development of selective and hybrid perception – involve all parties in an ongoing form of conceptual restructuring and repositioning. In the case of the former, participants were repositioned in relation to the object of their activity as different solutions were put forward to address the problem in hand. In the case of the latter, participants restructured their under-standing about the extent to which different suggestions constituted solutions to the problem in hand as they inferred what followed from those suggestions and, in the process, advanced their own understanding based on others' insights. What emerges from participants' use of the interplay between their and others' theoretical and work-based knowledge is a practical judgement about how to collectively support the lateral branching of practice (i.e. the creation of a new work-based curriculum and a solution to an architectural problem). This judgement has an epistemic dimension in the sense that it is informed by the contextual application of disciplinary concepts and experiences. Nevertheless, the judgement has been reached without all members of the interprofessional teams having necessarily fully grasped the meaning that the forms of knowledge (i.e. cultural tools), and the suggestions made on the basis of that knowledge, are likely to have for the specialist community from where they originated (Arievitch, 2004)[4]. Thus, we can see that there is an iterative relation between restructuring, repositioning and recontextualisation. Although they can be distinguished analytically from one another because they serve different purposes, they also have a relation to one another and, as such, are an integral feature of the process of learning.

The second issue to be considered here is that the link between reason, inference and action in both examples reveals how recontextualisation is integral to the development of that which both Knorr Cetina and this book have accepted as the cornerstone of the knowledge economy/society: namely a culture of epistementality to support practice in laterally branching out in slightly different ways. Returning to the case of the first example, it highlighted the imperative for curriculum planners and designers to formally make the criteria that they devised to select different types of knowledge explicit, so that lecturers could see that there were compelling reasons for that selection. They could then use these reasons as a resource to help them to sequence the teaching of different types of modules in such a way that it constituted a coherent learning programme. In the case of the second example, it highlighted the importance of collectively modelling and reasoning in a discursively explicit and representationally vivid way, so that all the specialists involved could contribute their expertise to the process.

What is common in both cases, however, is that the contributing parties to the recontextualisation process have actively sought to identify ways to make what is implicit in their practice explicit (i.e. to reposition others in relation to the object of their activity). They do this in order to accomplish common goals and persuade those parties of the value of their insights (i.e. to restructure their understanding of how to tackle the common problem), rather than engage in a zero-sum game based on the imposition of a particular disciplinary or professional solution to a common problem. What is missing from these examples, however, is why we create new activities and artefacts and what is distinctive about the form of learning that supports this process. This leads us to consider the relation between the second type of doubt and the final expression of mediation – reconfiguration.

Reconfiguration, reasoning and action. We defined the second type of doubt earlier as asking whether the reasons currently taken as authoritative with regard to the purpose of, and the social constitution of, an activity and practitioner's practice should continue to remain authoritative in the light of the identification of contradictions, tensions or concerns about them. We also defined reconfiguration as the way in which our response to the aforementioned tensions serves as a pivot or trigger for the development of new manifestations of activity and new artefacts. The common ground between the two terms becomes clearer when we return to the work of Engeström.

Engeström formulated his theory of expansive learning and his Developmental Work Research (DWR) methodology to support us to create new activities rather than, as is the case with most other theories of learning, to engage with humankind's accumulated cultural–historical heritage or to reflect on how to change ingrained habits. Moreover, Engeström maintained that, for these reasons, his theory and methodology constitute a way to address the type of challenges that are emerging in the knowledge economy, for example, to create new relations between producers and consumers, and to develop the heterogeneous capabilities required for the new forms of work, for example, knotworking, associated with these new working relations.

Engeström's DWR methodology, as we saw in Chapter 7, firmly locates the process of expansion in laboratory conditions. Specifically, he argues that a special space – a boundary-crossing laboratory – has to be established within a single or network of activity systems where a cross-section of the workforce can firstly, envision a new object, expressed in the form of a new concept (i.e. theoretically grasped practice) and articulate the reasons underpinning that concept. Secondly, members of one or more activity system(s) working in the boundary-crossing laboratory can then use those reasons to explain to other colleagues why they should, and how they can, contribute to process of realising the new object.

We can extrapolate a number of guidelines from Engeström's investigations in laboratory conditions of the way in which new activities and new modes of expertise are created. These guidelines will apply generally to the process of reconfiguration, irrespective as to the context where it occurs and the constituency of people involved in that process. The hallmarks of reconfiguration are firstly, recognising that the object of our activity has been constituted according to a set of reasons that may or may not be consciously articulated by those involved with that activity. Secondly, asking whether the reasons that are currently accepted as authoritative with regard to the purpose of, and the social constitution of, an activity and practitioner's practice should continue to remain authoritative in the light of the identification of contradictions, tensions or concerns about them. Thirdly, identifying a pedagogy process that we can use to assist us to radically rethink and/or create a new object of activity, and establish a new normative context (i.e. division of labour, community, rules) for that activity.

This recasting of Engeström's insights about expansive transformations of activity systems and expertise into a general set of guidelines may appear, at first sight, to be a regressive step. After all, Engeström (2007), and other researchers who have been influenced by him (Edwards et al., 2009; Engeström & Keruso, 2007), have consistently claimed that expansive transformations can only be accomplished through recourse to the interventionist DWR methodology. This is because the methodology helps to develop the forms of 'critical design agency' amongst all parties (i.e. researchers, managers, workers and clients) who are involved in the rethinking of their object of activity. The desire to develop critical design agency is a laudable goal in settings where there is both a commitment and funding to support this type of intervention; there are, however, examples of expansive transformation occurring and critical design agency being built without recourse to the DWR methodology.

One of the most widely celebrated examples of this is the development of Open Source Software (von Hippel, 2005). This development represents, on the one hand, the emergence of a new principle of production (i.e. object of activity) that does not conform to the widely held economic beliefs about economic behaviour, in other words, that it is concerned with a small group of people or company devising and selling products and services to maximise profit for themselves and their shareholders (Benkler, 2006); and, on the other hand, evidence of a move towards user-community-based innovation (i.e. activity system) through the development of distributed and shared expertise (von Hippel, 2005). The reason that this shift in economic logic and the locus of the development of expertise has happened is that, in the 'open' development model in software production, the source code of the software is kept freely available. According to licences based on the 'copyleft principle', users are invited to use, modify, and further distribute and develop the code (Miettinen, 2006).

The best-known example of the open-source model is Linux, where the core community comprises Linus Torvalds and over 120 maintainers, who are responsible for the modules of Linux. In addition, several thousand user–developers regularly participate in the reporting of bugs and the writing of new code. The hallmark of this community is that it offers users a way to informate their own and other's networks and organisations, and thus to escape from the financial and coding constraints associated with proprietary systems, such as those Microsoft offer to corporations. Moreover, the community of user–developers offer feedback to one another as regards the modification of code as well as to their networks. They do this in order to share the insights accruing from learning (i.e. recontextualise knowledge, operating protocols, etc.) via the open-source networks and so further develop capacity and capability within the wider Linux community.

Furthermore, some sectors of the economy are characterised by a continuing commitment to create new products and services and, as a consequence, are not characterised by a rigid adherence to an object of activity underpinned by deeply entrenched divisions of labour, communities and rules. The creative and cultural sector, for example, is increasingly characterised by network-based forms of work, and project teams that only come together for the life of a project and that actively involve stakeholder communities in such networks (Bilton, 2007; Deuze, 2007). The formulation and instantiation of new objects of activity in such settings is therefore a regular rather than an exceptional feature of work, and also occurs without any explicit reference to Engeström's theory of expansive learning or his interventionist methodology.

The existence of expansive transformations in the knowledge economy alerts us to the wider potential of Engeström's constellation of concepts and methods. At present, they are a 'closed' theoretical and methodological approach (i.e. primarily developed by Engeström and colleagues as part of the DWR programme). This restricts their use to settings where research budgets have been secured and companies have agreed to participate in a DWR programme. Arguably, Engeström's concepts and methods could become more 'open' resources that could be made available through different modes of PVWL to firms and networks in the private and public sector. This would enable members of such firms and networks to recontextualise Engeström's concepts and methods to help them to reconfigure their specific problems and concerns. Those involved in the reconfiguration process could use the notion of an 'object of activity' to explore the way in which different reasons underpin the forms of socially sanctioned activity they are involved with. The notion of 'expanding' an object of activity could be used to provide a language of description, for firms and networks to clarify why they are involved in a process of formulating and instantiating new products and services, and what they are aiming to accomplish (i.e. a new object). The 'cycle of expansive learning' could be modified contextually to facilitate active engagement in the social practice of giving and asking for reasons by providing a framework to the process of inference during the formulation and instantiation stage.

This recasting of Engeström's concept and methods allows us to see that although the reconfiguration is a slightly different type of unfolding process compared to recontextualisation, both presuppose a normative context, in other words, a space of reasons, that participants use to make their ideas and suggestions intelligible to one another. The concept of reason has always been a feature, albeit under-discussed, of operating in a boundary-crossing laboratory. Engeström and colleagues have deployed his conceptual constellation – activity system, cycle of expansive learning, double simulation, etc. – to support participants in the boundary-crossing laboratory to develop a working grasp of the interplay between those concepts and the formulation and instantiation of a new object. In doing so, they have provided a conceptually structured framework that enables participants to share ideas, understand the reasons that inform those ideas, infer what follows for the constitution of the new object and, as a result, reconfigure the division of labour, rule and community within the workplace. Hence, it is participation in this social practice that has gradually assisted those in the boundary-crossing laboratory to operate in an expanded space of reasons, even if they do not yet have a full grasp of all the implications of the connections that operating in this space may afford them.

Undertaking the process of reconfiguration outside 'laboratory' conditions predisposes teams to accept the responsibility for establishing the type of epistemic culture and pedagogic processes to formulate and instantiate a new object of activity. This is a very demanding challenge because it requires teams to establish and maintain the cultures and practices that will facilitate the creation of a new object. To do so, it is necessary for them to agree what working on a new object, to recontextualise one of Brandom's comments that we used earlier, commits them to, as well as what that commitment predisposes them to accept responsibility for. In the case of the former, it commits team members to strive to understand the thoughts of others who have very different modes of expertise and ideas about how their expertise can contribute to the formulation of the new object and its normative context (i.e. new constitution of the division of labour, rules, and community). In the case of the latter, to accept responsibility for establishing a space of reasons where competing and contending ideas and suggestions can be assessed in relation as to which offer more compelling reasons for choosing to follow one course of action rather than another. Because their goal is to create the new context in which expertise will be deployed, team members are involved in a process of making a series of collective rather than individual practical judgements. This requires them to act, to recast Bauman's (1987) terms, as 'interpreters' who form collective inferences and agreed courses of action as opposed to 'legislators' who make individual pronouncements and undertake insular actions[5].

CONCLUSION

We have shown in this chapter the distinctive and related contribution of the four mediated expressions of learning (restructuring, repositioning, recontextualisation and reconfiguration) and the three expressions of the development of practice (evolve, laterally branch and transform), which we identified from our analysis in Chapters 6, 7 and 8, add to our understanding of the learning challenge of the knowledge economy. Our conceptual reframing of Vygotsky, Leont'ev, Wertsch,

Lave and Wenger, and Engeström's insights, while respecting the integrity of their own concerns and important contributions to our understanding of learning, provides a new framework that can be used to identify the range of challenges for progra- mmes of PVWL to address.

We have done so by showing that the concept of reason, which is formed as we engage with and develop our accumulated cultural–historical inheritance, and the concept of action, which is formed as we use the different traditions of that inheritance (i.e. discipline, everyday, professional, workplace) to understand and transform the world, is central to each expression of mediation. The process of: (i) *restructuring* highlighted the way in which we use the reasons that underpin concepts to grasp aspects of the world that are often not susceptible to sensory perception; (ii) *repositioning* revealed the importance of inquiring about the reasons that underpin the current constitution of practice, or that are in play as we seek to rethink and redesign practice; (iii) *recontextualisation* revealed that we have to rethink the reasons that underpin our use of an existing tool if we are to use it to address a problem in another context; and finally (iv) *reconfiguration* reminded us that practice and context are inextricably intertwined, and that we have to attend to the reasons that tie both together if we want to embed any transformatory activity.

In doing so, we have accomplished two goals. The first is to re-establish the constant presence of the explicit and implicit dimensions of mediation that some neo-Vygotskians, for example Roth (2007), and some social practice theorists, for example Berducci (2004) and Billett (2009) have questioned through their interest in the notion of the 'im- or pre-mediate'. The problem with these positions is, as McDowell presciently observes in a conversation with Hubert Dreyfuss about our mediated relation with the world, that:

> We should not start with the assumption that mindedness, the characteristic in virtue of which I am the thinking thing I am, is alien to unreflective immersion in bodily life. If we let our conception of mindedness be controlled by the thought that mindedness is operative even in our unreflective perceiving and acting, we can regain an integrated conception of ourselves, as animals, and – what comes with that – beings whose life is persuasively bodily, but of a distinctively rational kind.

(McDowell, 2007b, p. 369)

Our four expressions of mediation offer us a way to flesh out what McDowell means by the phrase, 'persuasively bodily, but of a distinctively rational kind'. Put simply, McDowell means that our embodied and articulated actions are both concep- tually structured capabilities that are exercised in different ways from one another (for example, theoretical and practical reasoning), rather than radically different kinds of capabilities born of different kinds of engagement with the world. The common thread between them is that they are different modes of response to, and engage- ment with, the mediated world (i.e. a world created through human action and underpinned by reason) in which we live. The difference is that the former is normally a product of implicit mediation while the latter is a product of the interplay between implicit and explicit mediation.

The second goal is to establish the conceptual basis that allows us to rethink the conventional wisdom about the learning challenge of the knowledge economy, and to consider how PVWL can support us to address that new challenge. Based on the premises that we have articulated in this book, namely that we that we live in a mediated (i.e. humanised/idealised/conceptualised) world, it follows that learning entails understanding the constitution of the world and then using the ensuing knowledge to contribute to its continual transformation in one of three ways: evolving, laterally branching or transforming activity. What is common to each of these modes of modes of learning is that they are all based on a common starting point – the relation between mind and world, theory and practice, etc. – rather than the idea of two separate worlds of knowledge. Where they differ from one another is that they require different forms of pedagogic support and result in very different outcomes. Our contention that learning is a process of remediation offers, as we shall see, a way to address similarities and differences between forms of knowledge, rather than, as do the pedagogies of reflection, a way to affirm their difference.

NOTES

[1] We have drawn on Pinkard (1994) because he has clarified the different ways in which Hegel employed notions of reason in his *Phenomenology*. Given that Hegel and this particular text are central to CHAT, Brandom and McDowell, Pinkard's work constitutes an ideal vehicle for clarifying the role of reason in their work.

[2] The distinctions about different types of knowledge (i.e. 'vertical' and 'horizontal') and modes of recontextualisation (i.e. 'reclassificatory' and 'pedagogic') are based, respectfully, on Young's (2006; 2008) and Barnett's (2006) interpretation of Bernstein's (2000) concepts of 'horizontal' (i.e. local, segmented and context-bound) and 'vertical' (i.e. general, explicit and codified) discourses. Because we are already using the terms 'horizontal' and 'vertical' to refer to different processes of recontextualisation, we have refrained from introducing Bernstein's slightly different use of these terms, so as to not confuse the reader with alternative usages of the same terms within the space of a few lines.

[3] Hall *et al.* (2003) do not explicitly employ the terms 'recontextualisation' or 'cultural tools', nevertheless, it is clear from their descriptions of interprofessional practice that the terminology that they employ, for example, 'infrastructure' and 'representational devices' denotes their preferred term of reference rather than any fundamental difference of view. For the sake of consistency, we have therefore chosen to substitute the term 'cultural tool' for 'representational device'.

[4] Hall and colleagues (2003) tend to rely on the representational paradigm to justify their argument about the contribution that the 'representational infrastructure' makes to interprofessional collaboration. It is my contention, based on my interpretation of the evidence that Hall and colleagues present, that it is not professionals' use of the representations as such, but their ability to infer what follows from their appropriation of those representations, that allows them to communicate and advance social practice.

[5] The challenge of sustaining and developing new contexts is an issue that remains relatively under-discussed in Engeström's work. We can gain a sense of what is entailed from Felstead *et al.'s* (2009) notion of 'conjoined' working and learning practices, that is, practices that assist us to understand the reasons for the existing constitution of activity and to use those reasons as resources to develop that activity.

THE NEW LEARNING CHALLENGE OF
THE KNOWLEDGE ECONOMY

INTRODUCTION

We stated at the outset of this book that our intention was to outline an alternative account of the new role of knowledge in the economies of advanced industrial societies and the learning challenge that this development poses for those societies. This alternative view is set against the current conventional wisdom about the relative contribution of theoretical and tacit knowledge to economic growth and the importance of assisting a greater proportion of the population of all societies to attain higher-level qualifications. In light of these aims, our final chapter starts with a concise summary of all the strands of the alternative account of knowledge and learning that have been presented. We then show how a number of new tenets for learning emerge from this summary. We use these tenets, in conjunction with our mediated expressions of learning and the development of practice, to highlight how educational institutions and workplaces can reconfigure professional, vocational and workplace learning (PVWL), to support what we maintain is the hallmark of a knowledge economy/society: the development of epistemic cultures and objects.

Turning the Conventional Wisdom on its Head

Summary of the argument. We have established throughout the book that the prevailing consensus about the knowledge economy and its implications for educational policy is misplaced for a number of reasons. We first showed that the knowledge economy is being presented as, paradoxically, both an imaginary and a pre-given reality: so it can be both a way to talk about all the issues pertaining to the use of knowledge in the economy, and a new economic and social world that we have to adapt to. We then showed that the debate about whether theoretical or tacit knowledge is the most important form of knowledge in the economy has arisen as a result of the unacknowledged legacy of the two worlds of knowledge in the Social Sciences. We further showed that the invocation of Polanyi to justify the continuing acceptance of this split is a misinterpretation of Polanyi's position about theoretical and tacit knowledge. His famous comments about theoretical and tacit knowledge have been treated by social and management theorists as though they referred to separate types of knowledge, rather than – as Polanyi had presented them in *Personal Knowledge* (1958) – as two interdependent dimensions of theoretical knowledge.

This framing of the role of knowledge has pre-disposed social and management theorists to overlook an essential part of their own argument about the new role of knowledge in the economy: that knowledge economies/societies pre-suppose knowledge cultures. This has happened in part because social scientists have historically downplayed the contribution of culture to economic activity. It has also happened because social scientists who have taken a cultural turn tend to operate with a rather circumscribed notion of the cultural: culture as the context for economic activity (i.e. organisational culture), or culture as a special kind of economic activity (i.e. the creative and cultural sector), rather than culture as constitutive of practice, identity, knowledge and so forth. Hence it is hardly surprising that social scientists in general were also slow to detect that epistemic cultures and practices were spilling over into professional arenas and producer–consumer collaborations and, in the process, contributing to the growing knowledge texture, based on new forms of intra- and interprofessional collaboration, in some parts of advanced industrial societies.

The 'cultural' logic that informs our restatement of the argument presented in this book about the new role of knowledge in the economy, and the learning challenge that this poses for advanced industrial societies, implies: (i) a radically different conception of knowledge economies/societies to the current conventional wisdom that is enshrined in national policies for education and many scholarly and popularist texts; and (ii) a new purpose for PVWL. Instead of describing the national or the global economy *sui generis* as a knowledge economy, and assuming that because the forms of knowledge developed within PVWL have an 'applied' character these types of qualification constitute a proxy measure for employability in those economies, we have articulated an alternative position. The cornerstone of this position is that: (i) the term 'knowledge economy' should be reserved for those sectors or parts of sectors that are characterised by the spread of epistemic cultures and practices; and (ii) the new (i.e. re-mediated) aim of PVWL should be to support the development of epistemic cultures by assisting people to:

– restructure their thinking and acting by locating forms of knowledge and their associated practices in the space of reasons;
– reposition themselves by questioning the constitution of knowledge and practice in relation to their object of activity;
– recontextualise and/or reconfigure knowledge and practice to achieve new economic, political and social outcomes.

We derived these tenets for learning from a number of sources. The first source was Vygotsky, because he was the first scholar to specifically articulate how we learn that we live in a mediated world, and he did so in radical philosophical, psychological and pedagogic ways. Vygotsky's philosophical radicalism led him to show how cultural tools play a transformatory, rather than an additive, role in human development and action. In doing so, Vygotsky offered us a way not only to overcome the longstanding split between mind and world, and theory and practice, but also to escape from the idea that we are totally constrained by our biology, and enable us to appreciate that we are responsible for placing or not placing constraints on our freedom to act in the world. His psychological radicalism led Vygotsky to explain how the development of the higher mental functions results in the emergence of a mediated (i.e. a culturally and historically constituted) mind: a mind, moreover, that we continue to develop throughout the life-course by engaging with, evolving and transforming culturally and historically constituted tools and practice in educational and work contexts. His pedagogic radicalism resulted in Vygotsky offering us the first insight into the contribution of pedagogy to the development of mind. His concept of the zone of proximal development (ZPD) directed our attention to the way that experienced others can support us to conceptually restructure our existing theoretical and everyday concepts as we learn new theoretical concepts. In the process, Vygotsky paved the way for a unified conception of the development of mind from childhood and through adulthood.

Furthermore, we used Vygotsky's argument about the intellectual basis of perception, as well as the difference and relation between theoretical and everyday concepts – even though it was formulated before Polanyi wrote his treatise on tacit knowledge – to elaborate and extend Polanyi's insights about the two interdependent dimensions of scientific knowledge. In a nutshell, our argument is that once we understand mind as a culturally–historically constituted phenomenon, we are in a position to appreciate that our tacit perceptions are the explicitly or implicitly mediated outcome of: on the one hand, our continual engagement with a humanised or idealised world; and, on the other hand, our own prior knowledge and experience. This rebalancing of our understanding of the relation between theoretical and tacit knowledge enabled us to appreciate that the form of tacit knowledge required for economic development emerged as professionals mediated their disciplinary and work-based perceptions. As such, it constitutes the basis of the judgements they made about which individual or collective course of action to take in order to develop epistemic cultures and practices.

The second source was Leont'ev's concept of the object of activity. This helped us to develop the new tenets of learning in a number of ways. The first was to demonstrate that an object is a necessary condition for the development of any activity (for example, the organisation of educational institutions through to the organisation of epistemic cultures), and for the mental reflection that follows from that development. We demonstrated that the process of conceptual restructuring that occurs as we learn a new, albeit extant, theoretical concept is significantly enhanced if we ask questions about the socially constituted purpose and organisation of the field from whence that concept originates. Such questions enable us to reposition ourselves in relation to both the existing field of knowledge – for example, understanding why a concept has been developed, what issues it does and does not shed light on and how it might expand our options for acting in the world – as well as to position us to develop new fields of knowledge.

The second way was to reveal the implicit influence of the object of activity on the mediated basis of learning in educational as well as everyday activities, such as work. Specifically, we highlighted the way in which a socially accepted object of activity always underpins pedagogic conditions (for example, legitimate peripheral participation); access to tools (for example, the technologies of practice); and discursive abilities (for example, ventriloquating with different types of discourse) and how all three contribute to the implicit mediation of understanding and performance in different settings. In doing so, we identified another, albeit less profound, way that activity/social practice can develop: it can co-evolve as we act agentively to re-mediate habitualised routines and operations.

We pursued the implication of this issue by distinguishing between the two types of questions that could be asked about the existing social constitution of practice: questions that facilitated the collective development of a practice, often in new and startling ways, or the creation of a new practice. The former was explored through the notions of recontextualisation and lateral branching of practice. We showed how major modifications to practice and/or new expressions of an existing practice can occur as we use existing cultural tools, specifically modes of knowledge, in new ways. The implications of the latter type of question were explored through a third source of ideas about learning – the work of Engeström. His creation of a new collective unit of analysis – an activity system – and his linking of that unit of analysis to the mode of production (for example, co-configuration), provided us with a way to analyse the relation between object and practice, and his instruments of expansion – the CEL and boundary-crossing laboratory – provided us with a way to analyse the creation of a new object and new practices. In the case of the former, we highlighted how the concept of an activity system can be used to reveal the way in which the principle of production positions people to work and learn in different ways. In the case of the latter, we used Engeström's expanded conception of the ZPD (the distance between current and future activity) and his tool of expansion (the CEL) to show how heterogeneous communities can work together to envision a new object (i.e. product or service) and create the new modes of activity required to realise that object.

The fourth source was the concept of reason. We used McDowell's concept of the space of reasons to deepen our use of the aforementioned writers' ideas about learning. Specifically, we showed how learning to engage with an activity (for example, education), or use a cultural tool (for example, a theoretical concept), in any context, pre-supposes being inducted into the reasons that underpin and inform the normal meaning of that activity and its associated cultural tools. We then turned to Brandom's concept of giving and asking for reasons to develop the pedagogic implications of what it means to inhabit the space of reasons. This move enabled us to highlight the implicit hermeneutic and active dimension of conversing with any tradition. This led us to conclude that the creation of mind and hence our capacity to act is greatly enhanced as we understand the relation between concepts and practices; the development of such understanding implies inhabiting the space of reasons that gives and sustains their meaning and, moreover, the development or transformation of concepts and/or practices entails that we expand the space of reasons through establishing more heterogeneous and less homogeneous communities and activities.

In the course of articulating our conceptual position, we identified four mediated expressions of learning that were slightly under-developed within Vygotsky's and the post-Vygotskians' work and that shed light on vitally important aspects of learning. We used the notions of: (i) *restructuring* to conceptualise our continued refinement and development of our higher mental functions throughout the life-course; (ii) *repositioning* to make the implicit link between thinking, communicating and acting explicit; and (iii) *recontextualisation* and *reconfiguration* to pursue the implications of this link by providing a language of description for, in the case of the former, the creative use of existing cultural tools to refashion activity and, in the case of the latter, the creation of new activities. The net effect was the emergence of an iterative and nuanced conception of learning as a mediated process that places the concepts of reason and action as the unifying link between them. Each facet of mediation pre-supposes either understanding existing webs of reason, or generating and communicating the importance of developing more encompassing webs of reason and using such understandings to inform our subsequent action in the world.

Our final observation is that in the process of making the above argument we have referred to three expressions of the development of practice: the evolutionary (i.e. generated by our own agentic activity); the lateral branching (i.e. generated by our use of extant or new knowledge) and the transformatory (i.e. generated by a radical questioning of the object of activity). These terms represent a language of description for the way in which we have, on the one hand, delineated between these different expressions of the development of practice; and, on the other hand, related the development of practice to an explicit or implicit engagement with the object of activity.

The New Tenets of PVWL

Introduction
The preceding summary of the argument developed in this book about the new learning challenge of the knowledge economy has re-affirmed why the concepts of mediation, object, reason and action are central to the reformulation of PVWL that is being undertaken in this final chapter. These concepts are, as we have seen, very different from current thinking and practice in PVWL that is predicated on the notions of adaptation, reflection and qualification. This means that our reformulation of PVWL will involve a significant shift in thinking about its purpose, content and process.

Arguments about 'shifts', as noted in Chapter 5, can appear to imply either a decisive rejection of existing assumptions and practices as regards knowledge and learning, or that it is a fairly mechanical exercise to replace one set of assumptions and practices with another set. Clearly, from the mediated perspective developed in this book, neither outcome is true; rather our argument has been to show the deficiencies of existing assumptions and practices, to accept that the legacy of existing styles of thinking and acting will continue to influence both of those processes, and to identify how alternative ways of thinking expand our options for acting in the world. Hence, our assertion that the notions of mediation, the object of activity and reasons should replace reflection, adaptation and qualifications does not mean that the latter are irrelevant, merely that there are good, even compelling, reasons why they should no longer constitute the bedrock tenets for PVWL. To show why, we will discuss each of the above pairs of assumptions in relation to one another and, in the process, highlight the advantage of making this shift in emphasis. We will then consider the pedagogic implications of our argument.

The shift in the tenets for PVWL. The shift from adaptation to mediation, as we have seen from Chapter 6 onwards, constitutes a fundamentally different starting point for understanding our relation with our environment, and the cultural tools, both symbolic (forms of knowledge) and material (organised activities), that we encounter and use within that environment in general, and in educational institutions and workplaces in specific. The former assumption placed biological maturation and adaptation to external conditions at the centre of human development in Vygotsky's time and its legacy continues to do so today. Given that these ideas have taken root in our collective thinking and discourse, it is hardly surprising that policymakers casually invoke notions of, 'adaptation to the reality of a knowledge economy' as a justification for the formation of lifelong learning policies in general (European Commission, 2000) and as regards the merits of PVWL in particular. The result is that the knowledge economy is reified into a given condition, and policymakers proceed as though there is no other option for them and us other than to 'adapt' to that reality. The mechanisms of adaptation consisting of: higher-level qualifications and qualification frameworks that facilitate mobility between education systems and in the labour market.

The assumption that we work and learn in a mediated environment is predicated on a radically different conception of human development – and its relation to the environment – than the notion of biological adaptation. The cornerstone of a mediated conception of development has been succinctly summarised by Stetsenko (2004, p. 65) as follows:

> The collaborative processes of social practice (including development and passing on, from generation to generation, the collective experiences of people reified in tools, including language) represent a form of exchange with the world that is unique to humans – the social practice of labour, or human activity. In these social and historically specific processes people not only constantly transform and create their environment; they also create and constantly transform their life, consequently changing themselves in fundamental ways and, in the process, gaining self-knowledge about the world.

This quotation is a succinct restatement of one of the themes running through this book, namely that one of the characteristics, to borrow Arendt's (1958) term, of the 'human condition' has always been our capacity to formulate aspirations for, and identify courses of, action to transform our lives – and, in the process, to offer future generations a richer cultural inheritance. We might imagine that the ideas of creation and transformation of the environment will lose their philosophical and aspirational significance and take on a more instrumental orientation when linked to PVWL. This is, however, only the case if we continue to allow the notion of adaptation to a pre-given reality (i.e. knowledge economy) to unconsciously influence our sense of why acts of creativity and transformation are necessary, rather than following the counter-position developed in this book: namely that we have the potential to subjectively, materially and collectively co-evolve activities in ways that constitute better economic, social and political conditions for human life. Vygotsky ideologically and politically positioned himself and his work as an attempt to produce a 'revolutionary' psychology that reflected the turbulent social changes taking place in Russia. Bearing this in mind while working out his approach, our concern to rethink the purpose of PVWL from the Vygotskian-influenced position that we have developed may appear to many 'Vygotskians' as a rather modest, even conservative, engagement with his intellectual legacy.

This is not the case. We have identified three ways in which activity/practice may develop and shown how they pre-suppose different combinations of our expressions of mediation. The first and most common way that practice develops is the broadly anthropological argument that people, through their own *agentive* activity, have continually recontextualised the cultural tools that lie within their immediate environment. This has enabled them to support the forms of practice that they are engaged with to *evolve* and, in the process, to restructure their individual or collective understanding of their practice.

The second way recognises that we continually refine and develop our higher mental functions as we are enculturated into disciplinary and/or professional practices, in educational institutions as well as in workplaces. Such enculturation and development offers people, in principle, different types of contexts and resources that they can use to support practice to *laterally branch out*. This is more likely to happen when the contexts that we inhabit are characterised by epistemic cultures or where such cultures can be developed. This is because some resources – for example, cultural tools (i.e. concepts and methodologies) and cultural codes and conventions (i.e. peer review) – support the identification of problems, the pursuit of inquiries to address those problems and the warranting of findings. It is also because other resources, for example, cultural contexts (i.e. epistemic cultures) facilitate the dissemination of developments in clearly demarcated fields of professional activity. The significance of this lateral branching is, however, temporally contingent on its social recognition: sometimes new knowledge and/or artefacts are produced whose value unfolds over time, for example, the benefits from the Genome Project; on other occasions the value of new knowledge and/or artefacts is grasped more swiftly, for example, the Internet.

The third way is the *transformation* of practice based on the envisioning of a new mode of working and learning. This involves us continually refining and developing our higher mental functions and our practice. One way this can occur is when heterogeneous communities recontextualise extant pedagogic strategies (for example, offline spaces such as boundary-crossing laboratories), and extant tools (for example, the CEL), to generate new principles for the organisation of work, for example, 'co-configuration' and/or 'social production', as well as new products and services, for example, Open Source Software.

Our emphasis on the relation between learning and the development of practice anticipates our second shift – from reflection to the object of activity. This shift entails, firstly, recognising that social practices can be supported to continually unfold in creative – and individually and collectively beneficial – ways, rather than exercising an inhibiting influence on human affairs. This notion of the continual unfolding of social practice predisposes educational institutions and workplaces to replace their pre-occupation with using PVWL to develop a mental strategy to address the assumed theory/practice divide, with a concern to support the lateral branching or reconfiguration of practice. This move means that instead of assuming that our reflections are generated directly by contact with external artefacts, experiences and influences – and that authentic learning means converting direct experience into something more meaningful, most commonly in PVWL programmes, through the use of the pedagogies of reflection, we start from a different under- standing of our relation with the world.

The cornerstone of this position is to recognise that we develop our under- standing of the meaning of social practices that humankind has created, for example, education or work, through our contacts with the world of objects and our engagement with the reasons that underpin the connections and relations that shape the cultural manifestation of and practices associated with that object. The distinctive character of this contact is our engagement with the reasons that underpin the connections and relations, which in turn shape the cultural manifestation of, and practices associated with, that object. This object-related perspective allows us to appreciate the difference and relation between the objective and subjective dimensions of our experience, as opposed to trying to use reflection as a strategy to engage with an external world, and to make sense of our own and others' feelings and emotions about that assumed external world. Our focus on objects re-reminds us that socially sanctioned activities such as education may, on the one hand, take a particular institutional form for historical and pedagogic reasons – and that, if we want to change those institutional forms then we have to call into question the object that has given rise to their constitution; and, on the other hand, that our engagement with education in accordance with its existing manifestations leads us to personalise our experience and, in the process, value some and criticise other aspects of the current organisation of that activity.

Clearly, there is a reflective element running through our deliberations about how we respond to the objective and subjective dimensions of our experience, and the way we might use existing knowledge to call into question the current object of activity. Thus, we are not denying the enduring contribution of reflection to human activity in general and PVWL in particular. Rather, we are acknowledging that when we use the object of activity as the starting point to understand specific social practices and practitioner's practice associated with that practice, then we are less likely to reify reflection into a pedagogic strategy to resolve the theory/practice dilemma in the knowledge economy. Instead, we are more likely to ask whether the object of activity is pre-given: in other words, whether its purpose and the process we are offered to engage with that object has been determined by other parties, and there is little scope for us to vary or contest them, or whether it is a shared object. Moreover, a shared object constitutes the basis, as we saw in Chapter 7, for participants to work together to create an epistemic culture to foster the continuing development of that object and paves the way for the object and its associated concepts and practices to become a resource for others to recontextualise to serve different purposes.

Our discussion of the implications of adopting an object-related perspective has demonstrated that the extent to which we are able to create new objects and their corresponding epistemic cultures is influenced firstly by the principle of production that underlies the existing constitution of an activity. We saw, for example, that the principles of mass production and co-configuration influence the locus of, and scope for, agency in very different ways. The former offers us a very circum-scribed remit for varying or changing the object: the dominant mode of interaction is based on cooperation amongst team members and teamwork is secured through adherence to pre-given performance standards. In contrast, the locus of agency in co-configuration lies in the strong communicative relations that are built between producers and consumer, thus facilitating heterarchical modes of coordination based on collective agreements about the devolution of responsibility for decision-making to different constituencies. Secondly, it is influenced by the extent to which organi-sations have developed the type of epistemic cultures and practices that assist people to engage in the social practice of giving and asking for reasons. This practice is central to the four expressions of mediation, which, used in different combinations, facilitate the evolution, lateral branching or transformation of practice.

The link between objects, cultures and practices and the way in which they can facilitate or inhibit objects and epistemic cultures, rarely surfaces in the policy literature or much of the research literature about learning and the knowledge economy. This is partly because, as we noted in Chapter 1, the dominant policy and educational discourses are a concern for: (i) the way in which all forms of education can be used to foster social cohesion and economic competitiveness (Green, Preston & Janmaat, 2008); and (ii) for way in which qualification frame-works are promoted as the mechanism to support employability and inclusion in the knowledge economy, because they make qualifications more flexible, portable and transparent (Young & Alias, 2009).

Both are laudable goals. Policymakers' attempts to design transnational quali-fication frameworks to support employability and inclusion in the knowledge economy reflect a grain of truth about the relation between qualifications and employment: namely that there is a trade-off between the acquisition of higher-level qualifications and employment in professional fields. Nevertheless, a two-fold problem is masked in this assumption: that the notions of flexibility, portability and transparency are predicated on an assumption that knowledge and skill are discernible items that can be acquired and, as such, represent a proxy measure of our compe-tence to work in a particular field, and unproblematically transferred from one context to another; and that this predication unintentionally perpetuates an individual and mechanistic perspective on the use of knowledge in the economy, as aptly captured by the colloquial phrase, 'application of individual knowledge'. In the process, policymakers unintentionally over-promote the idea that it is ownership of a qualification, rather than engagement with the reasons, inferences and practices associated with a disciplinary or professional field, that will secure employability in the knowledge economy. Both notions are clearly at variance with the character of epistemic cultures and, as a consequence, unintentionally perpetuate miscon-ceptions about the 'knowledge and skill' required for working in such contexts.

To combat this misunderstanding about the nature of, and the knowledge and skill required for, work in the knowledge economy, it is necessary to make the third and final shift in PVWL that we identified above: a shift from qualifications to reasons, inferences and action. This shift means that policymakers should temper both their claim that qualification frameworks will support mobility in the knowledge economy, and their contention that 'outcome statements' actually specify the competence (i.e. forms of knowledge or skill) that people have developed and are required to have in that economy. This claim rests on a 'correspondence' and 'representational' view of the relation between knowledge and practice – which we have demonstrated throughout the book to be both a philosophical misconception of that relation and a misunderstanding of the nature of much work in the knowledge economy – and, as a corollary, either what qualities an employer may be looking for when recruiting or what forms of social capital people may require to create opportunities for themselves to gain employment (Guile, 2009).

A focus on reasons, inferences and action pre-supposes that policymakers rebalance and broaden the focus of their policies for lifelong learning. Policies for lifelong learning should affirm our engagement with the traditions associated with different fields of knowledge or professional/vocational practice as much as on the formal outcome of learning (a qualification). It is vitally important to stress the content (i.e. theoretical, professional and workplace elements) and the process (i.e. pedagogy) and as much as the outcome of learning, because it is our pedagogic immersion in the aforementioned traditions of knowledge that enable us to develop the ability to: (i) inquire by using the reasons that underpin disciplinary or professional fields why they have been constituted in particular ways, and why certain things are or are not the case from the perspective of that field; (ii) use theoretical concepts, allied to professional/vocational experience, as a resource to infer what follows from one's own or other people's processes of reasoning; and (iii) on the basis of discerning other people's intentions and understanding the conclusions that they have formed, act accordingly by offering support or challenging the conclusion and the action that is being proposed on the basis of that conclusion. In contrast, the tendency to break up knowledge into byte-size chunks severs its connection from its constituting tradition and handicaps us from understanding the relation between different modes of knowledge, reasoning and acting.

What emerges from our continual engagement with the traditions associated with different fields of knowledge and professional practice is a mediated mind, that is, a mind capable of forming and acting on the basis of judgements. By this we mean in general terms, responding to reasons, determining their relative worth in relation to the issue-in-hand, and attempting to persuade others about the validity of those reasons and their implications for action in educational or workplace settings. In specific terms, we mean forming judgements as: (i) learners engage with extant theoretical concepts; (ii) professionals work in fields that are primarily concerned with theoretical debates and developments, for example, philosophy and physics; and (iii) professionals work in fields that co-mingle theory and practice to address intra-and interprofessional concerns.

This constitutes a very different notion of an outcome of learning compared with policymakers' affirmation of qualifications as outcomes. Our idea is predicated on the development of the ability to reason, infer and act accordingly. It thus implies that educational institutions and workplaces should accord more attention to pedagogies that facilitate the development of these capabilities, rather than merely concentrating on increasing the 'stocks' of skills as represented by increasing the volume of the population that hold higher-level qualifications. This is because these aforementioned capabilities are a pre-condition to understanding why there are not two separate worlds of knowledge, and how to work collaboratively with others to conceive of new objects and to create new epistemic cultures to support their development.

Enacting the New Tenets for PVWL

Introduction

PVWL can encompass, as we saw earlier, two rather different modes of activity. In one mode, learning is the explicit objective. This mode, however, can take three forms. The classic form is the initial formation of professionals, such as architects and medics, through a formal programme of study and is based on an explicit partnership between higher education institutions (HEIs), professional/vocational institutes and work. The contemporary form is programmes of continuing professional formation to support the reformation of professional expertise and identity, and is based on similar partnerships. These have emerged to assist people to change their profession or to respond to changing economic conditions, and they are primarily led by educational institutions and supported through public funds. In the other mode of PVWL, the primary objective of an activity is the production of goods or services, rather than learning in an educational institution. Learning in this mode of PVWL is an implicit feature of the way in which, for example, architects or medics, work intra- or interprofessionally to solve problems on their own or in partnership with educational institutions (hereafter *curriculum-* or *work-led* PVWL). The next section outlines in ideal–typical terms the way in which our three new tenets for PVWL offer us a way to rethink both expressions of PVWL.

Converging and diverging issues for curriculum- and work-generated PVWL. Our starting premise is that the formulation and instantiation of the new object of activity for curriculum- or work-generated PVWL that we have outlined above pre-supposes the constitution of partnerships. This is hardly an earth-shattering observation: the creation of new activities in general, let alone PVWL programmes, are rarely designed by one organisation alone. From our perspective, the critical issue is that the locus of control as regards membership, purpose and assessment of the outcomes of PVWL should be determined by the partnership. This may not, on first hearing, seem to be a very radical suggestion because stakeholders have been actively involved in designing PVWL curricula for many years.

Our notion of partnership, however, is predicated on a subtle but significant difference from the conventional wisdom in the public policy process about the concept of stakeholder involvement. The latter operates on the basis of pre-given roles and responsibilities, where: national governments define mechanisms of accountability;

higher education institutions (HEIs) determine curricula structures, pedagogic processes and assessment frameworks; and professional/vocational associations/ bodies
determine regulatory issues. In contrast, our conception of partnership is predicated on
the type of 'communitarian' principles – that is, a commitment to forming values,
beliefs and courses of action in public space through debate and deliberation – that
Knorr Cetina and Engeström maintain are, respectively, the pre-conditions for the
development of the types of epistemic cultures that support the lateral branching or
transformation of practice. These principles play out, as we are about to see, rather
differently in curriculum-generated compared with work-generated PVWL.

Enacting the above principles in curriculum-generated PVWL implies, at a
minimum, a three-way dialogue between representatives from education, work and
associations/agencies – for example, professional bodies and/or trade unions, who
have a vested interest in supporting the process of initial and continuing formation.
A slightly different picture tends to emerge in work-generated PVWL. This aim of
this form of PVWL is usually to support continuing intra- and/or interprofessional
formation in a single organisation and/or network, with the result that partnerships
have considerable transactional freedom to determine the object of their collective
activity, and their modes of working and supporting one another to establish the
type of epistemic culture in the partnership to realise that new object.

From our perspective, the very mention of partnerships and the formulation and
instantiation of a new object of activity should, irrespective of the mode of PVWL,
put the relation between innovation and pedagogy centre stage. These issues, as we
saw in Chapter 9, have only recently been viewed in relation to one another. This
is because, on the one hand, the human capital justification for curriculum- and
workplace-generated PVWL has, as we have seen, tended to result in both modes
of PVWL concentrating on the development of stocks of skills, rather than the
facilitating the branching out or creation of new objects of activity in the workplace.
On the other hand, discussions of innovation have tended to focus either on the institutional conditions that facilitate macro-level innovation, or on the discernible
outcomes of an innovative process – for example, patents and intellectual property
rights (IPR) and, in the process, marginalise the contribution of epistemic cultures
and workplace pedagogies to innovation.

Our relational perspective on innovation and pedagogy, as we have shown from
Chapter 4 onwards, has demonstrated that new objects are unlikely to be formulated,
and new normative contexts instantiated for those objects, without consideration
being given to the processes that will facilitate such development. It is our contention
that either type of PVWL partnership could use our three expressions of the
development of practice and our four mediated expressions of learning, to clarify
the purpose of a new PVWL programme (i.e. innovation), and to identify the
processes required to accomplish that goal (i.e. pedagogy). Our distinctions would
provide partnerships with a language of description to help them to, respectively:
decide whether they are looking to support the evolution, lateral branching or
transformation of practice; agree the criteria of representation amongst stakeholders;
and agree the process of working and learning amongst themselves and amongst
those involved in delivering and participating in the new programme.

From our perspective, it is important to draw a parallel between the way in which the partnership and those involved in delivering and participating in the new programme operate. In the case of the former, having agreed the goal, mode of representation and process of working/learning in the partnership, the first step is for stakeholders to ensure that they reposition themselves so that attachment to their current object of activity does not influence the way they are supporting the lateral branching or transformation of practice. One way to achieve this goal is to modify contextually extant working and learning strategies, such as Engeström's cycle of expansive learning. Another way is to draw on the war stories and insights provided by social movements, such as the Open Source movement, who have generated their own repositioning, working and learning strategies.

As suggestions for the content and pedagogy of a new PVWL curriculum, or for working and learning practices in teams are put forward for consideration, the critical challenge for the partnership is to ensure that the reasons that inform those suggestions are made explicit. This process of making the implicit reasoning that lies behind a suggestion explicit will assist stakeholders to gradually develop a shared space of reasons to underpin their deliberations, inference and actions. The building block for this space of reasons is stakeholders' disciplinary, professional, policy, etc., traditions. These traditions provide resources, for example, concepts, heuristics, practices, that stakeholders will draw on to make suggestions about how to instantiate the new object. For these suggestions to co-mingle meaningfully with one another in relation to the new object, it will be vital for stakeholders accept the challenge of inferring what follows from someone else's ideas for their own views and then assess the merit of a suggestion, rather than reject them out-of-hand or because the ideas conflict with how their expertise positions them to respond. This process of collective reconstruction, problematisation and inference is critical to the establishment of a heterogeneous space of reasons (i.e. one that cuts across domains of expertise). This space of reasons will serve slightly different purposes in curriculum-generated compared with work-generated PVWL.

In the case of curriculum-generated PVWL, stakeholders will use the space of reasons to agree criteria to justify their decisions about the selection and recontextualisation of disciplinary and workplace concepts into a new PVWL curriculum. Once this has occurred, those involved with curriculum-generated PVWL are in a position at a later stage (see below) to convey the logic that underpinned their decisions to their colleagues, who will have different responsibilities for implementing the new curriculum in educational institutions and workplaces. This pedagogic process will support those parties to understand why: (i) certain forms of knowledge have been chosen to be recontextualised into the new curriculum; (ii) various pedagogic processes have been suggested to support learners to recontextualise that knowledge in relation to their starting points and interests; and (iii) certain modes of assessment – for example, written academic assignments or portfolios that contain examples of contributions that individuals have made to the development of practice in the workplace – have been recommended.

In the case of people with pedagogic roles in educational institutions and workplaces, they can use their understanding of the logic that lay behind the selection and inclusion of different forms of knowledge, with their different logics of reasoning, in a number of ways. One way is to rethink their existing assumption about the relation between theory and practice. As lecturers grasp the way in which different forms of knowledge have been recontextualised and embedded in practice, they are in a position to restructure their ideas about theory and practice. One form that this restructuring might take is to see theoretical and practical reasoning as different manifestations of conceptually structured judgements and actions, rather than as different kinds of cognitive and material activity. The reasons underpinning this new holistic conception of the theory–practice relation will provide lecturers with resources to support learners to reconsider, and conceivably restructure, their 'folk' notions about the relation between theory and practice. Another way is to support learners to appreciate the conceptualised nature of their work context and work practices, and why the content of the curriculum constitutes a resource for them to both understand and conduct inquiries about existing practice.

These inquiries will require different forms of support depending on whether they are intended to facilitate the lateral branching as opposed to the transformation of practice. Broadly speaking, the former require pedagogic strategies to support participants to recontextualise extant knowledge to facilitate the lateral branching of practice. Stated in minimalist terms, the process of recontextualisation involves: (i) selecting concepts that participants feel may be used to shed light on aspects of their practice; (ii) considering whether those selected need to be supplemented in order to make them more contextually relevant or nuanced as a resource to investigate practice; and, (iii) using the concepts to call into question aspects of practice that are generally taken for granted because they and their meaning appear to be easily apprehended by sensory perception. In contrast, the latter requires programmes of PVWL to support participants to create new knowledge to radically transform practice. The type of new knowledge will be akin to what Engeström (2004) refers to as 'theoretically-grasped practice, in other words, a new single concept or set of concepts that convey the purpose of the new form of practice, and guide decisions about how to implement that concept. The process required here would follow the guidelines we established above, based on Engeström's DWR methodology.

In the case of work-generated PVWL, members of work teams will use the space of reasons to assist one another to understand the reasons that underpin their respective suggestions and practices, rather than to assist them to comprehend the relation between curriculum content and workplace practice. This process of making what is implicit in a suggestion or practice explicit varies slightly depending on whether its aim is to support the lateral branching or transformation of practice. In the case of the former, the process that is most likely to be conducted discursively and animated by text, gestures, actions and sounds, is to support team members to understand why and how forms of knowledge that they are unfamiliar with are embedded in work practice, and how shared knowledge about the constitution of practice is a resource to facilitate change. In the case of the latter, the process that is likely to be conducted in a similar vein, is to support team members to formulate and instantiate a new object.

Our emphasis on a shared object of activity in both modes of PVWL pre-supposes a ZPD that embraces all contributing parties. This type of ZPD is essential because the lateral branching or transformation of practice consists of, as we have seen in Chapters 7 and 9, complex mediated processes. The hallmark of these processes is to support people to enlarge the space of reasons that they usually inhabit by actively participating in the social practice of giving and asking for reasons. The common challenge for curriculum- and work-generated PVWL partnerships is to provide all parties contributing to the formulation phase with opportunities to: (i) complete and form their understanding of a concept or practice they have recently been introduced to by playing back their understanding of the meaning and/or deployment of a concept or practice; (ii) use that understanding to infer what follows for the agreed object of our activity and share their inferences with other participants; and (iii) test out the agreed options.

This social practice is a transcontextual process of learning rather than a feature associated with, or restricted to, one type of context. The capability to give and ask for reasons, rather than attempt to impose a zero-sum solution on a problem, supports people to restructure their taken-for-granted assumptions and habituated responses by forming and communicating ideas about what should happen and why. This capability, as we have endeavoured to show in this book, heralds a rather different conception of expertise compared to long-standing ideas that expertise is characterised by outstanding performance (Chi *et al.*, 1988), or even more recent ideas that it is concerned with progressive problem-solving (Bereiter & Scardamalia, 1993). These conceptions of expertise still rest primarily on a Cartesian view of the world (for example, that knowledge is applied to unmediated environments), and on an individualistic notion of expert performance (for example, that the expert application of knowledge in undertaken in isolation from other experts and with minimal reference to context).

In contrast, the relational conception of expertise that we are arguing is critical to the new role of knowledge in the economy is predicated on a very different set of assumptions. They are that the content and process of any field of expertise are inextricably bound up with one another (for example, in the field of education, pedagogic knowledge is used to inform and guide learning and teaching practice), and that the hallmark of intra- and interprofessional activity is allowing others to understand the basis of one's judgements and actions. Thus we conclude by re-affirming that the development and enactment of expertise is a mediated process, and that the challenge for curriculum- and work-based PVWL is to support people to use their expertise to remediate concepts and practices at the individual and collective level.

CONCLUSION

The premise of this book was that the legacy of the Cartesian conception of the two worlds of knowledge in the social and management theorists' ideas about the new role of knowledge in the economy resulted in a debate about the relative importance of theoretical or tacit knowledge in the economy. From this perspective, the role of PVWL is to recognise and accredit these different types of knowledge.

In contrast, we have interwoven our interpretation of Knorr Cetina's ideas about epistemic cultures, our elaboration and extension of Vygotsky's theory of cultural mediation, and McDowell and Brandom's ideas about reason and action to present a very different conception of the learning challenge of the knowledge economy. Our conception is based on: (i) a philosophical position that acknowledges the difference and relation between forms of knowledge and also identifies the criteria for mediating between different forms of knowledge or knowledge embedded in practice; (ii) a sociological position that explains why epistemic cultures and practices are central to the understanding, lateral branching and/or transformation of knowledge and activity; and, (iii) a pedagogic position that explains why learning can require us to:

- restructure our thinking and acting by locating forms of knowledge and their associated practices in the space of reasons;
- reposition ourselves by questioning the constitution of knowledge and practice in relation to their object of activity;
- recontextualise and/or reconfigure knowledge and practice to achieve new economic, political and social outcomes.

AFTERWORD

This book, with its explicit focus on the constitutive role of culture to the formation of mind and development of social practice, has been written during a period when the scientific study of our nervous systems has undergone a significant increase – principally due to revolutions in molecular biology, electrophysiology and computational neuroscience – and without any reference to that development. The latter development has meant that it is now possible to understand, in much detail, the complex processes occurring within a single neuron. This scientific breakthrough has led many neuroscientists to claim that the last frontier of the biological sciences, namely understanding the biological basis of consciousness, will soon be within our grasp (Kandel *et al.*, 2000).

Although much is still to be learned about the contribution of networks of neurons to the production of intellectual behaviour, cognition, emotion and physiological responses, the value of neuroscientists' accumulating insights about the functioning of the brain has already seized the imagination of some psychologists and educationalists. It has led to the suggestion that these insights will ultimately help: firstly, psychologists to analyse the ways in which we are 'connected' to one another and how that connectedness influences the collective basis of our social life (Christakis & Fowler, 2010); and secondly, education to address the longstanding problem of how to support people to learn more effectively (Blakemore & Frith, 2005). In light of society seemingly being on the threshold of this scientific breakthrough, the cultural argument we have presented in this book about the nature of the learning challenge of the knowledge economy may strike some people as out-of-date. Nothing, however, could be further from the truth.

Writers such as Blakemore and Frith's zealousness to embrace neuroscience rests on their unproblematic acceptance of an assumption about the biological basis of consciousness that is held by neuroscientists and embraced by some eminent philosophers, for example, Dennett and Searle (Bennett *et al*, 2007). This assumption is that consciousness is a biological phenomenon caused by the brain's neural circuitry and, thus, it follows that neuroscientists can explain how people develop from mechanical parts. This ascription of psychological attributes to the brain has convinced Blakemore and Frith (2007, p. 15) that the fruits of neuroscientific research will provide, 'all sorts of new and radically different ways to increase the brain's potential to learn', and that the task of education will be to 'engineer' (2007, p.1) information into people's heads and implant skills into their bodies. They even go so far as to speculate that one day it may be possible to 'pop a pill to learn' (2007, p. 187).

The problem with the neuroscientists' assumptions, from the perspective we have advanced in this book, is that it rests on a view that our mental life consists of states, events and processes that exist in our brain. Whilst it is undoubtedly true that neuroscientists can identify the type of neural correlates, even to a high degree of detail, of our mental activity – for example, what is going on in our head when we see a red car – what neuroscience cannot observe and shed light on is the mental activity itself, in other words, what it was actually like for me or you to see the red car. By not grasping this issue, neuroscientific-inspired educationalists, such as Blakemore and Frith, end up defining the learning challenge as the education of brains rather than of people.

From our perspective, it is certainly reasonable to claim that establishing neural correlates justifies the idea that our brain enables our mindedness, but that falls a long way short of confirming that such functioning is actually constitutive of our minds. What the former disregards is that our mental states are not just collections of representations. Translated into Vygotsky's language, each concept that we learn has a place in a culturally and historically established and developing network of concepts and, moreover, we develop our appreciation and use of that network of concepts as we use them in different ways throughout our life-course. Our concepts help us to form therefore a unified, though not uniform, developing system of thought. Furthermore, we evaluate any new concept or belief that we encounter in relation to how it sheds additional light on or reveals limitations within existing conceptual frameworks and their associated modes of reasoning and acting. Hence, our mind is formed as we engage with different social practices and developed as we change social practices.

The difference between our view and the way that writers such as Blakemore and Frith (2007) interpret neuroscientific research hinges on the following issue. By treating us solely as biological creatures, Blakemore and Frith accept that thought and action can be explained through recourse to causal–scientific considerations. In contrast, the cultural–historical argument that we have presented in this book leads us to conclude that that although we are born mere animals we are 'transformed into thinkers and intentional agents in the course of coming to maturity' (McDowell, 1996, p. 125). What the former account of our mental functioning conveniently overlooks is that although our responsiveness to stimuli, irrespective as to whether they are symbolic or material, may start as a natural process, it undergoes a qualitative transformation throughout the lifecycle. It becomes a normative process, as we are enculturated into social practices and the different logics that have been responsible for their constitution. Thus our distinctive psychological powers reside, as we have maintained, in our responsiveness to reasons and, as a corollary, our development of the capacity for conceptual thought and conceptualised action is formed by operating in and contributing to the enlargement of the space of reasons.

Our conception of our mindedness allowed us to show that it is the norms of rationality in conjunction with neural circuitry that enable us to communicate with one another about (i) issues that have a universal purchase on our experience of the world, for example, Vygotsky's argument about how we learn the meaning of, and then learn to use, the concept of density to guide our thoughts and actions; and (ii) issues that trouble or excite us and, as a consequence, motivate us to, following Engeström, work collaboratively with others to re-think the object of our activity.

Furthermore, our normative account of the development of mind allowed us to show, in contradistinction to Blakemore and Frith's claim that the learning challenge is to engineer new information into learner's heads or implant skills in their bodies, the *mediated* nature of the learning challenge. We did this in two ways. One was to show that learning pre-supposes the ability to: probe why things are 'thus and so' by asking for reasons (i.e. being repositioned in relation to the object of activity); use those reasons to form inferences (i.e. beginning to restructure thought); then explain and convince existing constituencies of interest as to what follows for existing forms of activity (i.e. recontextualising extant cultural tools to support it to branch out); or mobilise new constituencies of interest to create new forms of activity (i.e. reconfiguring activity). The other was to demonstrate that the social practice of giving and asking for reasons constitutes the quintessential human resource for learning in educational and work contexts. Although the resources for this social practice may vary from one context to another – for example, disciplinary subjects rather than work practices – the ability to ask for reasons offers us a way to explore the relation between, for example, the significance of the concept of density in science and in materials used in a workplace.

In essence our argument is that the development of mind and the transformation of forms of activity that constitutes the context for our lives in the twenty-first century is a distinctively human endeavour. Moreover, this endeavour will be continue to be, as Bakhurst (2008), observes, grounded in an appeal to rational considerations based on entailment, probability and plausibility, despite the inevitable frustrations and contradictions associated with these processes, as recent geo-political debates about, for example, how to address the problem of global warning have shown. This position allows us to recognise that the insights that will flow from neuro-science will be an invaluable resource to our understanding of how our organism works and, as a result, are likely to further the development of medical science. Nevertheless, the insights are unlikely to help us to identify the problems that PVWL will have to address, or to devise the pedagogic processes in educational and work contexts to facilitate the resolution of those problems.

BIBLIOGRAPHY

Allen, J. (2002). Symbolic economies: The 'culturalisation of economic knowledge. In P. du Gay & M. Pryke (Eds.), *Cultural economy*. London: Sage.

Anderson, J., Ryder, L., & Simon, H. (1996). Situated learning and education. *Educational Researcher, 25*(4), 5–11.

Archer, M. (1988). *Culture and agency: The place of culture in social theory*. Cambridge: Cambridge University Press.

Arendt, H. (1958). *The human condition*. Chicago: Chicago University Press.

Argyris, C., & Schön, D. (1978). *Organizational learning: A theory of action perspective*. Reading, MA: Addison Wesley.

Arievitch, G. (2004). A potential for an integrated view of development and learning: Galperin's contribution to sociocultural psychology. *Mind, Culture and Activity, 10*(4), 278–288.

Arsneth, H.-C. (2008). A critical account of the concepts of practice and situatedness in relation to activity theory and Lave and Wenger's 'situated learning' – with special relevance to educational research. *Pedagogy, Culture & Society, 16*(3), 289–303.

Arrow, K. J. (1962). The economic implications of learning by doing. *Review of Economic Studies, 39*(80).

Bakhtin, M. (1981). *The dialogic imagination* (M. Holquist, Ed., C. Emmerson & M. Holquist, Trans.). Austin, TX: University of Texas Press.

Bakhtin, M. (1986). *Speech genres and other late essays*. Austin, TX: University of Texas Press.

Bakhurst, D. (1990). Social memory in Soviet thought. In D. Middleton & D. Edwards (Eds.), *Collective remembering*. London: Sage.

Bakhurst, D. (1991). *Consciousness and revolution in Soviet philosophy: From the Bolsheviks to Evald Ilyenkov*. Cambridge: Cambridge University Press.

Bakhurst, D. (1995). Lessons from Ilyenkov. *Communication Review, 1*(2), 155–178.

Bakhurst, D. (1997). Meaning, normativity and the life of the mind. *Language and Communication, 17*(1), 33–51.

Bakhurst, D. (2007). Vygotsky's demons. In H. Daniels, M. Cole, & J. Wertsch (Eds.), *The Cambridge companion to Vygotsky*. Cambridge: Cambridge University Press.

Bakhurst, D. (2007). *Life in the space of reasons: Mood, music, education and the philosophy of John McDowell*. Annual Conference, Philosophy of Education Society of Great Britain, Keynote Lecture.

Bakhurst, D. (2008). Mind, brains and education. *Journal of Philosophy of Education, 42*(3/4), 415–432.

Barnett, M. (2006). Vocational knowledge and vocational pedagogy. In M. Young & J. Gamble (Eds.), *Knowledge, curriculum and qualifications for South African further education*. Pretoria: HSRC Press.

Barnett, R. (1991). *The idea of higher education*. Buckingham: Open University Press.

Barnett, R. (1992). We're all reflective practitioners now. In R. Barnett (Ed.), *Improving higher education: Total quality care*. Buckingham: Open University Press.

Barnett, R. (1997). *Realising the university*. Buckingham: Open University Press.

Barnett, R. (1999). *Higher education: A critical business*. Buckingham: Open University Press.

Bateson, G. (1973). *Steps towards an ecology of mind*. New York: Basic Books.

Baudrillard, J. (1988). *Jean Baudrillard: Selected writings* (M. Poster, Ed.). Stanford, CA: Stanford University Press.

Bauman, X. (1987). *Legislators and interpreters*. London: Polity Press.

Beck, U. (1987). *The risk society*. London: Polity Press.

Beck, U., Giddens, A., & Lash, S. (1994). *Reflexive modernisation*. London: Polity.

Bell, D. (1973). *The coming of post-industrial society: A venture in social forecasting*. New York: Basic Books.

Bell, D. (1979). *Cultural contradictions of capitalism*. New York: Basic Books.

Bell, D. (1999). Foreword: The axial age of technology. In *The coming of post-industrial society*. [Special Anniversary ed.]. New York: Basic Books.

Benkler, Y. (2006). *The wealth of networks*. New Haven, CT: Yale University Press.

Bennett, M., Dennett, D., Hacker, P., & Searle, J. (2007). *Neuroscience and philosophy: Mind, brain and language*. Oxford: Blackwell.

Berducci, D. (2004). Vygotsky through Wittgenstein. *Theory & Psychology, 14*(3), 329–353.

Bereiter, C., & Scardamalia, M. (1993). *Surpassing ourselves: An inquiry into the nature and implications of expertise*. La Salle, IL: Open Court.

Bernstein, B. (2000). *Pedagogy, symbolic control and identity: Theory, research and critique*. London: Taylor and Francis.

Bernstein, J. M. (2002). Re-enchanting nature. In N. H. Smith (Ed.), *Reading McDowell: On mind and world*. London, New York: Routledge.

Bernstein, R. J. (1971). *Praxis and action*. Philadelphia: University of Philadelphia Press.

Bernstein, R. J. (2002). McDowell's domesticated Hegelianism. In N. H. Smith (Ed.), *Reading McDowell: On mind and world*. London, New York: Routledge.

Billett, S. (2002). Workplace pedagogic practice: Co-participation and learning. *British Journal of Educational Studies, 50*(4), 457–481.

Billett, S. (2007). Including the missing subject: Placing the personal within the community. In J. Hughes, N. Jewson, & L. Unwin (Eds.), *Communities of practice: Critical perspectives*. London: Routledge.

Billett, S. (2009). Conceptualizing learning experiences: Contributions and mediations of the social, personal and brute. *Mind, Culture and Activity, 16*(1), 32–47.

Bilton, C. (2007). *Management and creativity: From creative industries to creative management*. Oxford: Blackwell Publishing.

Bishop, C. (2007). *Installation art*. New York: Routledge.

Blakemore, S. J., & Frith, U. (2005). *The learning brain: Lessons for education*. Oxford: Oxford University Press.

Boisot, M. H. (1995). Is your firm a creative destroyer? Competitive learning and knowledge flows in the technological strategies of firms. *Research Policy, 24*(4), 489–506.

Boreham, B., Fischer, M., & Samurçay, R. (2002). *Work process knowledge*. London: Routledge.

Boud, D., & Soloman, N. (Eds.). (2001). *Work-based learning: A new higher education?* Buckingham: SRHE/Open University.

Boud, D., Cressey, P., & Doherty, P. (2009). *Productive reflection at work*. London: Routledge.

Bourdieu, P. (1977). *The logic of practice*. London: Polity Press.

Bowker, G., & Star, S. L. (2000). *Sorting things out: Classification and its consequences*. Cambridge, MA: MIT Press.

Bradbury, H., Frost, N., Kilminster, S., & Zukas, M. (Eds.). (2009). *Beyond reflective practice: New approaches to professional lifelong learning*. London: Routledge.

Brandom, R. (1995). Knowledge and the social articulation of the space of reasons. *Philosophy and Phenomenological Research, 55*, 895–908.

Brandom, R. (2000a). *Articulating reasons: An introduction to inferentialism*. Cambridge, MA: Harvard University Press.

Brandom, R. (2000b). Facts, norms and normative facts: A reply to Habermas. *European Journal of Philosophy, 8*(3), 356–374.

Brandom, R. (2002). *Tales of the mighty dead*. Cambridge, MA: Harvard University Press.

Brandom, R. (2009). *Reason in philosophy: Animating ideas*. Cambridge, MA: Harvard University Belknap Press.

Bridges, D. (2002). Back to the future: The higher education curriculum in the 21st century. *Cambridge Journal of Education, 30*(1), 37–55.

Brockbank, I., & McGill, S. (1998). *Facilitating reflective learning in higher education*. Buckingham: Open University Press.

Brown, P., & Lauder, H. (2003). Collective intelligence. In S. Baron, T. Schuller, & J. Field (Eds.), *Social capital: Critical perspectives*. Oxford: Oxford University Press.

Bruegger, U., & Knorr Cetina, K. (2002). Global microstructures: The virtual societies of financial markets. *American Journal of Sociology, 107*(4), 909–950.

Bruner, J. (1978). Prologue to the English edition. In L. S. Vygotsky (Ed.), *The collected works of L. S. Vygotsky: Problems of general psychology* (Vol. 1, including the volume 'Thinking and Speech'; N. Minick, Trans., R. W. Reiber & A. S. Carton, Eds.). New York: Plenum Press.

Bruner, J. (1986). *Actual minds, possible worlds*. Cambridge, MA: Harvard University Press.

Bubner, R. (2002). Bildung and second nature. In B. Smith (Ed.), *Reading McDowell*. London: Routledge.

Burgess, T. (1993). Reading Vygotsky. In H. Daniels (Ed.), *Charting the agenda: Educational activity after Vygotsky*. London: Routledge.

Burke, T. (1994). *Dewey's new logic*. Chicago: University of Chicago Press.

Calhoun, C. (2000). Resisting globalisation or shaping it? *Prometheus, 4*, 29–47.

Callinicos, A. (1989). *Against postmodernism*. Cambridge: Cambridge University Press.

Campbell, J. (1995). *Understanding John Dewey. Nature and cooperative intelligence*. Chicago: Open Court.

Castells, M. (1989). *The informational city*. Oxford: Blackwell.

Castells, M. (1996). *The rise of the network society* (Vol. 1. The information age: Economy, society and culture.). London: Macmillan.

Castells, M. (2000). *The rise of the network society* (Vol. 1. The information age: Economy, society and culture.) (2nd ed.). Oxford: Blackwell.

Caves, R. (2000). *Creative industries: Contacts between art and industry*. Harvard, MA: Harvard University Press.

Cazden, C. (1981). Performance before competence: Assistance to child development in the zone of proximal development. *Quarterly Newsletter of the Laboratory of Human Cognition, 3*, 5–8.

Chaiklin, S. (2008, November 29). *Lecture*. Institute of Education, London.

Chaiklin, S. (2003). The zone of proximal development in Vygotsky's analysis of learning. In A. Kozulin, B. Gindis, V. Ageyev, & S. Miller (Eds.), *Vygotsky's educational theory in context*. Cambridge: Cambridge University Press.

Chaiklin, S., & Lave, J. (1993). *Understanding practice: Perspectives on activity and context*. Cambridge: Cambridge University Press.

Chi, M., Glaser, R., & Farr, M. (1988). *The nature of expertise*. Hillsdale, NJ: Lawrence Earlbaum Press.

Christakis, C., & Fowler, J. (2010). *Connected*. New York: Harper Press.

Churchland, P. (1989). *A Neurocomputational perspective: The nature of mind and the structure of science*. Cambridge, MA: MIT Press.

Clark, A. (1997). *Being there: Putting brain, body and world together again*. Cambridge, MA: MIT Press.

Coase, R. (1937). The nature of the firm. *Economica, 2*(2), 386–405.

Colardyn, D., & Bjornavöld, J. (2004). Validation of formal, non-formal and informal learning: Policy and practices in EU-member states. *European Journal of Education, 39*, 69–89.

Cole, M. (1996). *Cultural psychology: A once and future discipline*. Cambridge, MA: Harvard University Press.

Committee on Higher Education (appointed by the Prime Minister under the chairmanship of Lord Ribbins). (1961–1963). *Higher education*. [Appendix 4: Administrative, financial and economic aspects of higher education.] London: HMSO.

Cook, D., & Seely Brown, J. (2000). Bridging epistemologies: The generative dance between organizational knowledge and organizational knowing. *Organizational Science, 10*(4), 381–400.

Cortada, R. (1998). *The rise of the knowledge worker*. London: Butterworth-Heinemann.

Cowan, R., David, P. A., & Foray, D. (2000). The explicit economics of knowledge, codification and tacitness. *Industrial and Corporate Change, 9*(2), 211–253.

Dall'Alba, G., & Sandberg, J. (1996). Educating for competence in professional practice. *Instructional Science, 24*(1.3), 411–437.

Dalton, T. (2002). *Becoming John Dewey: Dilemmas of a philosopher and naturalist*. Bloomington, IN: Indiana University Press.

Dancy, J. (2006). Acting in the light of appearances. In C. Macdonald & G. Macdonald (Eds.), *McDowell and his critics*. Oxford: Blackwell.

BIBLIOGRAPHY

Daniels, H. (2001). *Vygotsky and pedagogy*. London: Routledge.
Daniels, H. (2008). *Vygotsky and research*. London: Routledge.
Davenport, T., & Prusak, L. (1997). *Working knowledge: How organisations manage what they know*. Boston, MA: Harvard Business School Press.
Davydov, V. V. (1990). *Types of generalization in instruction*. Reston, VA: National Council of Teachers of Mathematics.
Davydov, V. V., & Radzikhovskii, L. A. (1985). Vygotsky's theory and the activity-oriented approach in psychology. In J. V. Wertsch (Ed.), *Culture, communication, and cognition: Vygotskian perspectives*. Cambridge: Cambridge University Press.
DCMS. (2001). *The creative industries mapping document 2001*. Retrieved from http://www.culture. gov.uk/global/ publications/archive_2001/ci_mapping_doc_2001.htm
de Certeau, M. (1984). *The practice of everyday life*. Berkeley, CA: University of California Press.
Delanty, G. (2001). *Challenging knowledge*. Buckingham: Open University Press.
Dennett, D. (1987). *The intentional stance*. Cambridge, MA: MIT Press.
Derrida, J. (1976). *Of grammatology* (G. Spivak, Trans.). Baltimore: John Hopkins University Press.
Derry, J. (2003). *Vygotsky and philosophy*. Unpublished PhD Thesis, Institute of Education, University of London, London.
Derry, J. (2008). Abstract rationality in education: From Vygotsky to Brandom. *Studies in Philosophy & Education, 27*(1), 49–62.
Deuze, M. (2007). *Media work*. London: Sage.
de Vries, W. (1996). Hegel on reference and knowledge. *Journal of the History of Philosophy, 26*, 297–307.
Dewey, J. (1887/1967). Psychology. In J. A. Boyston (Ed.), *John Dewey: The early works 1882–1898* (Vol. 2). Carbondale, IL: Southern Illinois University Press.
Dewey, J. (1910/86). How we think: A restatement of the relation of reflective thinking to the educative process. In J. A. Boyston (Ed.), *John Dewey: The later works 1925–1953* (Vol. 1). Carbondale, IL: Southern Illinois University Press.
Dewey, J. (1925/53). From absolutism to experimentalism. In J. A. Boyston (Ed.), *John Dewey: The later works 1925–1953* (Vol. 5). Carbondale, IL: Southern Illinois University Press.
Dewey, J. (1925/81). Experience and nature. In J. A. Boyston (Ed.), *John Dewey: The later works 1925–1953* (Vol. 1). Carbondale, IL: Southern Illinois University Press.
Dewey, J. (1929/88). The quest for certainty. In J. A. Boyston (Ed.), *John Dewey: The later works 1925–1953* (Vol. 4). Carbondale, IL: Southern Illinois University Press.
Dewey, J. (1938/89). Logic: The theory of inquiry. In J. A. Boyston (Ed.), *John Dewey: The later works 1925–1953* (Vol. 12). Carbondale, IL: Southern Illinois University Press.
DfES. (2003). *The future of higher education*. London: The Stationery Office.
Dosi, G. (1988). *Technical change and economic theory*. London: Pinter.
Dreyfuss, H., & Dreyfuss, S. (1986). *Mind over machine*. New York: Free Press.
Drucker, P. (1969). *The age of discontinuities*. London: Transaction Publications.
du Gay, P., & Pryke, M. (Eds.). (2002). *Cultural economy*. London: Sage.
Dyson, J. R. (1987). *Accounting for non-accounting students*. London: Pitman.
Ecclestone, K. (2004). *Understanding assessment and qualifications in post-compulsory education: Principles, politics and practice* (2nd ed.). London: NIACE.
Edwards, A. (2001). Researching pedagogy: A sociocultural agenda. *Pedagogy, Culture and Society, 9*(2), 161–186.
Edwards, A. (2004). *Let's get beyond community and practice: The many meanings of learning by participating*. [Paper circulated at the first 'Sharing Expertise – Work-related Learning' Workshop, University of Warwick, 18 October.]
Edwards, A. (2007). An interesting resemblance: Vygotsky, Mead and American pragmatism. In H. Daniels, M. Cole, & J. Wertsch (Eds.), *The Cambridge companion to Vygotsky*. Cambridge: Cambridge University Press.
Edwards, A., Daniels, H., Gallagher, T., Leadbetter, J., & Warmington, P. (2009). *Improving inter-professional collaborations: Multi-agency working for children's wellbeing*. London: Routledge.

Edwards, R. (2000). *Globalisation and pedagogy: Space, place and identity*. London: Routledge.

Edwards, R., & Usher, R. (1994). *Postmodernism and education*. London: Routledge.

Edwards, R., & Usher, R. (2000). *Globalisation and pedagogy*. London: Routledge.

Engeström, Y. (1987). *Learning by expanding: An activity-theoretical approach to developmental research*. Helsinki: University of Finland.

Engeström, Y. (1999). Activity theory and individual and social transformation. In Y. Engeström, R. Miettinen, & R.-L. Punamaki (Eds.), *Perspectives on activity theory*. Cambridge: Cambridge University Press.

Engeström, Y. (2001). Expansive learning at work: Toward an activity-theoretical reconceptualisation. *Journal of Education and Work, 14*(1), 133–156.

Engeström, Y. (2004). The new generation of expertise: Seven theses. In H. Rainbird, A. Fuller, & A. Munro (Eds.), *Workplace learning in context*. London: Taylor Francis.

Engeström, Y. (2008). *From teams to knots: Activity-theoretical studies of collaboration and learning at work*. Cambridge: Cambridge University Press.

Engeström, Y., & Keruso, H. (Eds.). (2007). From workplace learning to inter-organizational learning and back: The contribution of activity theory. *Journal of Workplace Learning, 19*(6), 336–342.

Engeström, Y., Miettinen, R., & Punamaki, R.–L. (Eds.). (1999). *Perspectives on activity theory*. Cambridge: Cambridge University Press.

Engeström, Y., & Miettinen, R. Introduction. In Engeström, Y., Virkkunen, J., Helle, M., Pihlaja, J., & Poikela, R. (1996). Change laboratory as a tool for transforming work. *Lifelong Learning in Europe, 1*(2), 10–17.

Eraut, M. (2004). Informal learning in the workplace. *Studies in Continuing Education, 26*(2), 247–273.

Etzkowitz, H., & Leydesdorff, L. (1997). *Universities in the global knowledge economy: A triple helix of academic–industry–government relations*. London: Cassell.

European Commission (EC). (1995). *Teaching and learning: Towards the learning society*. Brussels: EC.

European Commission (EC). (2000). *Memorandum on lifelong learning*. Brussels: EC.

Evans, K., Guile, D., & Harris, J. (forthcoming). Putting knowledge to work: Conceptual and practical issues. *Journal of Nursing Education*.

Felstead, A., Fuller, A., Jewsom, N., & Unwin, L. (2009). *Improving working as learning*. London: Routledge.

Florida, R. (2002). *The rise of the creative class*. New York: Basic Books.

Foray, D., & Lundvall, B.-Å. (1996). The knowledge-based economy: From the economics of knowledge to the learning economy. In *Learning and growth in the knowledge-based economy*. Paris: OECD.

Forrester, T. (1985). *The information technology revolution*. Oxford: Blackwell.

Foucault, M. (1970). *The order of things: An archaeology of the human sciences*. London: Tavistock.

Fukuyama, F. (1992). *The end of history and the last man*. London: Hamish Hamilton.

Fullan, M. (2001). *The new meaning of educational change*. London: Falmer.

Fuller, S. (1997). *Science*. Buckingham: SRHE, Open University Press.

Fuller, S. (2003). Can universities solve the problem of knowledge in society without succumbing to the knowledge society? *Policy Futures, 1*(1), 106–124.

Fulton, O. (1996). *Work-based learning and its accreditation: Can higher education deliver?* [Evaluation of the DfEE's work-based learning theme; final report.] Lancaster: CSET.

Gadamer, H. G. (1989). *Truth and method* (J. Weinsheimer & D. G. Marshall, Trans.). (2nd ed.). New York: Crossroad.

Garfinkle, H. (1967). *Studies in ethnomethodology*. Upper Saddle River, NJ: Prentice Hall.

Garrison, J. (1995). Dewey's philosophy and the experience of working: Labour, tool and language. *Synthese, 105*(1), 87–144.

Garrison, J. (2001). Dewey and Eros: A response to Prawat. *Teachers College Record, 103*(4), 722–738.

Garrison, J. (2002). An introduction to Dewey's theory of 'trans-action': An alternative paradigm for activity theory. *Mind, Culture and Activity, 8*(4), 275–296.

Garrison, J. (2006). The "permanent deposit" of Hegelian thought in Dewey's theory of inquiry. *Educational Theory, 56*(1), 1–37.

Geertz, G. (1973). *The interpretation of cultures*. New York: Basic Books.

Gergen, K. (1994). *Realities and relationships*. Cambridge, MA: University of Harvard Press.

Gibbons, M., Limoges, C., Nowotny, H., Schwartzmann, S., Scott, P., & Trow, M. (1994). *The new production of knowledge*. London: Sage.

Gibson, J. (1979). *The ecological approach to perception*. Boston: Houghton Mifflin.

Giddens, A. (1984). *The constitution of society: Outline of the theory of structuration*. Oxford: Polity.

Giddens, A. (1990). *The consequences of modernity*. Stanford, CA: Stanford University Press.

Gladwell, M. (2005). *Blink: The power of thinking without thinking*. Boston: Little, Brown.

Gokulsing, K., & de Costa, C. (Eds.). (1997). *Usable knowledge as the goal of university education*. Lampet: Edwin Mallen Press.

Goodwin, C. (1994). Professional vision. *American Anthropologist, 96*, 606–636.

Green, A., Preston, J., & Janmaat, G. (2008). *Education, equality and social cohesion: A comparative analysis*. London: Palgrave.

Guile, D. (2001). Work experience in the European knowledge economy. *Journal of Education and Work, 15*(3), 251–276.

Guile, D. (2006). What knowledge in the knowledge economy? In H. Lauder, P. Brown, J. A. Dillabough, & A. A. Halsey (Eds.), *Education, globalisation & social change*. Oxford: Oxford University Press.

Guile, D. (2007). Moebius-strip enterprises and expertise: Challenges for lifelong learning. *International Journal of Lifelong Education, 26*(3), 241–261.

Guile, D. (2009). *Research paper*. LLAKES Centre, Institute of Education.

Habermas, J. (2000). From Kant to Hegel: On Robert Brandom's pragmatic philosophy of language. *European Journal of Philosophy, 8*(3), 322–355.

Hage, J., & Powers, C. (1992). *Post-industrial lives: Role and relationships in the 21st century*. London: Sage.

Hall, R., Stevens, R., & Torroba, T. (2003). Disrupting representational infrastructure in conversations across disciplines. *Mind, Culture and Activity, 9*(2), 179–210.

Hanks, W. (1991). Foreword. In J. Lave & E. Wenger (Eds.), *Situated learning*. Cambridge: Cambridge University Press.

Haraway, D. (1989). *Primate visions: Gender, race and the nature of the world in modern science*. New York: Routledge.

Hartley, D. (1997). *Re-schooling society*. London: Falmer.

Hatchuel, A., & Weil, B. (1994). *Experts in organisations*. Berlin: Walter de Greyer.

Heckscher, C., & Adler, P. (2007). *The firm as a collaborative community*. Oxford: Oxford University Press.

Hedegaard, M. (2001). *Learning and child development*. Aarhus: Aarhus University Press.

Heidegger, M. (1962). *Being and time* (Re-translated by Joan Stambaugh). Albany, NY: State University of New York Press, 1996.

Hickman, L. (1990). *John Dewey's pragmatic technology*. Bloomington and Indianapolis, IN: Indiana University Press.

Hirschorn, L. (1987). *Beyond mechanization*. Cambridge, MA: MIT Press.

Holquist, D. (1990). *Dialogism: Bakhtin and his world*. London: Routledge.

Houlgate, S. (2006). Thought and experience in Hegel and McDowell. *Journal of Philosophy, 14*(2), 242–261.

Hoyles, C., Noss, R., Kent, P., & Bakker, P. (2010). *Improving Mathematics at Work*. London: Routledge.

Hughes, J., Jewson, N., & Unwin, L. (2007). *Communities of practice: Critical perspectives*. London: Routledge.

Hutchins, E. (1995). *Cognition in the wild*. Cambridge, MA: MIT Press.

Hyysalo, S. (2005). Objects and motives in a product design process. *Mind, Culture and Activity, 12*(1), 19–36.

Ilyenkov, E. V. (1977a). The concept of the ideal. In *Philosophy in the USSR: Problems of dialectical materialism*. Moscow: Progress Press.

Ilyenkov, E. V. (1977b). *Dialectical logic: Essays on its history and theory.* Moscow: Progress Press.

Jacob, M., & Hellstrom, T. (Eds.). (1999). *The future of knowledge production in the academy.* Buckingham: SRHE, Open University Press.

Jensen, K., & Lahn, L. (2005). The binding role of knowledge: An analysis of nursing students' knowledge ties. *Journal of Education and Work, 18*(3), 305–320.

Jensen, K., Lahn, L., & Nerland, M. (2010). *Professional learning in the knowledge society.* Rotterdam: Sense Publications.

Jessop, B., Fairclough, N., & Wodak, R. (2008). *The knowledge-based economy in higher education in Europe.* Rotterdam: Sense.

Jones, P. (2009). Breaking away from Capital? Theorising activity in the shadow of Marx. *Outlines, 1(1),* 45–57

Johnson, B., Lorenz, E., & Lundvall, B.–Å. (2002). Why all this fuss about codified and tacit knowledge? *Industrial and Corporate Change, 11*(2), 245–262.

Jonsen, A., & Toulmin, S. (1988). Theory and practice. In A. Jonsen & S. Toulmin (Eds.), *The abuse of casuistry: A history of moral reasoning.* Los Angeles: University of California Press.

Kandel, E. R., Schwartz, J. H., & Jessell, T. M. (2000). *Principles of neuroscience* (4th ed.). New York: McGraw-Hill.

Kant, E. (1929). *Critique of pure reason.* London: Macmillan.

Kaptelinin, V. (2006). The object of activity: Making sense of the sense-maker's mind. *Mind, Culture and Activity, 12*(1), 4–19.

Kerr, C. (1963). *The uses of the university.* Cambridge, MA: Harvard University Press.

Knorr Cetina, K. (1997). Sociality with objects: Social relations in post-social knowledge societies. *Theory, Culture and Society, 14*(4), 1–30.

Knorr Cetina, K. (1999). *Epistemic communities.* Harvard: Harvard Education Press.

Knorr Cetina, K. (2001). Transitions in post-social knowledge societies. In E. Ben-Rafael & Y. Sternberg (Eds.), *Identity, culture and globalization.* Leiden, Boston, Köln: Brill.

Knorr Cetina, K. (2006). Knowledge in a knowledge society: Five transitions. *Knowledge, Work & Society, 4*(3), 23–41.

Kolb, D. (1978). *Experiential learning: Experience as the source of learning and development.* Englewood Cliffs, NJ: Prentice Hall.

Koschmann, T., Kutti, K., & Hickman, L. (1998). The concept of breakdown in Heidegger, Leont'ev and Dewey, and its implications for education. *Mind, Culture and Activity, 5*(1), 25–41.

Kozulin, A. (1998). *Psychological tools: A Socio-cultural approach to education.* Cambridge, MA: Harvard University Press.

Kozulin, A. (1990). *Vygotsky's psychology: A biography of ideas.* Cambridge, MA: Harvard University Press.

Kumar, K. (1995). *From post-industrial to post-modern society.* Oxford: Blackwell.

Lahn, I. (2003, August 26–30). *Developmental transfer: A look from the outside.* Paper presented at EARLI 10th Biennial conference, Padua.

Langemeyer, I., & Roth, W.-M. (2006). Is cultural–historical activity theory threatened to fall short of its own principles and possibilities in empirical research? *Outlines: Critical Social Studies, 4*(1), 20–42.

Larmore, C. (2002). Attending to reason. In B. Smith (Ed.), *Reading McDowell.* London: Routledge.

Lash, S., Szerszynski, B., & Wynne, B. (Eds.). (1996). *Risk, environment and modernity.* London: Sage.

Lash, S., & Urry, J. (1994). *Economies of signs and spaces.* London: Sage.

Latour, B. (2000). When things strike back: A possible contribution of science studies to social studies. *British Journal of Sociology, 51*(1), 107–124.

Lave, J. (1988). *Cognition in practice: Mind, mathematics and culture in everyday life.* Cambridge: Cambridge University Press.

Lave, J. (1996). Teaching as learning. *Mind, Culture and Activity, 3*(3), 149–164.

Lave, J., & Wenger, E. (1991). *Situated learning: Legitimate peripheral participation.* New York: Cambridge University Press.

Layton, D. (1993). *Technology's challenge to science education.* Buckingham: Open University Press.

Leadbetter, C. (1999). *Living on thin air*. London: Viking.

Lee, B. (1985). Intellectual origins of Vygotsky's semiotic analysis. In J. Wertsch (Ed.), *Culture, communication and cognition*. Cambridge: Cambridge University Press.

Lemke, J. (1999). Meaning-making in the conversation: Head spinning, heart winning, and everything in between. *Human Development, 42*(2), 87–91.

Leont'ev, A. N. (1978). *Activity, consciousness, and personality*. Englewood Cliffs, NJ: Prentice-Hall.

Leont'ev, A. N. (1981a). The problem of activity in psychology. In J. V. Wertsch (Ed.), *The concept of activity in Soviet psychology*. Armonk, NY: M. E. Sharpe.

Leont'ev, A. N. (1959/81b). *Problems of the development of the mind*. Moscow: Progress Press.

Leont'ev, A. N. (1983). Activity, consciousness and personality. In V. Davydov, V. Zinchenko, A. N. Leont'ev, & A. Petrovskij (Eds.), *A. N. Leont'ev: Selected papers*. Moscow: Pedagogigika.

Lewin, K. (1984). *Resolving social conflicts: Selected papers on group dynamics*. New York: Harpers and Brothers.

Livingstone, D., & Sawchuk, P. (2003). *Hidden knowledge: Organised labour in the information age*. New York: Rowan and Littlefield.

Lundvall, B.-Å. (Ed.). (1992). *National systems of innovation: Towards a theory of innovation and interactive learning*. London: Pinter.

Lundvall, B.-Å. (1996). *The social dimensions of the learning economy*. Working papers; DRUID: Copenhagen Business School, Department of Industrial Economics and Strategy; Aalborg University, Department of Business Studies.

Lundvall, B.-Å., & Archibugi, D. (2001). *The globalizing learning economy*. New York: Oxford University Press.

Lyon, D. (2000). Net, self and future. *Prometheus, 4*, 58–68.

Lyotard, J.-F. (1984). *The postmodern condition: A report on knowledge*. Minneapolis, MN: University of Minnesota Press.

Machlup, F. (1962). *The production and distribution of knowledge in the United States*. Princeton, NJ: Princeton University Press.

Mason, G. (2002). High skills utilisation under mass higher education: Graduate employment in service industries in Britain. *Journal of Education and Work, 15*, 427–456.

Marx, K. (1977). *Economic and philosophical manuscripts of 1844*. Moscow: Progress Press.

McDowell, J. (1995). Knowledge and the internal. *Philosophy and Phenomenological Research, 55*, 877–893.

McDowell, J. (1996). *Mind and world* (2nd ed.). Cambridge, MA: Harvard University Press.

McDowell, J. (2002). Responses. In N. H. Smith (Ed.), *Reading McDowell: On mind and world*. London, New York: Routledge.

McDowell, J. (2007a). What myth? *Inquiry, 50*(4), 338–351.

McDowell, J. (2007b). Response to Dreyfuss. *Inquiry, 50*(4), 366–370.

McDowell, J. (2009a). *Having the world in view: Essays on Kant, Hegel, and Sellars*. Cambridge, MA: Harvard University Press.

McDowell, J. (2009b). *The engaged intellect: Philosophical essays*. Cambridge, MA: Harvard University Press.

Meshcheryakov, B. (2007). Terminology in L. S. Vygotsky's writings. In H. Daniels, M. Cole, & J. Wertsch (Eds.), *The Cambridge companion to Vygotsky*. Cambridge: Cambridge University Press.

Miettinen, R. (2000). The concept of experiential learning and John Dewey's theory of reflexive thought. *International Journal of Lifelong Learning*, Jan–Feb, 54–72.

Miettinen, R. (2001). Artifact mediation in Dewey and in cultural–historical activity theory. *Mind, Culture and Activity, 8*(4), 297–308.

Miettinen, R. (2005). Object of activity and individual motivation. *Mind, Culture and Activity, 12*, 52–76.

Miettinen, R. (2006a). Epistemology of material transformative activity: John Dewey's pragmatism and cultural–historical activity theory. *Journal for the Theory of Social Behaviour, 36*(4), 389–408.

Miettinen, R. (2006b). The source of novelty: A cultural and systemic view of distributed creativity. *Creativity and Innovation Management, 15*(2), 173–181.

Minick, N. (1985). *L. S. Vygotsky and Soviet activity theory: New perspectives on the relationship between mind and society*. San Diego, CA: San Diego University Press.

Minick, N. (1987). The development of Vygotsky's thought: An introduction. In L. S. Vygotsky (Ed.), *The collected works of L. S. Vygotsky: Problems of general psychology* (Vol. 1, including the volume 'Thinking and Speech'; N. Minick, Trans., R. W. Reiber & A. S. Carton, Eds.). New York: Plenum Press.

Moore, R., & Young, M. (2001). Knowledge and the curriculum: Towards a reconceptualisation. *British Journal of the Sociology of Education, 22*(4), 445–461.

Muller, J. (2000). *Reclaiming knowledge*. London: Falmer.

Muller, J. (2001). Concluding comments: Connectivity, capacity and knowledge. In J. Muller & B. Closete (Eds.), *Challenging globalisation*. Durban, South Africa: Maskew, Miller and Longman.

National Committee of Inquiry into Higher Education (NCIHE). (1997). *Higher education in the learning society*. London: HMSO.

Nelson, R., & Winter, S. (1972). In search of a useful theory of innovation. *Research Policy, 6*(1), 36–77.

Nerland, M. (2008). Knowledge cultures and the shaping of work-based learning: The case of computer engineering. *Vocations and Learning, 1*(1), 49–69.

Nerland, M., & Jensen, K. (2010). Objectual practice and learning in professional work. In S. Billet (Ed.), *Learning through practice: Models, traditions, orientations and approaches*. New York: Springer.

Nietzsche, F. (1976a). *The portable Nietzsche* (W. Kaufman, Ed. and Trans.). New York: Penguin.

Nietzsche, F. (1976b). *The will to power* (W. Kaufman & R. J. Hollingdale, Eds. and Trans.). New York: Vintage.

Noble, D. (1986). *Forces of production: A social history of industrial automation*. Oxford: Oxford University Press.

Nonaka, I., & Konno, N. (1998). The concept of 'Ba': Building a foundation for knowledge creation. *Californian Management Review, 40*(3), 40–54.

Nonaka, I., & Takeuchi, H. (1995). *The knowledge creating company*. New York: Oxford University Press.

Nowotny, H., Scott, P., & Gibbons, M. (2002). *Re-thinking science*. London: Polity Press.

O'Doherty, B. (1976). *Inside the white cube*. Berkeley, CA: University of California Press.

OECD (Organisation for Economic Co-operation and Development). (1996). *The knowledge-based economy*. Paris: OECD.

Orlinkowski, W. (1992). The duality of technology: Rethinking the concept of technology in organizations. *Organizational Science, 3*(3), 398–427.

Osborne, T. (1998). *Aspects of enlightenment*. London: University College London Press.

Packer, M. J. (2008). Is Vygotsky's psychology still relevant: Vygotsky's Marxist psychology. *Mind, Culture and Activity, 15*(1), 8–31.

Penrose, E. (1959). *The theory of growth of the firm*. Oxford: Blackwell.

Peters, M. (2007). *Knowledge economy, development and the future of higher education*. Rotterdam: Sense.

Piaget, J. (1970). *Genetic epistemology*. New York: Cambridge University Press.

Pinkard, T. (1994). *Hegel's phenomenology: The sociality of reason*. Cambridge: Cambridge University Press.

Pinker, S. (2007). *The stuff of thought: Language as a window into human nature*. New York: Penguin.

Pippin, R. (2002). Leaving nature behind: Or two cheers for 'subjectivism'. In B. Smith (Ed.), *Reading McDowell*. London: Routledge.

Polanyi, M. (1958). *Personal knowledge: Towards a post-critical philosophy*. London: Routledge & Kegan Paul.

Polanyi, M. (1966). *The tacit dimension*. London: Routledge & Kegan Paul.

Powell, W., Koput, K., & Smith, D. (1996). Interorganizational collaboration and the locus of innovation: Networks of learning in biotechnology. *Administrative Science Quarterly, 41*(1), 116–145.

Prawat, R. S. (1999a). Cognitive theory at the crossroads: Head fitting, head splitting, or somewhere in between? *Human Development, 42*(2), 59–77.

Prawat, R. (1999b). Constructivism and the process-content distinction as viewed by Vygotsky and the pragmatists. *Mind, Culture and Activity, 6*(4), 255–273.

Putnam, H. (2002). McDowell's mind and McDowell's world. In B. Smith (Ed.), *Reading McDowell*. London: Routledge.

Ratner, C. (2004). Introduction to Vygotsky's 'The high mental functions'. In R. Rieber & D. Robinson (Eds.), *Essential Vygotsky*. New York: Klumer Academic/Plenum.

Reck, A. (1984). The influence of William James on John Dewey in psychology. *Transactions of Charles S. Peirce Society, 20*(2), 87–117.

Redding, P. (2007). *Analytical philosophy and the return of Hegelian thought*. Cambridge: Cambridge University Press.

Reddy, M. (1979). The conduit metaphor. In A. Orton (Ed.), *Metaphor and thought*. New York: Cambridge University Press.

Reich, R. (1991). *The work of nations: Preparing ourselves for 21st century capitalism*. New York: Vintage Books.

Rescheler, N. (1987). *Scientific realism: A critical reappraisal*. Boston: D. Reidel.

Rheinberger, H. (1992). Experiment, difference and writing I: Tracing protein synthesis. *Studies in the History and Philosophy of Science, 23*(2), 305–331.

Rip, A. (1997). A cognitive approach to the relevance of science. *Social Science Information, 38*, 149–176.

Robbins, D. (1963). *Higher education: Report of the committee... under the chairmanship of Lord Robbins*. London: HMSO.

Robertson, S. (forthcoming). *'Producing' the global knowledge economy: The World Bank, the knowledge assessment methodology and education*.

Rockmore, T. (2000). Hegel and inference. *Journal of Philosophical Studies, 10*(4), 429–447.

Rodgers, C. (2002). Defining reflection: Another look at John Dewey and reflective thinking. *Teachers College Record, 104*(4), 842–865.

Romer, P. (1986). Increasing returns and long-run growth. *Journal of Political Economy, 94*(5), 1002–1037.

Rorty, R. (1979). *Philosophy as the mirror of nature*. Princeton, NJ: Princeton University Press.

Rorty, R. (1986). Introduction. How we think: A restatement of the relation of reflective thinking to the educative process. In J. A. Boyston (Ed.), *John Dewey: The later works 1925–1953* (Vol. 4). Carbondale, IL: Southern Illinois University Press.

Rose, M. (2004). *Mind of the American worker*. London: Penguin.

Roth, W. M. (2004). Activity theory in education: An introduction. *Mind, Culture, & Activity, 11*, 1–8.

Roth, W. M. (2004). What is the meaning of meaning? A case study from graphing. *Journal of Mathematical Behaviour, 23*, 75–92.

Roth, W. M. (2007). On mediation: Towards a cultural–historical understanding of the concept. *Theory & Psychology, 15*, 655–680.

Roth, W. M., & Lee, Y. J. (2007). 'Vygotsky's neglected legacy': Cultural–historical activity theory. *Review of Educational Research, 77*, 186–232.

Rothblatt, S., & Wittrock, B. (Eds.). (1993). *The European and American university since 1800*. Cambridge: Cambridge University Press.

Russell, D. (2001). Looking beyond the interface: Activity theory and distributed learning. In M. Lea (Ed.), *Understanding distributed learning*. London: Routledge.

Sawyer, R. K. (2002). Unresolved tensions in sociocultural theory: Analogies with contemporary social debates. *Culture & Psychology, 8*(3), 283–305.

Schiller, D. (1997). The information commodity: A preliminary view. In J. Davis, T. Hirschal, & M. Stack (Eds.), *Cutting edge technology, information capitalisms and social revolution*. London: Verso.

Schön, D. A. (1983). *The reflective practitioner: How professionals think in action*. London: Temple Smith.

Schön, D. (1987). *Educating the reflective practitioner*. San Francisco: Jossey Bass.

Scribner, S. (1992). Mind and practice. In E. Tobach, R. J. Falamange, M. Parlee, L. W. Martin, & A. Kapleman (Eds.), *Mind and social practice: Selected writings by Sylvia Scribner*. Cambridge: Cambridge University Press.

Seely Brown, J. P., & Duguid, P. (2000). Knowledge and organisation: A social practice perspective. *Organizational Science*, *12*(2), 198–213.

Sellars, W. (1997). *Empiricism and philosophy of mind*. Cambridge, MA: Harvard University Press.

Senge, P. (1990). *The fifth discipline: The art and practice of the learning organization*. New York: Doubleday.

Sfard, A. (1998). On two metaphors for learning and the danger of choosing just one. *Educational Researcher*, *27*(2), 4–13.

Shannon, C., & Weaver, W. (1963). *The mathematical theory of communication*. Chicago: University of Illinois Press.

Shapin, S. (1994). *A social history of truth: Civility and science in seventeenth-century England*. Chicago: University of Chicago Press.

Shapin, S., & Schaffer, S. (1985). *Leviathan and the air-pump: Hobbes, Boyle and the experimental life*. Princeton, NJ: Princeton University Press.

Shin, T. (1999). Change or mutation? Reflections on the foundations of contemporary science. *Social Science Information*, *38*(1), 149–176.

Shook, J. (2000). *Dewey's empirical theory of knowledge and reality*. Nashville: Vanderbilt University Press.

Shotter, J. (1993). Bakhtin and Vygotsky: Internalisation as a boundary phenomenon. *New Ideas in Psychology*, *11*(3), 379–390.

Silver, H. (1988). *A liberal vocationalism*. London: Methuen.

Simon, H. (1979). *Models of human thought*. New Haven, CT and London: Yale University Press.

Smith, B. (Ed.). (2002). *Reading McDowell*. London: Routledge.

Solow, R. (1957). Technical change and the aggregate production function. *Review of Economics and Statistics*, *29*, 411–450.

Spender, J.-C. (1998). Pluralist epistemology and the knowledge-based theory of the firm. *Organization*, *5*(2), 233–256.

Star, S. L., & Griesemer, J. (1989). Institutional ecology, translations and boundary objects: Amateurs and professionals in Berkeley's Museum of Vertebrate Zoology, 1907–1939. *Social Studies of Science*, *19*, 387–420.

Stehr, N. (1994). *Knowledge societies*. London: Sage.

Stehr, N. (2001). *The fragility of modern societies*. London: Sage.

Sternberg, R. (1990). *Metaphors of mind: Conceptions of the nature of intelligence*. New York: Cambridge University Press.

Stetsenko, A. (2004). Introduction to Vygotsky's 'The tool and sign in child development'. In R. Rieber & D. Robinson (Eds.), *Essential Vygotsky*. New York: Klumer Academic/Plenum.

Stetsenko, A. (2005). Activity as object-related: Resolving the dichotomy of individual and collective planes of activity. *Mind, Culture and Activity*, *12*(1), 70–88.

Stetsenko, A., & Arievitch, I. (2004). Vygotsky's collaborative project: History, politics and practice in knowledge construction. *International Journal of Critical Psychology*, *72*, 52–80.

Sypnowich, C. (2000). Egalitarianism renewed. In R. Beinder & W. Norman (Eds.), *Canadian political philosophy at the turn of the century*. Oxford: Oxford University Press.

Thompson, T. (2004). *John McDowell*. Chesham: Acumen.

Thorpe, C. (1999). Science against modernism: The relevance of the social theory of Michael Polanyi. *British Journal of Sociology*, *52*(1), 19–35.

Thrift, N. (2004). *Knowing capitalism*. London: Sage.

Thrift, N., & Amin, A. (2003). *The cultural economy reader*. Oxford: Blackwell.

Thurow, L. (1997). *The future of capitalism: How today's economic forces will shape tomorrow's world*. London: Nicholas Brearley.

Tomasello, M. (1999). *The cultural origins of human cognition*. Cambridge, MA: Harvard University Press.

Toulmin, S. (1978). *Human understanding*. London: Clarendon Press.

Toulmin, S. (2001). *Return to reason*. Harvard, MA: Harvard University Press.

BIBLIOGRAPHY

Touraine, A. (1969). *Post-industrial society: Tomorrow's social history*. New York: Random House.
Touraine, A. (2000). Global thinking: Information age. *Prometheus, 4*, 49–58.
Tuomi-Gröhn, T., & Engeström, Y. (2003). Conceptualising transfer: From standard notions to developmental perspectives. In T. Tuomi-Gröhn & Y. Engeström (Eds.), *Between school and work: New perspectives on transfer and boundary crossing*. Amsterdam: Pergamon.
Turner, S. (1994). *The social theory of practices*. London: Polity Press.
Universities UK. (2005). *Patterns of higher education institutions in the UK: Fifth report*. Retrieved from http://bookshop.universitiesuk.ac.uk/downloads/patterns5.pdf
van der Veer, R., & Valsiner, J. (1993). *Understanding Vygotsky: A quest for synthesis*. Oxford: Blackwell.
Vann, K., & Bowker, G. (2001). Instrumentalizing the truth of practice. *Social Epistemology, 15*(3), 247–262.
van Oers, B. (1998). The fallacy of decontextualization. *Mind, Culture and Activity, 5*(2), 135–142.
Victor, B., & Boynton, A. C. (1998). *Invented here*. Boston: Harvard Business School Press.
von Hippel, E. (2005). *Democratising invention*. Cambridge, MA: MIT Press.
von Krogh, G., Roos, J., & Klein, D. (1998). *Knowing in practice*. London: Sage.
Vygotsky, L. S. (1978). *Mind in society: The development of higher psychological processes*. Cambridge, MA: Harvard University Press.
Vygotsky, L. S. (1981). The instrumental method in psychology. In J. V. Wertsch (Ed.), *The concept of activity in Soviet psychology*. Armonk, NY: M. E. Sharpe.
Vygotsky, L. S. (1987). *The collected works of L. S. Vygotsky: Problems of general psychology* (Vol. 1, including the volume 'Thinking and Speech'; N. Minick, Trans., R. W. Reiber & A. S. Carton, Eds.). New York: Plenum Press.
Vygotsky, L. S. (1997a). *The collected works of L. S. Vygotsky: Problems of the theory and history of psychology* (Vol. 3, including the chapter on the crisis in psychology, R. van der Veer, Trans. and Intro., R. W. Reiber, & J. Wollock, Eds.). New York: Plenum Press.
Vygotsky, L. S. (1997b). *The collected works of L. S. Vygotsky: The history and development of higher mental functions* (Vol. 4, M. J. Hall, Trans., R. W. Reiber, Ed., J. Glick, Prologue). New York: Plenum Press.
Vygotsky, L. S. (1997c). *Educational psychology* (R. Silvermann, Trans.). Boca Raton, FL: St. Lucie Press.
Vygotsky, L. S. (1998). *The collected works of L. S. Vygotsky: Child psychology* (Vol. 5, R. W. Reiber, Ed., C. Ratner, Prologue). New York: Plenum Press.
Vygotsky, L. S. (1999). *The collected works of L.S. Vygotsky: Scientific legacy* (Vol. 6, M. J. Hall, Trans., R. W. Reiber, Ed., D. Robbins, Prologue). New York: Kluwer Academic/Plenum Publishers.
Warrender, J. (2008). *Robert Brandom*. Stocksfield: Acumen Press.
Ward, S. (1994). *Reconfiguring truth*. Lanham, MD: Rowan and Littlefield Publishers.
Ward, S. (1996). Being objective about objectivity: The ironies of standpoint epistemological critiques of science. *Sociology, 3*(1), 773–791.
Wartofsky, M. (1973). *Models*. Dordrecht: Dreide.
Waters, A. (1996). *Daniel Bell*. London: Routledge.
Weber, M. (1922/92). *Economy and society*. New York: Bedminster Press.
Webster, F. (1997a). Information, urbanisms and identity: Perspectives on the current work of Manuel Castells. *City, 7*, 105–121.
Webster, F. (1997b). Is this the information age? Towards a critique of Manuel Castells. *City, 8*(1), 71–84.
Weingart, P. (1997). From 'finalisation' to 'Mode 2': Old wine in new bottles? *Social Science Information, 36*, 591–613.
Wells, G. (1999). *Dialogic inquiry: Towards a sociocultural practice and theory of education*. Cambridge: Cambridge University Press.
Wenger, E. (1998). *Communities of practice*. Cambridge: Cambridge University Press.
Wertsch, J. (Ed.). (1981). *The concept of activity in Soviet psychology*. Armonk, NY: M. E. Sharpe.
Wertsch, J. V. (Ed.). (1985a). *Culture, communication, and cognition: Vygotskian perspectives*. Cambridge: Cambridge University Press.

Wertsch, J. V. (1985b). *Vygotsky and the social formation of mind.* Cambridge, MA: Harvard University Press.

Wertsch, J. V. (1991). *Voices of the mind: A sociocultural approach to mediated action.* London: Wheatsheaf.

Wertsch, J. (1995). Sociocultural action. In J. Wertsch, P. del Rio, & A. Alverez (Eds.), *Sociocultural studies of mind.* New York: Cambridge University Press.

Wertsch, J. (1996). The role of abstract rationality in Vygotsky's image of mind. In A. Tryphon & J. N. Voneche (Eds.), *Piaget–Vygotsky: The social genesis of thought.* Hove, UK: Psychology Press/Erlbaum (UK) Taylor and Francis Ltd.

Wertsch, J. (1998). *Mind as action.* New York: Oxford University Press.

Wertsch, J. (2000). Vygotsky's two minds on the nature of meaning. In C. D. Lee & P. Smagorinsky (Eds.), *Vygotskian perspectives on literacy.* Cambridge: Cambridge University Press.

Wertsch, J. (2007). Mediation. In H. Daniels, M. Cole, & J. Wertsch (Eds.), *The Cambridge companion to Vygotsky.* Cambridge: Cambridge University Press.

Wertsch, J., del Rio, P., & Alverez, A. (Eds.). (1995). *Sociocultural studies of mind.* New York: Cambridge University Press.

Wertsch, J., Tulviste, P., & Hagstrom, F. (1993). A sociocultural approach to agency. In E. Forman, N. Minick, & C. Addison Stone (Eds.), *Contexts for learning.* Oxford: Oxford University Press.

Westphael, K. (2007). Contemporary epistemology: Kant, Hegel, McDowell. *Journal of Philosophy, 14*(2), 275–301.

Winter, R., & Maisch, M. (1996). *Professional competence and higher education: The ASSET programme.* London: Falmer Press.

Wolf, A. (2002). *Education for democracy.* London: Penguin.

World Bank. (2003). *Lifelong learning for a global knowledge economy.* Washington, DC: World Bank.

World Bank. (2008). *Knowledge for development (K4D): Knowledge Assessment Methodology (KAM).* Retrieved from http://web.worldbank.org/kam/

Young, M. F. D. (2000). Bringing knowledge back in: Towards a curriculum for lifelong learning. In A. Hodgson (Ed.), *Policies, politics and the future of lifelong learning.* London: Kogan Page.

Young, M. (2006). Conceptualising vocational knowledge. In M. Young & J. Gamble (Eds.), *Knowledge, curriculum and qualifications for South African further education.* Pretoria: HSRC Press.

Young, M. (2008). *Bringing knowledge back in.* London: Routledge.

Young, M., & Alias, C. (2009). *Learning from the first qualifications frameworks: Employment working paper 45.* Turin: International Labour Office.

Ziman, J. (1984). *An introduction to science studies.* Cambridge: Cambridge University Press.

Ziman, J. (2000). *Rethinking science.* Cambridge: Cambridge University Press.

Zuboff, S. (1988). *In the age of the smart machine.* London: Heinemann.